AT THE EDGE OF LAW

For Oliver and Millie, with love

At the Edge of Law
Emergent and Divergent Models of Legal Professionalism

ANDREW FRANCIS
Keele University, UK

ASHGATE

Published by
Ashgate Publishing Limited
Wey Court East
Union Road
Farnham
Surrey, GU9 7PT
England

Ashgate Publishing Company
Suite 420
101 Cherry Street
Burlington
VT 05401-4405
USA

www.ashgate.com

British Library Cataloguing in Publication Data
Francis, Andrew.
  At the edge of law : emergent and divergent models of legal professionalism.
  1. Practice of law—England—History—20th century.
  2. Practice of law—Wales—History—20th century.
  3. Practice of law—England—History—21st century.
  4. Practice of law—Wales—History—21st century.
  I. Title
  340'.023'42–dc22

Library of Congress Cataloging-in-Publication Data
Francis, Andrew.
  At the edge of law : emergent and divergent models of legal professionalism / by Andrew Francis.
    p. cm.
  Includes bibliographical references and index.
  ISBN 978-0-7546-7744-4 (hardback : alk. paper) -- ISBN 978-0-7546-9479-3 (ebook)
  1. Lawyers—England. 2. Legal services—England. I. Title.
  KD460.F73 2011
  340.023'42–dc22

2011015340

ISBN 9780754677444 (hbk)
ISBN 9780754694793 (ebk)

Printed and bound in Great Britain by the
MPG Books Group, UK

Contents

Preface

By its nature, this book has developed out of collaboration and conversation with a number of colleagues and friends.

First and foremost, I would to like to thank Iain McDonald, Hilary Sommerlad and Matthew Weait. I have learnt a great deal through our collaborations on, respectively, Part-time Law Students, Access to Legal Work Experience and Activist Lawyers, and have enjoyed the process. I should, of course, make clear that the arguments and ideas developed in the book on the basis of data which emerged from our various joint endeavours are, nevertheless, my responsibility alone. Any errors and misjudgements are mine, and should not be taken as having been endorsed by Iain, Hilary or Matthew. Nevertheless, I am grateful to them all for their support in conducting the research, and for their agreement to allow me to draw on the data collected to advance my own arguments.

The development of this book has also benefitted enormously from being written in the supportive atmosphere of Keele Law School. I have been enormously lucky in being able to develop my ideas within such an environment. So thank you, to all Keele colleagues past and present, for your support and encouragement and in creating a vibrant intellectual and collegial place in which to work.

I would also like to thank my students, who are a testament to the mutually supportive relationship between research and teaching. A number of ideas which were first articulated in the classroom in response to student questions or comments have found their way into this book. I hope some of my ideas and findings have helped them along the way too.

A book of this nature would not exist were it not for the lawyers, academics, students and other professionals who generously gave up their time to participate in the research discussed here. I am indebted to them all. Particular thanks to Diane Burleigh at ILEX, Fiona Woolf and Bill Cox from the Law Society, David Harvey and Geoffrey Shindler from STEP and David Eby from the British Columbia Civil Liberties Association for help in securing access to various research sites.

The ideas in this book have been presented at various 'work in progress' seminars, including at Birmingham, Bristol and Keele universities, and at the annual conferences of the Law and Society Association, the Society of Legal Scholars and the Socio-Legal Studies Association and the UK Centre for Legal Education (UKCLE), and I would like to thank the participants in these sessions for their valuable comments. I would also like to thank all those who have participated in discussions about my work over the years including Rick Abel, John Baldwin, Dave Cowan, Rob East, John Flood, Martin Laffin, Bob Lee, Richard Moorhead, Donald Nicolson, Margaret Thornton, Julian Webb, Richard Young and many others. I owe a particular debt to John Flood, Marie Fox, Rosie Harding, Sajida

Ismail, Marie-Andrée Jacob, Iain McDonald, Hilary Sommerlad and Mathew Weait for reading, and then making characteristically insightful comments, on a number of the chapters.

I would also like to thank the Nuffield Foundation and UKCLE for research funding, and Keele University for a period of funded research leave which enabled me to conduct the empirical research for this book.

Thank you also to Alison Kirk and Sarah Horsley at Ashgate for encouraging the book and responding to my queries with promptness and clarity.

Earlier versions of some of the arguments presented in Chapter 4 have previously appeared in the following published form: Francis, A., 2002, Legal Executives and the Phantom of Legal Professionalism: The Rise and Rise of the Third Branch of the Legal Profession?, *International Journal of the Legal Profession*, 9(1), 5–25; and Francis, A., 2006, 'I'm not one of those women's libber type people but...': Gender, Class and Professional Power within the Third Branch of the English Legal Profession, *Social and Legal Studies*, 15(4), 475–93. I am grateful to the publishers for these permissions.

Last, but by no means least, I would like to thank my family and friends for their encouragement and distraction. My mum and dad, Sylvia and David, and my sister, Jenny, have been there from the outset, and latterly have assisted with the childcare. Oliver and Millie constantly remind me what is really important, and without Natasha's love, support and eye for detail, this book would not have been completed. Thank you.

Andrew Francis,
Keele
7 January 2011

Abbreviations

BIHR	British Institute of Human Rights
BIS	Department for Business Invention and Skills
BLD	Black Lawyers Directory
BSB	Bar Standards Board
CBA	Canadian Bar Association
CLLS	City of London Law Society
DCA	Department for Constitutional Affairs
HMCS	Her Majesty's Court Service
ILEX	Institute of Legal Executives
JASB	Joint Academic Stage Board of the Law Society and Bar Council
LCF	Law Centres Foundation
LSB	Legal Services Board
LSC	Legal Services Commission
RAB	Regulatory Affairs Board
SLS	Society of Legal Scholars
SLSA	Socio-Legal Studies Association
SMCA	Solicitors' Managing Clerks' Association
SRA	Solicitors Regulation Authority
STEP	Society of Trusts and Estates Practitioners

Chapter 1

Introduction: Lawyering at the Edge

Law is now practised by groups, individuals, and in settings, far removed from the core of legal professionalism. Despite widespread recognition of the changing ways in which the legal profession is organized and delivers its services, most studies still focus on readily recognizable sectors of the legal profession; for example legal aid (Moorhead 2004, Sommerlad 2001), family law (Eekelaar, Maclean and Bienhart 2000, Mather, McEwen and Maiman 2001) or corporate law firms (Empson 2007, Hanlon 1999, Heinz et al. 2005, Flood 2007). *At the Edge of Law* is an analysis of a range of actors not readily accommodated within the traditional conception of the collective legal profession. Nevertheless, these actors are an important dimension of the ways in which legal professionalism is developing, given its fragmented, heterogeneous and fluid nature. In studying the professional strategies of those at the profession's margins, this book contributes an additional perspective to the analysis of the changing nature of contemporary legal professionalism within England and Wales. Moreover, it develops the analysis of a core tension facing contemporary legal professionalism: the accommodation of *some* of these divergent visions of legal practice, while other patterns of occupational closure are reinforced.

The legal profession in England and Wales has faced significant changes since the mid-1980s (fragmentation, increasing fluidity of disciplinary boundaries, fractured relationship with the state, shifts in the regulatory environment and so on). In England and Wales the pace of such change has accelerated following the Legal Services Act 2007. While the study of Anglo-American legal professions has achieved a degree of consensus about the nature of these developments, there is greater uncertainty as to whether we are entering a period of post-professionalism (Kritzer 1999) or perhaps a new negotiated contract for legal professionalism (Paterson 1996). At the heart of these debates is the question of what survives. Is there a core of contemporary legal professionalism that transcends the emergent models of legal practice and those practitioners who operate in diverse sectors? Social homogeneity has long since faded in importance although, as Chapters 3 and 4 will highlight, some aspects of social closure demonstrate remarkable tenacity. There are also questions as to the degree to which consumers and government are receptive to claims of shared ethical values. Furthermore, is it possible to identify core legal knowledge, forming the foundation of a collective project of legal professionalism, in an age of multi-disciplinary and cross-jurisdictional practice?

This book deals with unfamiliar and under-researched terrain in addressing these questions. Its methodological approach brings together a series of case-studies, built upon original empirical research, which focus upon those operating at the margins of core legal professionalism, both in practice and those seeking to enter the profession. Some of these groups, such as legal executives, have a long history and a growing contemporary presence. Others, like the multi-disciplinary professionals represented and accredited by the Society of Trusts and Estates Practitioners (STEP) and the lawyer-activists of the Pivot Legal Society, have emerged more recently. 'Outsider' law students have, on the other hand, always struggled to secure access to the legal profession and continue to experience difficulties today. My analysis of these case-studies is informed by a theoretical framework which develops from a market-control understanding of legal professionalism (Larson 1977, Abel 1988), tempered by the important contribution that writers such as Royston Greenwood, Michael Lounsbury, Roy Suddaby and others have made to our understanding of organizational change and institutional entrepreneurship. Given the identification of patterns of closure running alongside these emergent models of legal professionalism I argue, in Chapters 2 and 3, that Pierre Bourdieu's work on cultural reproduction (1977) informs the analysis of the continuing existence of social closure, without the supports (or perhaps imperatives) ascribed by the market control theorists.

In presenting a close analysis of individuals, groups and sectors on the margins of legal professionalism, I argue that it is possible to identify a range of individual *and* collective models of legal professionalism in operation. Through looking at those at the edge, we can learn much about the core values of a field (Abbott 1995: 861–2, Nelson and Trubek 1992a: 214). I argue that the stories of those operating at the margins of traditional legal professionalism highlight the embeddedness of exclusionary practices at the same time as other emergent models of legal professionalism orbit at the edge of the traditional core. Thus, the challenge becomes one of attempting to identify which strategies of professional advancement may be deployed by which actors and in what context.

Current Issues: A Profile of the English Legal Profession

The following section establishes some of the core issues facing the English legal profession in order to provide a framework for the discussion which follows in later chapters. Although this book does refer to the barristers' profession, its primary focus is on the largest legal profession in England and Wales, solicitors. Notwithstanding the importance of the changes which confront barristers (Flood and Whyte 2009, Zimdars 2010), and related issues facing practitioners within Northern Ireland and Scotland (The Lawyer 2010), the focus on English and Welsh solicitors attempts to capture the centrality and influence of key professional actors within the UK (Abel 1988, Galanter and Roberts 2008).

Fragmentation

There are approximately 115,000 solicitors in England and Wales with practising certificates (Cole 2009: 5). These lawyers work in a variety of private practice firms and in-house organizations. These range from the 4,500 sole practitioners to the largest corporate law firms – the Magic Circle, comprising Allen & Overy, Clifford Chance, Freshfields Bruckhaus Deringer, Linklaters and Slaughter and May (Galanter and Roberts 2008). The smallest High Street firms typically deliver a wide range of generalist legal services, predominantly, but not exclusively, in the private client field (Franklin and Lee 2007), and historically have been heavily involved in publicly funded work (Moorhead 2004). The largest law firms deliver a broad range of legal and professional services, often to FTSE 100 corporations, including work in Mergers and Acquisitions, Banking and Finance (Flood 2010).

While there are approximately 10,000 private practice law firms, just 0.57 per cent of these firms have over 81 partners (Cole 2009: 24). 70 per cent of these firms are located in the City of London (Cole 2009: 24). While nationally small in number, they employ 25 per cent of all solicitors in private practice (Cole 2009: 25). Their turnover is huge, with the largest firms reporting turnover in excess of £1 billion per annum, dwarfing the income of their professional association, let alone their fellow professionals in the High Street. The financial disparity is particularly acute within the legal aid sector, where falling salaries are given as a key reason why people are leaving the sector (Sommerlad 2001, Moorhead 2004). Whereas small firms, in particular those in rural areas (Franklin and Lee 2007), stress their connection to the locality, the largest corporate firms operate in a global marketplace. Thus, they have offices in the main financial and legal centres of the world (Galanter and Roberts 2008), and in the future may outsource legal work to jurisdictions like India, alongside their North American rivals (Timmons 2010).

Globalization, of course, means that we are increasingly interconnected (Flood 1996: 173), and this is particularly pronounced within the professional services field (Dezalay 1995, Dezalay and Trubek 1994). Thus, many of the developments explored in this book may have an impact in other jurisdictions (Davis 2010), notwithstanding contextual differences (for example, in legal education or in partnership structure), given the interconnectedness of global professional service markets (Flood 2008) and the commonalities of Anglo-American professions (Freidson 1994: 16).

Access to the Profession

The main route into the solicitors' profession is an undergraduate degree in Law (or non-law degree followed by the one year, Graduate Diploma in Law), followed by the 9-month Legal Practice Course (LPC) – or Bar Professional Training Course (BPTC) for those wishing to join the Bar. Aspiring solicitors are required to secure and complete a two-year training contract with a law firm, or in-house provider. Notwithstanding the importance that Larson accorded to universities in

their role as a site for professional socialization (1977: 45), as with North America
(Manderson and Turner 2006: 666), the relationship between legal education and
the profession within the UK has veered between good, bad and indifferent over
the last 100 years (Cownie and Cocks 2009). The debate will be revisited from
February 2011, following the announcement of a wide-ranging review of legal
education by the legal professional regulators (BSB 2010), which is likely to see
further calls for greater professional oversight of the academic stage.

Although it is commonly accepted that approximately 50 per cent of law
undergraduates do not enter the legal profession (Hunt 2009: 88), it is less clear
whether this is through choice, or through a failure to realize what are, at the outset
at least, largely vocational aspirations (Pitcher and Purcell 1998: 185). Thus, while
in 2008 there were 13,803 Graduates in Law (Cole 2009: 32),[1] and 9,337 students
enrolled on the LPC in 2009 (Cole 2009: 39), the training contract remains the
key hurdle for those wishing to enter the profession. In 2008/2009 5,809 new
traineeships were registered with the Society. This represents a decrease (7.8 per
cent) on the level recorded in the previous year, when trainee registrations stood at
6,303. In response to growing concern within the profession about unrealistic and
uninformed student aspirations about the ease with which training contracts can
be secured, the Law Society campaigned in 2009 to bring these issues to greater
prominence (Chellel 2009).

The largest firms dominate recruitment to the profession. Thus, 28.7 per cent of
all traineeships are in the City, with a further 21.9 per cent in the rest of London.[2]
Although 61.7 per cent of all traineeships registered are women, men are more
likely to hold a traineeship in the City; 34.8 per cent of male trainees had City
traineeships in contrast to 25 per cent of women. Similarly, 34.9 per cent of all
traineeships are in firms with 81 plus partners (again an increase on the previous
year), and again men are more likely than women to have traineeships within these
firms: 39.6 per cent of men were in such a position in contrast to 31.9 per cent of
women (Cole 2009: 39–40). Notwithstanding the significance of these numbers,
I argue, in Chapter 3, that the influence of these firms on the broader sector is
greater than the numbers they directly employ (Boltanski and Chiapello 2006:
162). Thus, the attributes of early work experience, excellent academic record and
a well-rounded personality, valorized by this sector (Lee 1999: 32–6), increasingly
become the expectation in other sectors as well.

Diversity within the Legal Profession

The problems of diversity in relation to 'Access to the Profession', particularly
around gender, ethnicity and socio-economic background (Halpern 1994: 77–81),

---

    1   This does not include all graduates with Qualifying Law Degrees – for example,
combined honours, part-time and so on.
    2   The North West was the next most significant region with 11.4 per cent of all
traineeships.

continue to be experienced more widely within the profession. Perhaps oddly for a book concerned about those operating at the edge of law, there is no specific case-study of the experiences of women and lawyers from black and minority ethnic (BME) backgrounds (or indeed issues around age, sexuality, religion[3] and disability). I do not want to deny the pernicious disadvantage experienced by these groups. I simply wish to draw attention to actors at the edge of law whose experiences have received relatively less scrutiny to date. Class is a key stratifying factor (Milburn 2009) that often intersects with these other issues, and it is a theme which runs throughout Chapters 3 and 4.

Nevertheless, major problems remain for women and BME lawyers. Women now account for 45.2 per cent of solicitors with practising certificates. Whereas the total number of solicitors holding practising certificates has grown by 51.3 per cent since 1999, the number of women holding practising certificates has increased by 86.9 per cent (Cole 2009: 5). However, beyond the positive story at the point of access, as careers progress, men continue to secure greater access to senior posts and higher remuneration (Sommerlad and Sanderson 1998: 115); 77.8 per cent of men are partners or sole practitioners compared with only 49.2 per cent of women with 10–19 years of experience (Cole 2009: 16). Sommerlad and Sanderson argue, in the context of women within the solicitors' profession, that

> employees [are seen] as autonomous subjects, equal before the law, and requiring minimal legal intervention;… the legal workplace is represented as an arena in which equal subjects will be treated with impartiality, and where such individuals can make certain choices, whilst in reality it is soaked in the prejudices which underpin gendered difference. (1998: 103)

Similarly, in the context of BME lawyers, Nicolson, in reviewing a series of research studies, notes the ongoing problems that lawyers from these groups have faced in securing City trainee contracts, and subsequently partnerships (Nicolson 2005: 207). Vignaendra, Williams and Garvey highlight the particular difficulties that black men face (2000: 127). Major diversity initiatives have been in place since the mid-1990s (Braithwaite 2010). Nevertheless, the most recent major research study in this area (funded by the Legal Services Board) summarized its findings as follows:

> despite important advances towards greater openness and diversity, the profession is nevertheless perceived as inherently masculine in character in the sense of its working patterns and general culture, and, further, characterised by (possibly unwitting) biases against non-white professionals and those drawn from lower socio-economic groups. (Sommerlad et al. 2010: 6)

---

3   The sectarian dimension is a key issue which should be considered in the context of Northern Ireland, and, perhaps to a lesser extent, Scotland (Tsang 1999).

The Legal Services Board subsequently published plans to require firms and chambers to publish diversity data about its workforce, and it will be interesting to see how the profession responds to this latest initiative (LSB 2010d).

The Legal Services Act 2007

The Legal Services Act 2007 (LSA) will be discussed in more detail throughout the book, and particularly in Chapter 7, but it is important to establish some of its central features at the outset. Key factors leading to the legislation were recurrent consumer criticism about self-regulation in the legal profession (M. Davies 1999) and Office of Fair Trading concern about restrictive practices in professions (OFT 2001). The main features of the legislation are the establishment of the oversight regulator of legal services, the Legal Services Board (LSB) (s.2), and the clear articulation of regulatory objectives and professional principles (s.1). The continued role for Front-line Regulators such as the Law Society and the Bar Council is on condition that they separate their representative and regulatory functions to the satisfaction of the LSB (s.30). Thus, the Law Society established its regulatory arm, the Solicitors Regulation Authority (SRA) to comply with the legislation. The Act also establishes a single independent Office for Legal Complaints (s.114) and, perhaps most significantly for the legal marketplace as a whole, lays down the framework which will eventually lead to non-lawyer owners and managers of organizations providing legal services through Alternative Business Structures (ABSs) (ss.71–111). As a precursor to the ABSs, Legal Disciplinary Practices (LDPs) have been permitted since March 2009, which allow partnerships of lawyers (for example barristers, solicitors and legal executives) to be formed, with up to 25 per cent of non-lawyers (s.9A(2)(a) Administration of Justice 1985). As such, the legislation not only provides new challenges for the way in which professional bodies organize their regulation, but also for the market in which their members deliver their services.

Publicly Funded Legal Work within England and Wales

Following the publication of the Rushcliffe Report on Legal Aid in 1944 and the subsequent Legal Aid and Advice Act 1949, the legal profession co-opted the legal aid scheme (Goriely 1996) and it formed a significant body of work for the profession as a whole (Abel 1988). Since the late 1980s, successive Conservative, Labour and now Coalition governments, have attempted to restrict the profession's control over the scheme, improve the co-ordination of services and above all control costs (Abel 2003). Legal aid lawyers have come under increasing pressure, with many leaving the sector (or the profession entirely) in a response to falling income, a reduction in professional autonomy and diminished prestige in the eyes of both colleagues and the wider public (Moorhead 2004, Sommerlad 2001). The Access to Justice Act 1999 removed large areas of work from the scope of the legal aid scheme, and the Ministry of Justice has continued this direction of travel in its response to the austerity measures in the Coalition Government's October 2010 Comprehensive Spending Review (MoJ 2010). Other recent developments such as the Community Legal Service established following the Access to Justice Act 1999 to administer civil legal aid (which attempts to bring not-for-profit and for-profit agencies into closer collaboration) were welcomed with a level of optimism (Francis 2000). these developments have had an impact upon other, more radical, approaches to the delivery of legal services to the poor (Robins 2008).

Given the scale of these changes, the core of mainstream legal professionalism has been presented with a challenging set of circumstances, any of which may prompt shifts in the jurisdictional settlements within the system of the professions. My approach in this book, however, is to consider the experiences of those at the edge of mainstream legal professionalism in order to develop our analysis of how, when and by whom professional strategies may be deployed in the future.

Why the Edge?

This book's focus is upon a range of actors who are either positioned, or who choose to position themselves at, what I term, 'the Edge of Law'. As I explain more fully in Chapter 2, the notion of 'the edge' is used as a metaphor and analytical device in a number of ways. Many of the actors considered in this book are 'cutting edge' in the work that they do, challenging accepted practices and patterns of behaviour in the field – the 'institutional logics' (Lounsbury 2002: 255). Others are 'edgy', displaying status anxiety or identity dissonance about their place in the professional field (Costello 2005: 127). Fundamentally, however, I use 'the edge' to refer both to the internal stratification of the legal profession, and the horizontal orbit occupied by those moving away from the core of mainstream legal professionalism and potentially closer to actors in environing professions.

Although there is a wide range of literature considering changes within the legal profession, and indeed work that addresses the outsider experience (see, for example, Thornton 1996), most of this literature focuses on relatively familiar sectors of the profession. The case-studies explored here, which draw on original empirical research, analyse the structures and strategies of those at the edge to reveal the ways in which legal professionalism within England and Wales is responding to the challenges it faces in the early twenty-first century. This is particularly relevant in the context of an increasingly fluid, fragmented and heterogeneous legal profession.

Greenwood, Suddaby and Hinings (2002: 59) and Gieryn (1983) argue that neither behaviours nor boundaries within professional fields are fixed. Thus, as Abbott suggests, jurisdictional moves made by one profession can impact upon the position of another profession (1988: 86). Bucher and Strauss argue that 'most leadership is associated less with the entire profession than with restricted portions of it. ... Leadership, strategies and the fates of segments deserve full focus in our studies of professionalization' (1961: 334). Thus, rather than looking at the centre of professions, where we might find the embedded core of mainstream legal professionalism and its institutional leadership (the Law Society), Gieryn (1983) and Abbott's later work (1995: 863–5) directs us towards the boundaries, and the segments located there. It is in looking at the processes of change, how differences emerge between groups and how points of difference are shared between other groups, that we can more fully understand the emergence of new social entities, like professions (Abbott 1995: 869).

Of course, professions have always been concerned about boundaries, for example between themselves and other occupations (Sugarman 1995a). However, there is relatively little work that analyses the experiences of actors, who operate on these boundaries (whether by choice, or marginalization), and yet remain within the orbit of a weakened collective mobility project (Abel, 2003, Francis 2004, Kritzer 1999). As Abel suggests, we should be interested in the fringes of professionalism because that is where, just as in Arts Festivals, innovation, change and experimentation can emerge (1985: 6). Thus, new organizational forms developed at the edge, such as multi-disciplinary practices in accountancy, may become more widely accepted (Greenwood and Suddaby 2006), in much the same way as parts of the Edinburgh Fringe Festival are now mainstream (Sturges 2002). More broadly, Sharpe, drawing on Bauman, suggests that a society defines itself against 'outsiders' (2007: 209). Thus, in analysing the experiences of professional actors at the edge of law, we may add to an understanding of the core values of, and enduring ties binding actors to, mainstream legal professionalism.

I have previously argued that future conceptions of legal professionalism require detailed accounts of individual and collective models of professional advancement (Francis 2004: 347–8). The selected case-studies are an attempt to highlight just some of the many examples of professional advancement within the fragmented contemporary system of the legal professions. Inevitably this selection ignores a great deal. This book's core focus is not, for example, on the 12,000 barristers within England and Wales. There are obviously also other case-studies which could have been selected which would provide further insights about the current and future directions of legal professionalism; for example, claims management firms, unregulated will-writers and immigration advice providers. Nevertheless, the case-studies selected here all represent different examples of the way in which 'the edge' operates as a feature of contemporary legal professionalism.

Outsider students, discussed in Chapter 3, highlight the ways in which the patterns of social closure within the profession demonstrate remarkable tenacity, notwithstanding the apparent loss of the profession's capacity to exert collective control over entry. The in-depth analysis of legal executives, a largely ignored branch of the legal profession, demonstrates the attempt of an aspirant occupational group to deploy many of the traditional strategies of professional advancement and yet remain locked at the edge. The Pivot Cause Lawyers' relationship to the core of Canadian legal professionalism provides us with fresh perspectives on the disciplinary ties of Law (Chapter 5). Moreover, the limited potential for the direct applicability of their model to English progressive lawyers is important in emphasizing the key role of the state as an actor and the need to take account of context. STEP was chosen as a case-study, precisely because it is an attempt to articulate a new jurisdictional claim which transcends both disciplinary and international boundaries. Chapter 7's detailed analysis of the post-LSA landscape highlights not only the move to the edge of the professional field by the large corporate law firms, but their concurrent influence over the profession and enduring disciplinary ties. It also confirms an ongoing role for the Law Society as an organizational support for traditional, collective models of professional advancement.

Methodology

Factual information about the data collection methods is set out at the beginning of each of the chapters which follow. The following section is a broader explanation of the methodological approaches adopted.

The analysis within this book draws on a grounded theory approach in developing the theoretical insights from the themes, processes and evidence identified in the data collected (Glayser and Strauss 1967). Silverman notes that it is 'increasingly accepted that work becomes scientific by adopting methods of study appropriate to its subject matter' (1993: 144). Different objectives underpin each case-study. Thus, for example, there was little known about the demographic characteristics of part-time law students (Francis and McDonald 2005), thus it was appropriate to distribute a large-scale questionnaire which sought detailed information about their backgrounds. In contrast, the aim to explore the underlying assumptions of professionalism amongst the leaders of professional associations such as STEP, the Law Society and ILEX, meant that in-depth semi-structured interviews represented the most appropriate methodology.

The data itself was collected through the use of 'multi-method research techniques' (Denzin and Lincoln 1994: 2) combining both qualitative and quantitative research methods to identify not simply empirical facts, but the underlying reasons and motivations of the actors involved (Miller et al. 2002: 1). It involved large-scale questionnaires (online and paper), focus groups, in-depth semi-structured interviews, and analysis of minutes, policy documents and the official reports of the professional bodies.

As Jacob argues, the 'seemingly mundane ways of knowing such as paperwork, files, and committees' proceedings and procedures ... are important to study, precisely because they remain unquestioned and implicitly agreed upon' (2009: 99). Eliciting the 'official version' of the professional strategies set out in these documents was a key aim in itself (Dingwall 1997: 62). Gieryn argues that examining the '"stylistic resources" of ideologists', such as professions, is fruitful in highlighting the ways in which boundaries are drawn between themselves and other professional groups (1983: 791). Moreover, the public sphere within which these documents are used, for example Law Society responses to Government

White Papers, is a key arena within which claims for professional jurisdiction are made (Abbott 1988: 62). In drawing on a broader conception of grounded theory, which takes account of not simply the immediate dataset, but also a wider understanding of the processes and changes within the field (Layder 1993: 19), I was able to exercise judgement when assessing the claims made by elite actors in this material (Binns 1987: 227).

Qualitative methods of interviews and focus groups were deployed in relation to each of the case-studies. Moyser and Wagstaffe note that the use of interviews when studying elites is particularly useful for it can reveal 'information about underlying attitudes, interactions and intentions' (1987: 18, see also Crewe 1974: 43). Each of the case-studies was subject to institutional ethical approval and anonymity was, of course, assured to all the interviewees, and maintained in the presentation of the results (SLSA 2009: 6). I have included some contextualizing descriptors in my presentation of the data, but have kept these to a minimum, given the relatively closed environments of the organizations studied.

Dingwall sees the interview as a social construct between interviewer and respondent (1997: 59), and generally sees participant observation as offering greater insight and validity than interviews (1997: 64).[4] The basis of the semi-structured interviews and focus groups are indicated at the beginning of each substantive chapter to give the reader some guidance as to the 'interactional cues ... given off by the interviewer' (Dingwall 1997: 59), but all followed the typical format of beginning with a series of general biographical questions to put the interviewee at ease (Fontana and Frey 1994: 371), before covering broad themes over the course of 45 minutes to two hours. Silverman also cautions the interviewer against simply accepting the uniqueness of the interviewee's position, for then it is difficult to move beyond a purely common-sense interpretation of events. However, he also reminds us of the valuable insights that are gained in understanding how interviewees demonstrate their perceptions of reality (1993: 197).

Silverman notes that interviews are necessarily fragmentary in the way that they are represented to the reader and therefore, 'the critical reader is forced to ponder whether the researcher has selected only those fragments of data which support his argument' (1993: 162).[5] I attempt to demonstrate the plausibility and credibility of the evidence presented in a number of ways throughout the book (see Silverman 1993: 152). Thus, the broader context of the research has been set out in this chapter, and the specific context of each case-study is explained in the relevant chapter. I have also attempted to identify the incidence of deviant cases in my discussion and to give some indication of the relative weight of the qualitative data

---

4   The nature of the research questions meant that this was not appropriate for these case-studies. Although I did (briefly) consider subjecting myself to the processes of vacation scheme recruitment (see Chapter 3), ethical, practical and methodological problems meant that this simply was not feasible.

5   Dingwall also notes that in an interview study 'we can pick and choose the messages that we hear and that we elicit' (1997: 64).

through 'simple counting exercise[s]' (Silverman 1993: 162). The data itself was subjected to thematic analysis (Braun and Clarke 2006), and then, the 'informed coding and extraction of quotes to highlight relevant processes, practices and constraints' on the actors involved (Faulconbridge and Muzio 2008: 12). Denzin and Lincoln also caution against interpretative bias on the part of the researcher (1994: 14–15). The reader must be aware not only of the context of the interviews, but also of my role in the collection and the interpretation of the data, as a white, thirtysomething, university-educated male who has been writing about and working with lawyers for ten years as a full-time legal academic.

Three of the case-studies also rely on large-scale quantitative surveys (Part-time Law Students, Work Experience Project and STEP membership). The questionnaires all used different question formats to generate a full picture of the backgrounds, issues and concerns facing each sample (for example, Likert scale, multiple choice, ranking, true/false, 'free text' and so on). The design of the questionnaires and analysis of the data follows the broad positivist tradition of Durkheim which suggests that 'social behaviour which seems to be highly individualistic and idiosyncratic from the point of view of a lone individual in fact conforms to quite regular and predictable patterns if the occurrence of the behaviour is looked at for a large aggregate of people' (Miller et al. 2002: 3). In truth, however, much of the quantitative data presented is simply empirical presentation of the facts emerging from the studies.[6] Thus, for example, 55.4 per cent of the overall sample in the Work Experience study had some form of legal work experience by the November of the second year of their law degree.

However, more complex statistical analysis was used when appropriate. For example, the data did generate statistically significant associations between some variables, when cross-tabulation analysis was conducted. One way in which this is presented in the text is through the citation of a residual value. A residual value represents the difference between the 'expected frequencies and the observed frequencies' (Miller et al. 2002: 132). I have followed the accepted practice of giving special attention where the adjusted residual value is greater than 2 or less than −2 (Miller et al. 2002: 133). Thus, for example, the frequency with which lawyers, stated that 'I am a lawyer (or accountant, IFA and so on) first, and a trusts and estates specialist second', produced an adjusted residual of 7.2 when compared with the expected frequency of responses to that question, on the basis of the responses of other professional groupings within STEP.

This and subsequent chapters outline how I have attempted to ensure the validity and accuracy of the evidence on which my conclusions are based, by clearly documenting my research approach (Silverman 1993: 146). In addition, the Bibliography provides a full list of sources and the locations of the archive and online materials which would enable any subsequent researchers to check my findings.

---

6 However, information is given about the representativeness of the sample in relation to the broader population in each case-study.

Overview of the Book

In Chapter 2 I set out the main theoretical framework for the analysis of the case-studies in the following chapters. I argue that field location is central in understanding the capacity of different actors to deploy professional strategies and establish professional structures. Thus, location at the edge of mainstream legal professionalism can be indicative of a capacity to change the existing patterns of behaviour within the field, or can confirm marginalization and domination. The capacity of any actors to deploy these strategies will not only be contingent upon the field location of these actors, but also market needs and regulatory demands. The chapter also includes a diagrammatic representation of the different ways in which I use the framework of the edge of law.

Chapter 3 draws on two recent research studies, which focus on the student experience at the margins of legal education and the difficulties that 'outsider' students face in securing access to the profession. In doing so, it confirms the continuing existence of exclusionary patterns of cultural reproduction. This indicates the ongoing prevalence of social closure across the different sectors of the legal profession, notwithstanding the weakening of the collective strategies for control. Chapter 4 develops this analysis through consideration of another occupational group located at the vertical edge of law – legal executives. This third branch of the legal profession has made considerable strides in their professional project since 1998. However, they remain collectively subordinate to the solicitors' profession in important ways. Although the institutional logics of the field have been challenged by a number of actors, the constraining nature of a traditional legal professionalism continues to restrict the ambitions of legal executives.

Chapter 5 draws on research conducted on the Pivot Legal Society, a not-for-profit legal advocacy and community organization in Vancouver. I am clear that these lawyers' experiences and their relationship to the organized Canadian Bar are not directly analogous to the developing patterns of legal professionalism within England and Wales. The distance and differences are too great. Nevertheless, given the common heritage of the Anglo-American professions (Larson 1977) and the inter-connectedness of globalization, the discussion of the agency exerted by these lawyers in consciously (and strategically) positioning themselves at the edge of mainstream legal professionalism supports the analysis of the ways in which the traditional core might accommodate divergent models of professionalism. Moreover, in recognizing the limits of the applicability of the Pivot model to, for example, UK Law Centres, it also underlines the importance of context and the contingency of legal professionalism.

Chapter 6 presents the first academic analysis of the Society of Trusts and Estates Practitioners (STEP). STEP is a multi-disciplinary and cross-jurisdictional professional association representing and educating lawyers, accountants, bankers, trusts specialists and independent financial advisors working in the field of trusts and estates. In exploring the extent to which a new professional entity struggles to yoke these marginal groups within existing professions (Abbott 1995: 871–2),

I highlight the enduring disciplinary pull of Law for even those marginalized within its field. This suggests a model for making and sustaining claims of expert specialized knowledge separate from, but not in challenge to, the originating discipline of Law.

Chapter 7 is the final substantive chapter and covers the professionalization strategies deployed by a range of actors (both individually and collectively) in the events leading to, and following, the Legal Services Act 2007. It highlights the boundary-bridging power of the largest firms who are able to articulate a divergent model of legal professionalism in their own interests. However, their engagement with the traditional collective profession is partial and contingent upon a range of factors (although often on their own terms). The chapter argues that although the Law Society remains heavily constrained by the institutional logics of the field, it retains relevance and influence. Thus, I argue that the traditional collective profession-wide model of advancement appears to operate alongside (and contingently with) an increasing emphasis on individualized models of advancement. This argument is developed further in Chapter 8, which pulls the main themes of the book together and sets out an agenda for future work. Legal professionalism has continued its evolutionary path (Faulconbridge and Muzio 2008: 8, Paterson 1996), but there is still much to learn from those at the edge of law.

Chapter 2

Theorizing Professional Change and Advancement in Legal Services

Introduction

Classically, professions were analysed as collective entities supported and directed by a professional body which patrolled the clear boundaries of its jurisdiction, maintained control over entry and preserved the 'licence and mandate' with the state to secure its relative autonomy (Hughes 1981, Johnson 1972, Abbott 1988, Sugarman 1995a, 1996). However, this model was dependent upon the historically specific conditions identified by Larson (1977) which are, now, no longer available, or at least not in the same way (Abel 2003, Francis 2004, Kritzer 1999). In place of this model, we see an increasing focus on organizations as agents of change within the professional services field (Cooper and Robson 2006, Faulconbridge and Muzio 2008).

To understand change it is important to account for the institutional logics of a field (Lounsbury 2002: 255), which ensure that actors are habituated to the practices that have gone before them (Bucher and Strauss 1961: 331, Nelson and Trubek 1992b: 212). Notwithstanding these structuring properties, change and evolution have been identified within the professional field, whether driven by the profession collectively (Sugarman 1996, Paterson 1996), or by organizational actors (Greenwood and Suddaby 2006, Flood 2010). The practices and properties of the field may also shape the permissible choices of individual actors (Bourdieu 1990: 11). This is important in terms of new entrants seeking access to the profession, but also in terms of the ways in which the 'social status' of individuals affects their capacity to exert agency (Battilana 2006). We, therefore, need to develop a framework that takes account of agency while acknowledging the constraining power of the field (Giddens 1984). This must include a nuanced understanding of the implications of field position (Battilana 2006: 656) in order to understand how and when particular actors are able to deploy strategies of professional control (see, in particular, Chapter 7).

This chapter presents the main theoretical frameworks which inform the analysis of the case-studies and the developing picture of a complex and contingent professionalism. My understanding of the historic processes of professionalization is influenced by the work of Magali Larson (1977) (and the application of her model to the English legal profession by Richard Abel (1988)) and the development of a system of professions locked in jurisdictional competition by Andrew Abbott (1988). After this discussion of 'Professionalization and the Collective Mobility

Project', I review more recent theoretical advances, arising out of management studies, which place far greater importance on the organizational actor (Cooper and Robson 2006). Not only does this address archetype change within organizations (Greenwood and Hinings 1993), it also enables us to consider the organizations' relationship to the traditional core of the profession (Greenwood and Suddaby 2006). I conclude this chapter with a diagram, which seeks to clarify the relevance of field position, in terms of professional advancement and the 'edge of law'.

Professionalization and the Collective Mobility Project

The first studies of the professions (Carr-Saunders and Wilson 1933, Millerson 1964) were a 'largely sterile attempt to define what the special "attributes" of a profession are' (Johnson 1972: 10). These key traits include expert knowledge, education and training, a professional association, code of conduct and an adherence to an altruistic ideal. Subsequent studies (loosely, 'power' theories (MacDonald 1995: 5)) focused on the processes and strategies of professionalization; how professions secure autonomy over their work, engage in jurisdictional competition with other professions and control entry. This later work emphasized the collective nature of the professional project.[1] Within this, the importance of a well-organized professional association which provides leadership and structure to the claims of the wider profession is clear (Larson 1977: 69–70, Abbott 1988: 106); not simply as a signifying trait of the profession, but as a key way in which professionalization occurs – a fulcrum of professional advancement.

These successful professionalization projects were historically specific. Johnson argues that 'professionalism' arises only in certain circumstances; including a heterogeneous client group, a fiduciary one-to-one producer–client relationship and a homogenous occupational community with a low level of specialization (1972: 51–4). Larson also contends that the professions emerged as a result of the conditions generated by the industrial revolutions and growth of capitalism during the 'great transformation' of the nineteenth century within the UK and USA (1977: xiv, Perkin 1990). The key factors were the growth of scientific knowledge (and a growth in the recognition of its superior legitimacy[2] over traditional aristocratic claims of privilege (Larson 1977: 70)[3]) and the existence of the free market (Larson

---

1   However, some emphasize the interaction of different segments or arenas of the profession, in generating profession-wide norms and values (Bucher and Strauss 1961, Nelson and Trubek 1992b).

2   Gieryn (1983) provides an illuminating analysis of the strategies that science deployed to secure this legitimacy during this period.

3   Perkin describes a professional society as being 'one in which people find their place according to trained expertise and the service they provide rather than the possession or lack of inherited wealth or acquired capital'. However, he also notes that many of the first professionals were younger sons of landed gentry (1990: 359–60).

1977: 47–9). The necessary market conditions included a heterogeneous clientele, an uncompetitive market (although a competitive market will drive a profession to monopolize) and an affinity with the dominant ideology (Larson 1977: 15).[4] In the context of the legal profession, Abel asserts that it is a historically specific social phenomenon, 'that found its clearest expression in the last half of the nineteenth century and the first half of the twentieth century' (1988: 308); thus, the Law Society secured its second Royal Charter in 1845.[5] Paterson similarly locates the emergence of a traditional (albeit negotiated) legal professionalism, in the years leading to the 1930s, with the significant changes in the 'contract' between the profession and society only evolving since the beginning of the 1980s (1996: 145).[6] While I argue, throughout the book, that the collective emphasis of the professionalism of Larson and Abel is likely to be less significant in the early part of the twenty-first century, I also suggest that the strategies and processes they set out remain important because it is possible to identify their continuing use by individuals and organizations (Faulconbridge and Muzio 2008).

There are, therefore, a number of key themes which contribute to our understanding as to how professions emerged and in the case of the Law Society came to be, by the 1890s, 'the role model for would-be professional associations', with a central place in society (Sugarman 1996: 98). These are the importance of standardized knowledge base, control over entry and the internal structure of the profession and the role of the professional associations in maintaining the façade of homogeneity and sustaining the profession's relationship with the state.

Expert Knowledge, Market Control and Jurisdictional Competition

Prominent among the 'complex set of characteristics' identified by Carr-Saunders and Wilson was 'specialised intellectual training' (1933: 284). Although Eliot Freidson was sceptical about the substantive claims of professional expertise (1970: 80), he argues that the claims of expertise were, nonetheless, an important dynamic in a profession's drive to secure autonomy (1970: 337). Echoing these themes of professional control, Johnson argues that a 'social distance' exists between the producer (with the specialized occupational skills and knowledge) and the consumer (without the specialized occupational skills). Critically, power

---

4   Burrage also notes that the social and political conditions in which the solicitors profession emerged were key to establishing its autonomy, in contrast to the control of professions exerted by the state in the wake of the French and American Revolutions (1996: 62–6).

5   The Institute of Chartered Accountants of England and Wales (ICAEW) emerged from a series of mergers to be awarded its Royal Charter in 1880.

6   In these terms, then, Abel's identification of legal professionalism as historically specific could be seen as the historical specificity of a particular moment of legal professionalism – a relatively stable period of Paterson's evolving notion of professionalism (1996: 140).

determines whether the uncertainty produced by this distance is resolved in favour of the producer or the consumer (1972: 41). The professional power emphasized by Freidson and Johnson is a far cry from Carr-Saunders and Wilson's identification of 'an admirable sense of responsibility' and 'pride in service ... rather than ... personal profit' among the professions (1933: 471).

The existence of a standardized formal knowledge base was central to Larson and Abbott. Larson saw the existence of standardized knowledge as a specific resource element upon which professions were able to draw to further their collective mobility projects of market control and status gain (1977: 208). The cognitive structure had to be standardized 'in order to clearly differentiate their identity and connect them in the minds of consumers' (1977: 14), and bestows the profession with scientific legitimacy. The rationality of the profession's knowledge also suggests to society that the profession's knowledge is objective and transcends the personal preferences of practitioners (1977: 40). Additionally, it has democratic appeal, because it appears accessible to all. This credibility is further enhanced by the state's legitimization of the knowledge base and broader professional project (Larson 1977: 15, 40, Freidson 1970: 72).

However, once knowledge is standardized it is vulnerable to being seen as lacking the 'special skill' that sets the professions apart from the laity (Jamous and Peloille 1970: 111–19) and ensures a profession's 'aura of mystery' (Wilensky 1964: 149). There is, thus, a need to maintain the 'optimum abstraction' of the knowledge base (Abbott 1988: 102) as the 'optimal base for professional practice' (Wilensky 1964: 148). Professions assert that their abstract knowledge is most appropriate to resolve a particular set of human problems and seek exclusive rights over that area of work (Abbott 1988: 59). Thus maintaining optimum abstraction of professional knowledge becomes a key way in which jurisdictional claims are made and defended (Abbott 1988: 102). The indeterminate 'professional knowledge' becomes 'a means of defence, exclusiveness, self-perpetuation' (Jamous and Peloille 1970: 116). Conversely, occupations that challenge dominant 'professions' without this level of indeterminacy are, therefore, subordinated as technicians (Jamous and Peloille 1970: 117).[7]

Larson similarly notes that professionalization is frequently 'a struggle waged ... against rival occupations rather than across class lines' (1977: 157). Thus, it is in professional society's very nature to set up rivalries between different professions (Perkin 1990: 475) and this competition, a 'mutual disdain between the different professions, [together with] individual arrogance [and] collective condescension towards the laity', has been the 'Achilles heel' of the professions, preventing them achieving the class-based homogeneity of the old ruling classes (Perkin 1990: 390). Abbott argues that the professions make their claims for jurisdiction within

---

7 The challenge of maintaining optimum abstraction, and the special status of professional knowledge, will become even more acute if law firms adopt elements of Susskind's vision of commoditized legal services with a greater routinization of some tasks (2008). See further Chapter 7.

three different arenas; public, legal and workplace. The reconciliation of the dichotomous images of the profession within these different arenas is a central feature of the profession's struggle to maintain full jurisdictional control (1988: 66). The state is a critical audience to which the profession must make its claim given that, 'once state-backed monopoly is obtained, it represented the ultimate sanction of market control by a group of professional "producers" and a proved means, thereafter of protecting themselves against "undue" interference from the state' (Larson 1977: 53).

Boundaries (for example between professions) are, thus, not fixed, but change over time, often in response to strategies of demarcation invoked by the professions themselves (Gieryn 1983: 781–2). For example, professional protectionism played a strong role in supporting some of the early reservations of monopolized legal activities (Mayson 2010b: 45). Notwithstanding the divisions between the Law Society and the wider membership, the Law Society took a strong lead nationally (and particularly through its relationship with government) in its establishment of the accepted limits of solicitors' jurisdiction and the development of a profession-wide model of legal professionalism. The long-standing conveyancing monopoly held by solicitors,[8] arose fortuitously for the solicitors' profession. The Law Society's predecessor opportunistically took advantage of Pitt the Younger's need to raise taxes for the Napoleonic Wars and secured state support for the monopoly in return for the taxation of the relevant fees (Sugarman 1996: 89). The conveyancing monopoly was important to solicitors and Hanlon identifies the varying strategies (from litigation to legislation) invoked against their competitors – scriveners, the bar and certified conveyancers (1999: 47–50). Conveyancing was important to solicitors because it brought with it associations with land and the landed gentry and enhanced the status dimensions of the collective mobility project (Burrage 1996: 51, Sugarman 1995a: 230). While conveyancing was the major area of work over which solicitors had exclusive control, they have been continually engaged with other occupations holding overlapping work jurisdictions in a battle to establish full control of their work jurisdictions (Abbott 1988: 247–79). At one time estate agents, debt collectors, auctioneers, general agents, law stationers, barristers, arbitrators and many other public officials all competed with each other and solicitors over certain fields of work (Sugarman 1995a: 228 and Abel 1988: 185–9). More recently, Dezalay suggests that with growing internationalization

---

8   The solicitors' profession lost this following the Administration of Justice Act 1985, which created Licensed Conveyancers. This did not initially produce a major disruption to solicitors' formal control – it was a shared jurisdictional settlement (Abbott 1988: 69). However, Sherr (1994) notes that the spirit of competition engendered following the removal of the conveyancing monopoly, even prior to arrival of licensed conveyancers, in practice saw prices fall by 30 per cent during the mid to late 1980s. This increasingly uncontrolled competition did ultimately disrupt the internal organizational structures of the profession (Francis 2004: 335–7).

we need to conceive of a more complex system of the professions, capable of crossing international, as well as jurisdictional, boundaries (1995: 335).

The Bar and accountants were key competitors in the jurisdictional battle for solicitors, although solicitors initially looked to the Bar for their model of what a profession should be (Burrage 1996: 51). Abbott suggests the relative rigidity of English lawyers prevented them from extending their jurisdiction, in contrast to the 'structure of long tenuous boundaries' that allowed accountants to extend their influence (1995: 878). However, the popular picture of ascendant accountants (Hanlon 1999: 51–4) is provided with nuance by Sugarman's arguments about the pervasiveness of the ideology of law, which ensured that accountants looked to lawyers for the model of a professional association and operated within legal regulatory and cultural frameworks (1995a: 226, 234). Nevertheless, the Law Society took a strong lead. It first secured legislative protection (see also Larson 1977: 53), and then publicized prosecutions against those giving legal advice for financial reward (Sugarman 1995a: 229); that is, those who challenged the exclusivity of the work jurisdiction of solicitors (Abbott 1988: 59). Thus, the Law Society asserted the boundaries between different disciplines and superiority of legal knowledge to resolve the particular problem.[9]

Larson frames professionalization 'as the process by which producers of special services sought to constitute and control a market for their expertise' and 'as a collective assertion of special social status and as a collective process of upward social mobility' (1977: xvi–ii), and sees these goals as mutually reinforcing (1977: 79). Thus, the professions argued that their innate altruism safeguards society's interests as well as their own clients and militates against the power asymmetries created by the monopolistic project (Larson 1977: 56–63). Competition was also restricted internally, for example the undercutting of fees was proscribed by the Law Society in 1934 (Abel 1988: 193–6). This helped increase the status of the solicitors' profession and consolidated their claims that commercial pressures would not detract from their loyal service to the client and to justice. Thus, the profession restricted competition through price fixing in conveyancing work and there was a long prohibition on advertising for legal services (Abel 1988: 295). When advertisements about services did occur, for example alerting the public to the legal aid scheme, the advertising campaign was conducted on a profession-wide basis rather than by individual firms (Zander 1978: 43–6). These strategies preserved material gains by preventing excessively pernicious price competition but also recognized that 'even capitalist societies display considerable ambivalence about the explicit pursuit of material gain' (Abel 1988: 293).

Standardization of professional knowledge does not secure this 'distinct and recognizable' identity with consumers directly, but is achieved through the training

---

9   See Gieryn on science versus engineering (1983: 785–6), and Dezalay and Garth (1996) on jurisdictional competition over international commercial mediation and Alternative Dispute Resolution (ADR).

of the producers (Larson 1977: 40). Jamous and Peloille also argue that an important way in which this indeterminacy of professional knowledge is controlled is in 'the institutions and the organizations which turn out these "professionals"' (1970: 114). It is to these institutions, which trained the next generation of producers and legitimated the expert knowledge of the professions, that we now turn.

Controlling Entry to the Profession and Status Gain

As the codification of the profession's knowledge develops, formal training in universities supersedes the older apprenticeship model of training (Larson 1977: 44). These institutions produce a professional membership who share the standardized cognitive base, and are socialized to accept the existing model of internal professional stratification. Larson concludes that 'the standardization allowed by a common and clearly defined basis of training ... *is in fact, the main support of a professional subculture*' (1977: 45, Larson's emphasis).

The professions' claim to control the market and enjoy higher status was 'on a new basis, that of competence, defined and measured by a [standardized] system of testing ... Elite status was no longer claimed on the basis of identification with the extraneous stratification criteria of "aristocratic" elites' (Larson 1977: 70). However, the educational institutions tightly controlled the numbers and type of people allowed access to the profession's standardized knowledge (1977: 52), despite the rhetoric of equal access to education (1977: 136). Indeed, it was ideologically necessary that access to education should appear open (1977: 51). The institutions where the producers are produced, equip the profession with standardized objective knowledge, appear accessible to all, and serve as vital site of socialization for the future members of the profession (1977: 51, see also Kennedy 1998, Manderson and Turner 2006).

The importance of education was critical to the solicitors' profession and it initially took responsibility for training itself, before the universities took centre stage (Sugarman 1995b: 9, 1996: 92). However, rather than foster the development of good educational standards, it seems that much of the early system of examinations were part of an attempt to maintain social class homogeneity within its ranks (Abel 1988: 139–64, 286). The testing of Virgil, Homer, Latin, history and science was, for example, conceived as a 'remedy for the influx into the profession of persons of a lower social class' (The Law Times 1854, cited in Sugarman 1996: 108–9). Abel, however, accepts that (particularly for solicitors) there was some link between the entry requirements and practice: 'I am arguing not that entry requirements were irrelevant to practice (for then they would be too hard to justify) only that they cannot be understood entirely in such instrumentalist terms' (1988: 286). The operation of the entry barriers had two important effects, both central to the professional project – material and status gain. By limiting the numbers of suppliers of legal advice, in the face of increasing demand for their services, they were able to charge monopoly level fees for their services, free from excessive competition. However, the profession also enjoyed status as the elite minority provider of expert services (Abel 1988: 298). Moreover, the control of the number of solicitors entering the profession also affected its social composition.

The entry requirements of the profession produced both direct and indirect exclusions. Witz argues that 'one force for cohesion or basis for collective action has been gendered solidarity' (1992: 206), and insists that professionalization, as well as being historically specific, must also be seen as a gendered concept, within which professional exclusionary strategies are 'mediated by patriarchal power relationships' (1992: 42). Thus, in the context of the legal profession, women were prevented from entering the profession until 1919.[10] However, there was also a considerable class (and race) bias, and white, middle-aged, middle-class men dominated the profession (Abel 1988: 169–76).[11] Perkin notes that much of the professions' origins and interests were not far removed from existing class privileges (1990: 89–91, 141). Similarly, in the early stages of professionalization, professions still had to make appeals to 'gentlemanly' values, before the new values of competency became accepted (Larson 1977: 63). This social homogeneity assisted the profession in its collective mobility project (Larson 1977: 66), and preserved an image of the profession as a gentlemanly institution, which reflected the status quo within society (Burrage 1996, Sugarman 1996). The Law Society's elite origins and membership also enabled it to cement its voice as the profession's representative voice (Sugarman 1996: 95, see also Larson 1977: 70, Bucher and Strauss 1961).

Internal Stratification, the Façade of Homogeneity and the Centrality of the Professional Association

Although the aims of the professional project are fundamentally individualistic – that is, greater social prestige for individual practitioners – the means by which these aims are achieved are collective. Larson insists that analysis of social prestige begins with the analysis of the collective unit. The collective credit rating is determined by the success of the profession's organizational efforts (Larson 1977: 69). An indication of a profession's organizational strength is the emergence of a professional association, recognized as the representative voice of the profession, both internally by the profession and externally by the state. Thus, in the context of the solicitors' profession, the Law Society's efforts raised the collective status of the profession as a whole (Sugarman 1996: 108). As highlighted above, the state's legitimization of this process was critical (Larson 1977: 70).

A well-organized profession with a strong national association is better equipped to make claims that its knowledge base is the most appropriate to solve a

---

10   Women who have secured access to the profession now face difficulties in progression (Sommerlad and Sanderson 1998).

11   Despite the turmoil in the profession predicted by Abel (1989), there remain real problems with the diversity of the legal profession (Braithwaite 2010). See Chapters 1 and 3.

particular set of tasks (Abbott 1988: 82–5) and to support the academic work that legitimates its knowledge base (Abbott 1988: 52–7, Sugarman 1996). Moreover the profession with a strong internal structure was far better able to accommodate internal stratification while maintaining the façade of homogeneity (Abbott 1988: 106), necessary to reconcile the 'profound differences' in terms of professional boundaries within the workplace, public or legal arenas (1988: 66). Such internal stratification, whether on the basis of clients (1988: 122), work specialization (1988: 123) or, most importantly, between 'routine and non-routine elements' of the work (1988: 125), masks the reality of professional life when a particular image is presented to the public (1988: 117). Abbott argues that, crucially, it is 'internal stratification [which] provides the basic mechanism that keeps the public picture of professional life separate from the workplace one' (1988: 134). The other aspect of the strong organizational structure is the establishment of a subordinate jurisdiction – essentially paraprofessionals performing routine tasks with the profession's knowledge and under its control. Often a subordinate settlement will have been created following an unsuccessful claim for a full settlement, as in the case of nursing (Abbott 1988: 72, Manley 1995, Witz 1992). The accounts of the professionalization efforts of legal executives are also prime examples of a subordinate jurisdictional settlement (Francis 2002, Johnstone and Flood 1982, Johnstone and Hopson 1967).

Professions are too loose a group, with too diverse a set of interests to form 'a community of fate' (Larson 1977: 69). Nevertheless, through its professional association, a well-organized profession, such as solicitors, was able to present a façade of homogeneity to support its collective mobility project (Abel 1988, Sugarman 1996). Given that there is always a choice between 'things to be explained and things to be ignored' (Abbott 1988: 135), it is also important to acknowledge the relationship of the different segments of the profession to profession-wide norms and structures.

Bucher and Strauss develop the idea of 'professions as loose amalgamations of segments pursuing different objectives in different manners and more or less delicately held together under a common name at a particular period in history' (1961: 326). Abbott similarly invokes this notion, seeing a 'profession as a set of turf battles yoked together in a single defensible position' (1995: 860). Bucher and Strauss caution us that '[professional] associations are not everybody's association but represent one segment or a particular alliance of segments (1961: 331). However, the 'spurious unity' that they identify the elite associations being able to present (1961: 331–2) is strikingly similar to the façade of homogeneity, undercut by internal differentiation, stressed by Larson (1977: 69–71) and Abbott (1988: 106). Nelson and Trubek also stress the divergent visions of professionalism within different arenas (professional association, educational institutions, workplaces and so on). They emphasize 'contradiction and complexity where ... [other] accounts describe unity and coherence' (Nelson and Trubek 1992b: 184). While legal professionalism is contingent upon the arena within which lawyers operate and is not necessarily shared by the wider profession, the production of professional ideology in one arena may influence other arenas (Nelson and Trubek 1992b: 186). Notwithstanding these divisions, it is still possible for the professional body to present a vision of homogeneity and avoid exposing internal divisions when making claims in the public arena (Nelson and Trubek 1992b: 195–8).[12] Indeed, Van Hoy argues that, in respect of contentious profession-wide issues such as 'regulation', it is difficult for the organized profession to present anything other than a vision of homogeneity (1993: 107). Despite fragmentation within the solicitors' profession, for example between City of London practitioners and their regional brethren (Sugarman 1996: 102), by the early part of the twentieth century the Law Society had legitimate claim to represent the majority of solicitors (Sugarman 1996: 105 and Abel 1988: 242–7 and 444–7).

Thus, solicitors ensured social and work homogeneity, restricted internal and external competition and secured autonomy from the state (Abel 1988). The Law Society's role in this collective project is central to Abel's account. However, as noted above, Abel identifies the rise of the legal profession as a historically specific phenomenon. The environment which the legal (and other) professions found so conducive to their strategies for market control no longer exists, thereby leaving the profession with a potentially catastrophic balancing act to perform on the 'tightrope stretched between market and state' (Abel 1989: 285). These changes demand a new framework to account for the legal profession's advancement.

Structure, Agency and Post-Professional Advancement

There was a backlash against the rise of professional society towards the end of the twentieth century. This was characterized by a reduced acceptance of the professions' claims to special status by a public less deferential to establishment institutions in general, and the ideological antipathy of the Conservative Government of Margaret Thatcher (1979–90) to controlled markets of any form (Perkin 1990: 476–77). This reduced the effectiveness of the traditional supports of professionalism to such an extent that Abel foresaw the decline of professionalism (1989), and, moreover, professionalism, like 'Humpty Dumpty: once broken … cannot be reconstituted' (2003: 480). In particular, Abel identifies the declining homogeneity of the profession (in terms of both its work and social composition), the dangers of monopsany leaving the profession vulnerable to the demands of large powerful clients (1989: 315),[13] and increased pressure from the state.

---

12   See Halliday on the strategies and resources that professional associations deploy to achieve this (1987: 101–18).

13   In Johnson's terms, the uncertainty created by the social distance between the producer of knowledge and the consumer would now be resolved in favour of the consumer. 'Patronage', as a model of occupational control, occurs in its fullest form 'where consumers have the capacity to define their own needs and the manner in which they are catered for' (1972: 65).

Kritzer (1999) further highlights the pressures facing traditional legal professions in responding to greater fluidity in the way expert knowledge is claimed and markets for expertise are regulated. Thus, the current upheaval is evidenced by the profession's loss of exclusivity, increased segregation of specialized knowledge, globalization and a fractured (and fractious) relationship with the state. Kritzer suggests that legal professional associations have 'avoided coming to grips with this "brave new world"' (1999: 732), and in an earlier piece, I also explore the structural problems constraining the Law Society's responses to this new environment (Francis 2004: 347). Similarly, the crisis of professionalism is seen in the context of the bureaucracy and market imperatives of large global professional service firms, including law (Leicht and Lyman 2006: 32).

Professionalism's ability to evolve or transform itself is stressed by Paterson (1996), Friedson (2001) and Faulconbridge and Muzio (2008). However, the capacity of professional actors to exert the agency required to affect change will not be equally distributed (Bourdieu 1990, Battilana 2006). Greenwood and Hinings stress the temporal context when assessing the potential for change within organizations (1993: 1074). The current fluidity and flux of contemporary legal services, set out in Chapter 1, is similarly central to understanding whether legal professionalism is capable of this evolution.

Many of the changes in expert knowledge (Dezalay 1991, 1995, Kritzer 1999) are part of the broader conditions of late-capitalism in the late twentieth and early twenty-first century (Fournier 1999), which are marked by the tensions and opportunities generated by globalization (Beck 2005). Boltanski and Chiapello argue that capitalism has the capacity to embrace and incorporate its critics to reconstitute its support (2006). Thus, notwithstanding the crisis of global capitalism following the collapse of Lehman Brothers, models of 'social democracy' failed to secure popular purchase within the UK, partly as a product of the cultural emphases on middle-class universality and the individualization stressed through the 'consumer choice' rhetoric of the Labour Government (1997–2010) (Castree 2010: 197). This is reinforced by an emphasis on consumption and lifestyle,[14] within which the potential for identity to be defined by material consumption (whether that be of an Ipad or an outsized Louis Vuitton handbag) is emphasized. This stresses our capacity to 'choose who we may want to be' (Sweetman 2003: 530). The fluidity of knowledge, identity, borders and ideology combined with political, economic and cultural turbulence generates uncertainty for actors and organizations; thus Sweetman, drawing on Beck (1994), argues 'nothing can be taken for granted' (2003: 540). Critically, however, not everyone is appropriately positioned within the field to respond to these uncertain conditions (Sweetman 2003: 530 and see further below). Bauman argues that it is only the elites who experience 'lightness, detachment, hovering, leapfrogging, prancing, surfing and gliding' within the fluidity of these uncertain fields (2005: 135).

---

14   This was exemplified in the UK during the mid 1990s through the political and musical synergies around 'Britpop' and 'Cool Britannia' (Harris 2003).

In the professional services context, this fluidity can be seen in construction of and competition over expert knowledge, within which the 'internationalization of the market for professional expertise' is a key driver (Dezalay 1995: 235, Flood 1995). Lawyers, accountants and management consultants compete to define the nature of their work in an effort to extend their jurisdiction, and are both released and constrained by international boundaries, depending on how they are able to define their expertise (Dezalay and Trubek 1994, Dezalay and Garth 1996, Dezalay and Garth 2004). Abbott suggests that changes to the objective properties of a profession's cognitive base may disrupt the system of the professions (1988: 39), but the 'the subjective qualities of a task arise in the current construction of the problem by the profession currently holding the jurisdiction of that task' (1988: 40). Gieryn (1983) was also clear that boundaries between disciplines were not fixed, but were capable of change, and that the professions themselves were key actors in enforcing and defining these boundaries. Thus, the edges of the legal profession's boundaries are subject to change, and are arguably even more so during this time of uncertainty. Thus, following Abbott (1995), it is perhaps in looking at the boundaries, in identifying differences, where we can identify how and where the evolution and transformation of professionalism is taking place (Paterson 1996, Faulconbridge and Muzio 2008). Abel argues that 'whereas traditional professions shielded individual practitioners from market forces by controlling entry, in the future productive units will protect those temporarily sheltered within their walls' (2003: 477). It is these productive units, the organization, upon which we now focus.

The Organizational Focus

Leicht and Fennell argue, in the light of the contemporary pressures on professions, 'that researchers should study multiple professional groups interacting with each other and with non-professional groups in the same organizational settings' (1997: 225). Such is the impact and influence of the Big Four accountancy firms on the development and production of professional identity and regulation (Cooper and Robson 2006: 432), that there must be far greater focus on these 'relatively unaccountable and opaque centres of power' (Cooper and Robson 2006: 436), than either academics, the public or politicians have hitherto given. Thus, Marquis and Lounsbury chart the actions of national US banks which sought to extend their reach into new communities (2007: 813–15) and Marcos (2000) focuses on the moves by Spanish Audit firms into the delivery of legal services.

Abbott emphasizes the importance of knowledge in the jurisdictional competition in which the collective profession was engaged (1988: 98), however Greenwood and Suddaby argue that that the size and global reach of the Big Five (as was) accountancy firms and their capacity to internalize knowledge commodification processes requires a different model (2001: 948). Rather than jurisdictional disputes being resolved by professional associations and regulators, 'colonization and commodification practices appear to be the direct result of the increased tendency of professional services to be delivered by large complex organizations' (2001: 950). Similarly, expatriation is deployed as 'a business system for transnational knowledge development and diffusion' (Beaverstock 2004: 172), whereby the production and transfer of knowledge within firms is facilitated through the movement of the firm's workers across international borders. Professional training and socialization also increasingly takes place within large corporate law firms (Muzio, Faulconbridge and Cook 2010). It is within these organizations that Hanlon identifies the emergence of a 'commercialised professionalism'. This involves radical changes to previously uncontested features of lawyering, including a transformation of the lawyer–client relationship (Hanlon 1999: 123–63).

Greenwood and Hinings (1993), highlight the importance of 'archetypes' in organizational change, in shaping existing structures and providing a model around which new structures can coalesce. By 'archetype' they refer to the relationship between the patterns of organizational structures and management systems and the ideas, values and beliefs which underpin these systems – 'an archetype is thus a set of structures and systems that reflects a single interpretative scheme' (1993: 1052). Archetype theory suggests that organizations move to new archetypes in order to cement a stable, coherent interpretative scheme to produce efficiency in market and organizational coherence (1993: 1056). Kirkpatrick and Ackroyd note that the adherents to archetype theory highlight the role that professional agents may play in developing changes which often involves negotiation with other actors and organizations within the specific institutional context (2003: 735). However, the importance of the dynamics and momentum of change leading to organizational coherence remains central in such approaches (Greenwood and Hinings 1993: 1071). Drawing on archetype theory, Cooper et al. (1996) highlight the emergence of, what they describe as, the Managed Professional Business, within which management imperatives and structures are prioritized over the traditional professional archetype of the classic partnership model of a law firm (see also Hanlon 1999). Boltanski and Chiapello identify a similar transformation, and argue that 'that a new representation of the firm has emerged, featuring an organization that is very flexible; organised by projects; works in a network; features few hierarchical levels; where a logic of transversal flows has replaced a more hierarchical one, etc.' (2006: 165). An individualized responsibility for career development and jobs security takes the place of structured career progression (2006: 166).

Kirkpatrick and Ackroyd (2003) question the emphasis within 'archetype theory', upon the gravitational pull towards stability and coherence as drivers for change. They also cast doubt on the suggestion that the models are generalizable beyond the initial case-studies of law and accountancy (2003: 738). In its place they argue that a more nuanced approach to structure and agency (Giddens 1984) is required, and highlight the 'morphogenic theory' of Margaret Archer (1995), within which 'groups' relative resources and power are the indispensable key to understanding change' (2003: 741). In the context of organizational change, therefore, they also argue that greater attention needs to be paid to the insights from the sociology of the professions (see above) in understanding which groups of professionals are able to exert occupational control and generate change within organizations (2003: 742–4).[15]

In exploring data from Law Society statistics on firm sizes and structures, Muzio and Ackroyd attempt this synthesis of organizational and sociological theory. They argue that notwithstanding the shift towards larger and larger law firms, with a more commercialized ethos (Hanlon 1999, Cooper et al. 1996), that a defensive professionalism survives (Muzio and Ackroyd 2005: 641). In particular, 'management ideas and procedures are subservient to professional conceptions of policy and practice' and 'professionalism remains recognizably the basis of legal practice to which other institutional logics are subordinated' (2005: 620, see also Pinnington and Morris 2003). Thus, professionalism survives, and strategies of closure (for example, gendered closure, Bolton and Muzio 2007) are deployed internally by the partners of law firms, rather than by the profession on an occupational basis (Muzio and Ackroyd 2005: 618–19). Similarly, Faulconbridge and Muzio, in asserting the evolution of an 'Organised Professionalism', note the importance of professionalism as a form of occupational control in the organizational context, with 'professionals organizing professionals' (2008: 14). While these insights are important, this narrow focus simply addresses the changes within the largest, global law firms (2008: 8). Notwithstanding the power and influence of these firms, they remain only part of the continuing story of professionalism. Other, more marginal, stories also need to be told. Professionalism, if not necessarily along the lines laid out by Larson and Abel, remains capable of influence in wider legal sectors, and indeed in other occupations (Fournier 1999: 298).

Notwithstanding this organizational focus, it is important to note the ongoing importance of professional associations in this landscape. Van Hoy (1993) and Nelson and Trubek (1992b) note the continuing importance of the professional association as a site in which the tensions and disparate interests of a fragmented profession can be managed (Bucher and Strauss 1961: 331). Professional associations may retain influence for three reasons: as an arena within which the profession interacts collectively, a means through which interaction with other communities is facilitated, and as a mechanism through which compliance with either normatively or coercively sanctioned rules is monitored (Greenwood, Suddaby and Hinings 2002: 61–2). Lounsbury, in his analysis of the transformation of the Financial Services sector from regulatory to market driven logics, similarly notes the importance of the professional association, as 'a specific way in which an occupation can formalize its identify, make claims about its occupational status and participate in a field of governance' (2002: 256).

Despite the importance of organizations as actors in professionalization (Cooper and Robson 2006), the organized profession-wide structures and norms

---

15   Lounsbury similarly argues that greater synthesis of organizational theory and the sociology of the professions enhances understanding of organizational change (2007: 303).

remain relevant, and are often invoked at points of jurisdictional conflict (Dezalay and Garth 1996: 305). Suddaby, Gendron and Lam note, somewhat in surprise, that the 'majority of accounting professionals are relatively highly committed to their profession' (2009: 424), and even the representatives from the Big Four Firms, hold 'contradictory', rather than 'uniformly oppositional' views about professionalism (2009: 422). If, therefore, professionalism retains importance, how does change occur and which actors and organizations are situated in positions which enable them to generate change?

Institutional Logics and Professional Advancement

Organizations and actors operating within a particular institutional field are subject to the structuring properties of 'institutional logics'. These are the 'organising principles that govern the selection of technologies, define what kind of actors are authorized to make claims, shape and constrain the behavioural possibilities of actors and specify criteria for effectiveness and efficiency' (Lounsbury 2002: 255). Practices which reflect the ideology of previous generations are embedded within the institutional setting, 'accepted as … inherent' (Nelson and Trubek 1992b: 212) and 'taken for granted' (Bourdieu 1977: 80). Moreover, 'Professionalism', itself, is an institutional logic (Suddaby, Gendron and Lam 2009: 410). It operates as a disciplining discourse capable of shaping an employee's conduct, even when they are not necessarily subject to formal control (Fournier 1999: 290). Mutch, Delbridge and Ventresca emphasize that the structuring and constraining properties of these institutional logics operate in similar ways to the properties of fields identified by Bourdieu (1990); thus the actions of organizations 'produce and reproduce the world they inhabit' (2006: 608). It is important within both these frameworks to account for actions of actors and their relationship to the structures within which they are located (Leca and Naccache 2006). Although Bourdieu's agents have been described as 'bearers of unconscious processes of interest calculation' (Honneth, Kicbya and Schwibbs 1986: 42), this fails to address the complexity of the agency/structure relationship he presents. Bourdieu's actors do possess agency to the extent that habitus is not simply a fixed product but may change over time, sometimes in response to the actions of agents. Habitus is thus 'durable, but not eternal' (Bourdieu and Wacquant 1992: 133).

Giddens (1984) attempts to develop a framework that integrates structure and agency. Similarly, Archer's work on 'morphogenic theory' highlights the reciprocal way in which although agents may produce structures, these structures will subsequently influence the activities of actors within the field (1995: 247–93). Battilana also reminds us that 'those who are most often constrained by institutions and those who initially created those institutions are not the same' (2006: 654–5). Crucially, it is this difference in location within the field (Mutch, Delbridge and Ventresca 2006: 616), which I argue permits the 'repertoire of the possible' (Beagan 2001: 600) for organizations and actors seeking professional advancement and institutional change.[16]

Organizations and Institutional Entrepreneurship

In analysing the capacity for institutional change to be generated by entrepreneurial actors, Greenwood and Suddaby seek to answer what they describe as the 'paradox of embedded agency' (2006). Essentially, they explore 'why and under what circumstances are embedded elites enabled and motivated to act as institutional entrepreneurs in highly institutionalized contexts' (2006: 26). Although her focus is on individual actors, Battilana is similarly clear that it is the willingness and ability to act which is necessary, and, moreover, this will be linked to the position within the field (2006: 659–60). Greenwood and Suddaby stress that existing models of institutional change 'suggest that central organizations within an organizational field are embedded within, and privileged by, prevailing institutional logics; therefore they are neither open to alternative logics nor motivated to introduce them' (2006: 42). Under this framework, it is those at the periphery who have the capacity to drive forward changes, given that they have a reduced attachment to the central value systems (Shils 1975: 10). Central organizations, such as elite law or accountancy firms or professional associations, would seem too deeply embedded within the field to challenge institutional logics. Yet, given the difficulties that the dominated face in resisting their own domination (Bourdieu and Wacquant 1992: 24), it is important to remember the distinctions between horizontal and vertical stratification within the profession (Abbott 1988: 134).

Maturity within a field, for example accountancy or indeed law, produces stratification within that field (Greenwood and Suddaby 2006: 28). In emphasizing internal stratification, or social position, within a field, we are therefore able to develop a model within which elite actors drive institutional change, and in so doing, become peripheral to the central value systems. They are at once central and peripheral. As Sherer and Lee also argue, there is a need for greater account to be taken of the 'role for elites in initiating change' (2002: 116). In contrast, subordinate peripheral players will continue to be bound by the structuring properties of the field, given they possess a more limited range of permissible choices and expectations (Reay 2004: 433).

Greenwood and Suddaby analyze the development and embedding of a new, 'cutting edge', organizational form – Multi-Disciplinary Practices (MDPs) – within the field of accountancy. They argue that the Big Five Accountancy firms (as

---

16   Professional advancement, for example by a collective professional association acting as the fulcrum of the collective mobility project, may occur along traditional lines in line with the prevailing institutional logics. Although institutional entrepreneurship is a form of professional advancement which challenges the institutional logics, professional advancement does not have to involve institutional entrepreneurship.

was) challenged institutional logics in their instigation of the new organizational form because of 'a combination of four dynamics: adverse performance, boundary bridging, boundary misalignment and resource asymmetries' (2006: 35). The pull towards archetype coherence (Greenwood and Suddaby 1993) and the rewards which may follow from change (Kirkpatrick and Ackroyd 2003: 745, Greenwood and Suddaby 1993: 1056, Greenwood and Suddaby 2006: 35) explain the willingness to engage in institutional entrepreneurship. However, it is the 'boundary bridging' and the 'boundary misalignment' that give the ability to change. Greenwood and Suddaby argue that it is these factors that reduce the effectiveness of the institutional pressures (2006: 42). Thus, the global scale and client reach of the largest firms enables them to transcend the boundaries of the field of accountancy and identify new opportunities. Similarly this work removes them from the fixed, national focus of the professional body. However, it is important to note that, in contrast to Battilana's suggestion that challengers to institutional logics tend to be those 'less favoured by existing institutional arrangements' (2006: 661), the elite accountancy firms were already privileged (as are elite law firms, Galanter and Roberts 2008, Flood 2010). Their challenge to the institutional logics was designed to reinforce their position, so that 'underlying patterns of privilege ... remain[ed] untouched' (Greenwood and Suddaby 2006: 43). Thus, in international legal practice, Dezalay notes that the 'elites endeavour to reconvert their domination of national structures ... into a mastery of this nascent international market of legal-financial expertise' (1995: 332, Flood 1995, 1996).

Individual Agency in the Professional Fields

Pierre Bourdieu's work highlights the importance of the structuring properties of particular fields, for example the juridical field (Bourdieu 1987). An actor's habitus is a product of their individual family, educational and social histories and collective experiences; actors are, thus, 'products of [their] conditioning' (Bourdieu 1990: 59). The habitus is the durable ways of 'speaking, walking and thereby of feeling and thinking' (Bourdieu 1990: 70), required to demonstrate that the agent is 'objectively compatible' with the properties of the field (Bourdieu 1990: 54). These ways of enacting and understanding the legal field are 'habitual and pre-reflexive' (Sommerlad 2007: 194) and instinctive – they can play the game (Fowler 1997: 18). Bauman, citing Boltanski and Chiapello (1999), suggests that this 'savoir faire' is being displaced by '"savoir-être", the knowing-how-to-move-in-the-world, means more than anything else the quality of being well connected, capable to communicate easily and to have a wide circle of similarly well-connected people with whom to communicate' (2005: 134).

Within professional services we have seen the emergence of the 'networked professional' with a tacit understanding of 'how things work' (Anderson-Gough, Grey and Robson 2006: 238). Those with an instinctive understanding of how to move within the field enjoy the 'ease of a comfortable situation ensuring an easy life' (Bourdieu 1984: 255–6). Those without the appropriate habitus have their possibilities for action severely constrained (Bourdieu 1990: 68).

There have been criticisms about the role of agency in Bourdieu's framework, for example his analysis of the capacity of women to resist patriarchal power has been described as 'bleakly pessimistic' (Lovell 2000: 43). However, as discussed above, he did allow for agency, and other writers have developed explanations of the way in which agency and structure interact (Archer 1995, Giddens 1984). Central to Bourdieu's framework is the position of individual actors within the field. Thus, notwithstanding the potential for agency from some actors, 'only in imaginary experience (in the fairytale, for example) which neutralizes the sense of social realities does the social world take the form of a universe of possibles equally possible for any possible subject' (Bourdieu 1990: 64). Battilana argues that in order to act as institutional entrepreneurs (that is, to challenge institutional logics or the structuring properties of the field), individuals need both a willingness to act and an ability to do so. Crucially that ability to do so is linked to their social position in a field (2006: 659). In particular, an assessment of their ability to engage in institutional entrepreneurship requires attention to be paid to the social status of an organization and of the individual within it (2006: 661–2).

While Sweetman argues that reflexivity is demanded within the post-modern world in order to think our own advancement, critically not all actors within a field are positioned to be able to do so (2003: 537). Thus 'reflexivity losers' face a double disadvantage, 'not only performing routine manual work, but the lack of opportunity to develop the habitual reflexivity in higher status occupations, may further disadvantage such lower status groups in social and economic terms' (2003: 544). The internal stratification within the legal profession has accelerated (Faulconbridge and Muzio 2008). Now partners of elite, corporate law firms reserve the rewards of professionalism to themselves, rather than lawyers more generally (Muzio and Ackroyd 2005, Wilkins and Gulati 1998). In this context some lawyers lack the capacity for institutional entrepreneurship. Thus, the 'relative resources and power [of groups and actors] are the indispensable key to understanding change' (Kirkpatrick and Ackroyd 2003: 741). Many aspirant entrants to the profession will also lack the necessary habitus and cultural capital (Sommerlad 2007) to secure comfortable access to and passage within the legal professional field and are, thus, 'edgy' about their professional status. I argue (particularly in Chapters 3 and 4) that powerful forces of cultural and social reproduction continue to shape the nature of power relationships within the profession (Dezalay 1995: 340), even if formal exclusionary controls (Witz 1992: 44) are, now, no longer as prominent.

Looking at boundaries or differences can indicate where new social entities, such as professions, may emerge (Abbott 1995: 863). These differences may be 'yoked' to create entities (Abbott 1995: 872), which may over time endure to 'originate social causation' (Abbott 1995: 873–4), for example in invoking strategies of professional advancement or institutional entrepreneurship. However, the work discussed above cautions us that not all actors may be able to connect their differences, and even if they achieve this, may not thereafter be able to deploy strategies of professional advancement. The differences between elite actors (such as corporate law firms) and the rest of the legal profession (sketched out in Chapter 1) are important. Given their field position, such actors may be capable of generating institutional change. However, the differences between themselves and the rest of the profession may not be so pronounced that there is no longer any notion of collective professionalism at all. We also need to account for the structuring properties of the field. Not only may these reinforce the internal stratification of the profession, but potentially may confirm to those from lower status backgrounds that the profession is 'not for the likes of us' (Bourdieu 1990: 56). This is a complex and extremely contingent narrative of the possibilities of professional advancement. The following diagram is an attempt to clarify the implications of being located at the edge of the field of law for a range of actors and organizations. See Figure 2.1.

Conclusion

The contingency of the framework that I develop in this book is not nervousness about nailing my colours to the mast of a grand narrative. 'Critical realism' is an approach which takes the observable field positions seriously (Mutch, Delbridge and Ventresca 2006: 611). The complexity highlighted in the literature above and stressed in the following chapters is based on observable patterns and behaviours within the divergent and emergent models of legal professionalism.

This book addresses those actors and organizations who are situated or who choose to situate themselves at the edge of the law. In different ways, they are distanced from mainstream legal professionalism – which emphasizes traditional profession-wide values and knowledge, and is articulated by the professional association, for example the Law Society within England and Wales. However, I argue that peripheral location can be indicative of agency (and potentially institutional entrepreneurship), or can confirm marginalization and domination.[17] In more closely exploring the professional projects of those located at the edge of law, I develop an analytical model of something that we might describe as 'contingent professionalism'.[18] Contingent professionalism may be conceptualized as a model of professionalism that shifts and changes according to the market's/field's needs at any one time; a model of complexity (Webb 2004: 94–5). Moreover, particular organizations and actors may be better positioned and resourced to support their own professional advancement independently of the profession at large. It thus 'both recognizes and explores the constraining and enabling character of social

---

17   It could be argued that women lawyers in elite corporate law firms may occupy both marginal and central positions.

18   Teodoro (2010) also invokes the term, but uses it to refer to the professionalism of public sector bureaucrats being contingent upon mobility between different employers.

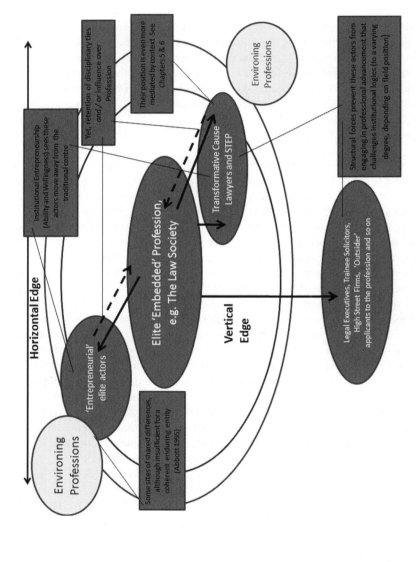

Figure 2.1

structures and the prospects of agency on the part of social actors' (Mutch, Delbridge and Ventresca 2006: 622). A key aim of this book is therefore to explain and understand how and when professionalization strategies can by invoked by different models of professional advancement.

What is striking in exploring the wider literature and the case-studies in Chapters 3 and 4, is the ongoing reinforcement of privilege within this evolving and complex model of professionalism. Thus, from Perkin's sons of the aristocracy (1990) to Dezaley's discussion of elite players in international professional services markets (1995), the elites have always been able to reinforce and protect their models of privilege. When assessing the capacity of non-elite players who seek either to access, or make market claims or status gains within, the profession we need to acknowledge the importance of habitus in order to comfortably pass within the field. The next chapter, which explores the experiences of 'Outsider' students and entry to the legal profession, appears to confirm Mutch, Delbridge and Ventresca's bleak conclusion that 'life chances [are] determined to a significant degree by … involuntary positioning' in the field (2006: 617). These actors are located at the edge of law, and will struggle to move from this position.

Chapter 3

Outsiders in Legal Education and Beyond: Marginal Students, Professional Identity and Access to the Legal Profession

Introduction

Notwithstanding, the (ideologically necessary) rhetoric of equal access to education, a profession tightly manages the numbers and types of people it allows access to its knowledge (Larson 1977: 52), and the legal profession was historically dominated by white middle-aged and middle-class men (Abel 1988: 169–76). This social homogeneity supports the professional project in reinforcing collective ties and signalling high status (Larson 1977: 66). However, there have been dramatic improvements in terms of socio-demographic diversity within the solicitors' profession since the 1970s (Braithwaite 2010), and the profession's collective control over entry has weakened (Abel 2003). The flux and fluidity within the legal professional field (see Chapters 1 and 2) should, theoretically, give new opportunities for actors and organizations to make claims and challenge pre-existing institutional logics. Yet, despite some welcome progress, concerns continue to be voiced about the accessibility of the profession (Sommerlad et al. 2010), with class a key issue (Milburn 2009). Non-traditional students face continuing problems in their attempts to secure access to the legal profession (Sommerlad 2007, Thornton 1996).

This chapter draws on the findings of two recent studies which focus explicitly on the student experience on the margins of legal education and the difficulties that non-traditional, or outsider, students[1] seemingly face in being able to demonstrate the appropriate professional identity in order to pass in the professional field. The shifts in the way that access to the solicitors' profession is organized are also a critical context in understanding these processes. While Larson (1977) and Abel

---

1   It is difficult to find an appropriate term for aspiring solicitors who come from a social group lower in status to that of the normative solicitor. Carbado and Gulati (2000; 2003) refer to outsiders and insiders. There is a similar difficulty when referring to students drawn from a group which has previously not attended Higher Education and who do not fit the occupational norm or are otherwise marginalized. The usual term is 'non-traditional'; however this can be read as pathologizing them and constructing them as responsible for their prior absence from these fields. Nevertheless, in view of the difficulty of finding appropriate alternatives, I use these terms here.

(1988) discussed control over entry in the context of the collective profession, it is the large corporate law firms that are now the primary gatekeepers to the profession (Hanlon 1999, see Chapter 1). Boltanski and Chiapello note that the largest international firms' 'impact on the global sphere is much higher than suggested by the proportion of private sector workers ... who are directly employed by them' (2006: 162, see also Greenwood and Suddaby 2006: 42–3). I would also argue that the influence of the large corporate firms extends across the profession (Flood 2010 and Chapter 7).[2] Their recruitment practices privilege a normative identity for an aspirant entrant, who has a followed a clear, instantly recognised path to the profession – '[they're] becoming bog standard, pretty much, because that's what the profession demands' (Interview 10, Female Graduate Recruitment, Large Corporate).[3] However, this is increasingly the normative identity and narrative for all sectors to the profession. While market forces and sector status mean that the insistence of straight-A A-levels, for example, is toned down in some regional firms, the general pattern of early work experience, excellent A-level performance, attendance at pre-1992 institutions,[4] further work experience at the end of the first year of a law degree, followed by vacation placement and subsequent recruitment to a training contract two years in advance, is the normative narrative of recruitment to the profession.[5] Clearly this is not a universal picture and there are successful entrants who do not follow this pattern; however, they are the exception. Outsider students who deviate from this recognizable pathway, by virtue of their background, experiences and histories, struggle to secure access to the profession (McLeod-Roberts 2010). I do not argue that firms do not accept applications from students who depart from this pathway, or discriminate against candidates from particular backgrounds, but it is easier for firms to recognize an entrant who demonstrates the normative professional identity and has followed a recognizable pathway. Consequently, it is easier for students who can readily demonstrate this identity and have followed this path to present themselves as a serious candidate. As subjects with the appropriate habitus for this social field, they experience the 'ease of a comfortable situation ensuring an easy life' (Bourdieu 1984: 255–6).

---

2   Some students, of course, reject this dominance and aspire to work in family and/ or publicly funded areas (see Chapter 5). However they are a minority (Norman 2004: 32).

3   This acceptance, that students follow a readily recognizable path, highlights the profession's contradictory requirements of individuality and conformity (Collier 2005: 69).

4   A commonly used term to refer to those institutions whose status as 'universities' dates from the removal of the distinction between universities and polytechnics under the Further and Higher Education Act 1992. See, for example, Webb (1999: 232).

5   See, for example, Law Careers Net (2006) *Cobbetts' Award Profile – Best Vacation Scheme* http://www.lawcareers.net/Solicitors/Assets/758/AwardProfile06.pdf [accessed: 23 April 2008]. Higgs and Sons, a smaller (27 partner, although clearly ambitious) firm, while stressing the different experience that they provide, also appears to offer a similar process (and representative trainees) to many of the larger firms (www.higgsandsons.co.uk [accessed: 23 January 2011]).

I begin with a brief overview of the two projects from which the data for this chapter is drawn. I then argue that, notwithstanding new possibilities opening up for participation within the legal services market, exclusionary practices of cultural reproduction persist. Despite the rhetoric of diversity, the regulatory objectives enshrined in s.1(1)(f) LSA 2007 and the promises of wider participation in both higher education and the legal profession, the edge of law is still one marked by disadvantage in terms of socio-economic background and educational opportunities. Outsider students are willing to challenge the logics of the field, but their field position restricts their ability to readily do so (Battilana 2006: 660).

The Case-Studies – Part-Time Law Students and Access to Legal Work Experience

The Part-Time Law Students Project[6] (conducted with Iain McDonald) provides the first in-depth analysis of a cohort of students previously ignored in academic literature and by policy-makers (Francis and McDonald, 2005, 2006 and 2009). In the context of 'outsider' participation in legal education and the profession, the part-time law student cohort offers an important case-study. In particular they reveal ways in which Law Schools are responding to an educationally and socially diverse range of students and, moreover, are an important yardstick against which the profession's claims of equal access can be measured.

The study ran from March 2003 until the beginning of 2005. All providers of part-time law degrees were invited to participate in the study and asked for detailed numbers of those on their programmes. Thirteen institutions agreed to participate and in total 255 students from these institutions responded to our questionnaire (just over 5 per cent of all part-time students registered on face-to-face law degrees in England and Wales). Follow up focus groups were conducted in May and November 2004 in two institutions.[7] Part-time law students are likely to find themselves at the intersection of *multiple disadvantages*. While the average age at entry to the solicitors' roll by direct entry is 28 (Cole 2009: 48), the majority of our sample was over 30, with 38 per cent of respondents aged between 31 and 40, and a further 18 per cent over 41. Part-time students are more likely to be from an ethnic minority background; a third in our sample compared with a quarter of all law graduates in 2003 (Cole 2004: 34). They are also much more likely to have attended a new university and to have had a broken educational background, with over 20 per cent not possessing educational qualifications above that of GCSE. Over 80 per cent of our sample did not have relatives in the profession.

The 'Access to Legal Work Experience Project' (conducted with Hilary Sommerlad) began with a series of questions inserted into the Law Society annual survey in 2007. The Law Society Research Team, following discussion with the

---

6   Nuffield Foundation Grant Reference SGS/00932/G.

7   For full methodology see Francis and McDonald (2009: 222–4).

authors, conducted telephone interviews with a sample of 600 firms, weighted on the basis of 2007 figures for partner count and region, in which they asked key individuals about the incidence of different types of work experience offered by their firm. Funding was subsequently secured from the UK Centre for Legal Education (UKCLE) for a two-year project to explore the role of Legal Work Experience as a mediating factor for access to the legal profession and as a process of identity formation. By work experience I refer both to informally arranged work experience (from as early as Year 10 at secondary school onwards) and Formal Vacation Schemes, typically aimed at undergraduate law students between their second and third year. The Formal Schemes fit centrally within firms' recruitment strategies, in similar ways to the Summer Associate Programmes run by the elite US law firms (Ginsburg and Wolf 2004: 931).

This phase of the project deployed a mixture of survey and qualitative methods with two samples: students and employers. The students were drawn from two institutions: a pre-1992 university and a post-1992 university.[8] In the first year of the project the students were in the second year of their law degree. The response rates were as follows:

Pre-1992 Law School: 135/280 = 48 per cent
Post-1992 Law School: 135/200 = 67.5 per cent

A sample of 50 firms was surveyed (26+ partners located in the principal legal markets served by the participating institutions). Unfortunately, the response rate was very low – only eight firms.[9] The survey was followed up by interviews with an illustrative sample of 16 Graduate Recruitment Managers and Partners based in a range of firms from elite corporate multinationals to 19 partner regional practices. The material provides the basis for the legal profession's expectations in recruitment.

The students were surveyed during the November/December of their second year – before they would have undertaken formal placements. The primary focus therefore was on the students' informally arranged work experience and the extent to which that experience successfully positioned them for the formal vacation schemes. We returned to the students in their third year to conduct follow-up questionnaires to chart their successes during a difficult recruitment cycle and to further explore some of the emerging issues in a focus group. The response rate of the third year students was lower than in the previous year, which may also be a product of the students' bruised experiences in the legal marketplace – 60/280

---

8   This is obviously a crude distinction, but does capture some of the key concerns about the stratification of legal education and Higher Education in general (Webb 1999: 232).

9   Limited resources inhibited intensive follow-up efforts. It seems possible that the financial crisis, which has clearly affected recruitment (see below), may have dampened respondents' enthusiasm for engaging with the research.

(21 per cent) pre-92 and 57/200 (28.5 per cent) post-92. All other demographics were consistent with the previous year of the study. In terms of sex and minority ethnic background, the demographic profile of the student sample broadly mirrors that of the national undergraduate cohort (Cole 2009: 29–32). There are, however, some demographic differences between the student bodies at the two institutions: for instance, the post-1992 institution contains more students from a BME background and more mature students, a finding which corresponds to that of other research on access to Higher Education and disadvantaged groups (Reay, David and Ball 2005).

At the Edge of Legal Education

The stratification of higher education, by which new, post-92, universities are rendered 'inauthentic spaces' (Archer 2007: 641) at the bottom of the 'largely unspoken prestige structure', continues to permeate legal education (Webb 1999: 232). Moreover, it is likely that such stratification will become more pronounced and potentially more visible following the increase in, and greater variability of, the fees charged by universities (Browne 2010, Willets 2010).

Notwithstanding the legal profession's traditional rhetoric of equal access to all (Larson 1977: 136), and more recent assertions by recruiters that they are 'open to everyone', regardless of institution attended (Clifford Chance 2007: 18 and Slaughter and May 2008: 22), it appears that the reputational capital of the institution attended is used as a proxy for the quality of the applicants to be found within them. This is compounded by the profession's increasingly vocal concerns about what it sees as the variable quality of Qualifying Law Degrees (JASB 2002a: 10, Law Society 2010b, CLLS 2010a).

> [We] get ... to diverse groups of students, different ethnic minorities, and the redbrick ones, a complete range ... We have ten. Oxford and Cambridge, Nottingham University ..., then we have Bristol, Durham, LSE, Kings, UCL, Manchester, Birmingham ... . (Interview 12, Female Graduate Recruitment, Large Corporate)

> We do have a number of institutions, 13 this year, that we have gone out to and have a more active, on-campus presence. And they are traditionally, well they are more your redbrick ones, and ones renowned for strong [academics]. (Interview 3, Female Graduate Recruitment, Large Corporate)

A number of firms, including one Magic Circle firm, adopt broader strategies in targeting institutions. Overall, however, the firms were clear that the decision to visit a particular campus was driven by resource considerations. In simple terms they visited institutions where they expected to find the most likely applicants.

Recruiters, interviewed as part of the Work Experience study, felt that students from some institutions were less well prepared for what was required in applications and in engaging with the profession. Thus one interviewee made it clear that 'there are some universities better geared up to giving [the students] the information that's needed' (Interview 6, Female Graduate Recruitment, Magic Circle), and at some institutions 'there is a resonance in the air' about what to do and say (Interview 11, Male Partner, Magic Circle). The institutions visited are those that require entry qualifications which most closely match the firms' own selection criteria. However, for many students, the institution attended may also be a matter of cultural imperatives to live close to home, poor advice from school or family, or simply prior educational and family background constraining their opportunities for A-level success (see further below). Goldthorpe highlights the importance of proximal factors in constraining choices and outcomes for 'non-traditional' students (2003, Hanley 2007).[10] To some extent, firms recognized this. Thus, the recruiter at the Magic Circle firm with the broadest on-campus reach justified their strategy in the following terms: 'there are some very talented people out there at very different institutions, that just don't have the opportunities to get access to the legal profession' (Interview 1, Female Graduate Recruitment, Magic Circle). However, the broad picture is that attendance at a less prestigious university Law School is not simply a marker of 'outsiderdom', but entrenches that status.

Part-time law students are disproportionately located in this sector given that, of the 45 universities offering part-time LLB programmes in England and Wales, 38 of these are post-92 institutions.[11] Part-time legal education was denoted as a second-class option from its inception (Marsh 1983: 89). Moreover, there are distinctive problems which derive from the part-time status of these students. The recruiters, above, noted how important it was for the students to have access to the right information at university. However, part-time law students had little exposure to careers advice. Thus, 42.5 per cent of respondents thought access to Careers Services was 'OK' at best, with 30 per cent thinking 'less than OK'. During one focus group, it became clear that there was a widespread lack of understanding about the two-year recruitment cycle among the larger law firms. The anger about the absence of such support is expressed well by the following student:

> This careers information should be available to us from the very start. Why aren't we being told? ... The University could do a heck of a lot more to say

---

10   Reay, David and Ball caution that 'choosing to go to university is not really a choice at all for the middle class students. It is about staying as they are and making more of themselves, whilst for the working classes, it is about being different people in different places, about who they might be, but also what they might give up' (2005: 161).

11   http://www.sra.org.uk/students/courses/qualifying-law-degree-providers.page [accessed: 24 January 2011].

'look there are these huge walls and barriers, but we're going to give you a stepladder'. (Male, 9B)

Part-time law students are more broadly marginalized in their experience of legal education (Francis and McDonald 2009). They reported significant difficulties in combining work with study, maintaining relationships with family and friends and often struggled with the associated costs of part-time legal education: childcare, transport, books and so on.[12] This may contribute to the high levels of attrition that part-time law students experience (Smith and Saunders 1991: 33–4, Francis and McDonald 2009: 230–1). The complex problems faced by the part-time law students appeared to be reinforced by their perceptions of institutional neglect and indifference. Thus, 55 per cent of the part-time law students studying the 'evening only' route stated that the provision was better for full-time students and 29.3 per cent reported that they did not have a personal tutor. Nearly 40 per cent of 'evening only' students reported that they relied on other students for their most significant source of pastoral care. Students believed that they were denied the 'opportunities that full-timers receive' (Resp. 9) or more explicitly, that full-timers were seen to have 'longer hours and more revision' (Resp. 151) or 'more handouts and support' (Resp. 153), which led many to feel 'like a second class citizen' (Resp. 135) or a 'forgotten population within the university' (Resp. 253). In the words of one focus group participant, 'there just seems to be a bit of an attitude or a mind-set that we're secondary; that we come after the full-time students' (Male, 7A).

Other students are increasingly affected by the challenges of having to maintain their studies alongside paid employment (Curtis and Shani 2002) and the Work Experience study suggests that this will be more likely within the post-92 sector (see further below). The proposal within the Browne Review (Browne 2010: 36), to move towards greater equalization of the fee regime of part-time and full-time students, is to be welcomed. However, it seems unlikely that the range of providers will significantly expand to give part-time law students easier access to institutions with enhanced reputational capital and more established connections with the recruiting profession. Moreover, for those non-traditional participants not put off by the fee repayment package, the need to work may leave these students similarly disadvantaged within legal education, particularly if legal education providers continue to take a traditional and increasingly outdated model of the typical student as their starting point (P. Davies 1999, Francis and McDonald 2009, Maynard 1992).

---

12   Under s41. Higher Education Act 2004, part-time students do not receive the same support, in terms of loans for up-front fees, as received by full-timers. One of the Browne recommendations is to address this disparity (2010: 36).

Professional Identity, Entry Requirements and Social Closure

Abel argues that the entry requirements imposed by the profession had only tenuous connections with the reality of assessing competence to practise (1988: 286, Larson 1977: 52). Access to the legal profession is, today, heavily managed and mediated by teams of HR professionals who stress openness to all, objectivity and psychometrically assessed neutral competencies (Galanter and Roberts 2008: 154, Braithwaite 2010). However, the reality appears to be that the normative entrant, capable of enacting the appropriate professional identity and having followed a recognizable pathway, is one they expect to encounter more readily. As Morley found, employers, generally, tend to hold normative and situated views about what constitutes the ideal graduate and construct career trajectories in a 'linear, traditional way' (2007: 205), and law firms appear to follow this pattern.

Despite each firm's insistence that they were a different firm, with a distinctive culture and, of course, the wider fragmentation within the legal profession, there was convergence about what they were looking for, and indeed who they actually saw. The firms reported being presented with example after example of students who would be 'yet another of our over-achieving trainees' (Interview 6, Female Graduate Recruitment, Magic Circle) and conceded that 'to a certain extent, they are all the same. They're all bright young law graduates' (Interview 8, Female HR, 19 partner regional commercial).[13] Essentially, all the firms (with little variation) looked for excellent 'academics', a well-rounded personality evidenced by a wide range of extracurricular activities, previous legal work experience and an ability to 'fit' within the firm – usually evidenced during their performance on an assessed Formal Vacation Scheme or at interview.

'Academics': From 'Virgil and Homer' to A*

The firms' insistence on strong A-level performance and predicted 2(i) degree classification[14] or better is, of course, objectively neutral and economically rational. They want the brightest possible applicants. Moreover, the firms have relatively little upon which to base their decision when the majority of their intake applies during the second semester of the second year of an undergraduate law degree. In

---

13   Duff, Shiner and Boon (2000) identify the possession of the Graduate Diploma in Law (GDL) as key variable for success. The strengths of GDL applicants were discussed by the firms. However, they appeared to look for a broad mix of law and non-law backgrounds, if not necessarily working to a specific target for each.

14   A 2(i) grade in an individual module represents a mark between 60 and 69 per cent. While, there is some variation in university algorithms used to calculate overall degree classifications, most institutions require either a majority of marks at 2(i) level or an average of marks at 2(i) level or some combination of this in order for a candidate to secure an overall 2(i) classification (QAA 2007). Given this variation, recruiters increasingly ask for a full module breakdown of university marks.

this context, therefore, A-Levels feature very heavily. The firms generally set high standards for A-levels. In responding to the questionnaire, all firms were 'extremely unlikely' to consider grades below BBC, but the interviewees generally spoke in terms of straight-As, or ABB at the outside. In terms of university performance, most firms were looking not just for a predicted 2(i), but a 'comfortable 2(i)', with '75 per cent of marks at 2(i) level'. Firms were also relatively traditional in terms of the subjects covered at A-level – 'academically rigorous subjects, so things like History, Politics, English, Business Studies [and Science and Languages]' (Interview 1, Female Graduate Recruitment, Magic Circle).

Outsider students face difficulties in meeting these requirements. Thus, part-time law students typically come from broken educational backgrounds; just over 20 per cent of the sample possessed qualifications no higher than GCSE. The legal executives discussed in Chapter 4 face similar challenges. Moreover, the problems that part-time law students experience during the course of their degree (Francis and McDonald 2009: 231–3), appear to contribute to a weaker academic performance. Harris and Beinart report that 54 per cent of full-time law students achieved 2(i) degrees compared to just 37 per cent of part-timers. Perhaps unsurprisingly the biggest differences were in the post-92 part-time sector (2005: 333). Of those students participating in the Work Experience study, 33.5 per cent had grades below BBC. More starkly, 62.3 per cent of post-92 students and 7 per cent of pre-1992 students had grades below this, which, admittedly, confirms some of the firms' expectations about traditional markers of achievement to be found at pre-92 institutions. However, there were statistically strong associations between Work Experience at Years 10/11, securing 360+ UCAS points,[15] attending the pre-1992 institution (which was more likely to be a student's first choice) and engaging in multiple forms of work experience and family and friends within the profession. This appears to indicate that 'those who have escaped elimination [from entry to Higher Education] have [not] completely escaped, once and for all, the effects of disadvantaging factors' (Bourdieu and Passeron, *Les étudiants et leurs études* (1964: 13), cited in Robbins (2005: 24)).

Archer argues that lower A-level grades and attendance at less prestigious universities ('bronze ...inauthentic' institutions), should not, however, be seen as a signifier of the 'productive capacities of individuals' (2007: 641). There also appears to be a similar failure to contextualize the generally better educational credentials that those from a more middle-class background have achieved, which are instead simply read as evidence of merit providing a legitimate justification for their selection. As Morley argues, 'socio-economic privilege appears to be transferred onto the production and codification of qualifications and competencies,

---

15 'The UCAS Tariff is the system for allocating points to qualifications used for entry to higher education. It allows students to use a range of different qualifications to help secure a place on an undergraduate course.' http://www.ucas.ac.uk/students/ucas_tariff/ [accessed 17 January 2011]. An A at A-level equals 120 points, a B equals 100 points and so on.

[ensuring that] social gifts are treated as natural gifts' (2007: 205). Similarly Dezaley highlights the ways in which the increasing universality of educational qualifications led the middle class to greater involvement in professional education and training, 'according academic status to qualifications transmitted essentially by the social milieu' (1995: 342 and see also Brown 1990: 77).

All firms in the Work Experience study emphasized that they were open to mitigating circumstances being offered as an explanation for weaker 'academics'. However, the recruiters were hardened to what they described as the 'bog standard ones, grandparents dying during exam periods, parents splitting up, glandular fever etc.' (Interview 10, Female Graduate Recruitment, Large Corporate), and generally expected something catastrophic or 'tragic' to have occurred, because 'in the workplace, lawyers have to work through some of the most horrific personal issues, but they do it because it's client driven' (Interview 10). The firms were also generally aware of the problems of socio-economic disadvantage. However, most felt it was too difficult to make distinctions based, for example, on a challenging secondary educational environment. Therefore, they generally limited their interventions to encouraging children from disadvantaged backgrounds to work hard and aspire to enter the legal profession, through schemes such as those run by Sponsors for Educational Opportunity (SEO), the Black Lawyers Directory (BLD) or to extend the range of Higher Education institutions with which they worked.

Moreover, a number of the firms also undercut their insistence on excellent 'academics' with an acknowledgement that it was often 'personality' or 'commercial awareness' that was just as, or more, important. The reality is that firms wanted both – 'personable geniuses' (Interview 15, Female Partner, Large Corporate), stressing that:

> You can have the best academic record in the world but if you can't hold a conversation in an interview, then that's no good. So, specifically we are looking for communication skills, motivation and drive, work ethic, ability to organise and plan; ability to work in teams, to use one's own initiative, to present coherently and succinctly, passion for law and for this firm, business savvy / commercial awareness and attention to detail. Showing a passion for the firm and making your application stand out are absolutely crucial. (Interview 7, Male Graduate Recruitment, Large Corporate)

Moreover, their conception of a well-rounded personality and the ways in which students could demonstrate this, also underline the difficulties that face many non-traditional students in seeking to negotiate the professional field, which fundamentally does not expect to see 'the likes of [them]' (Bourdieu 1990: 56). It is doable, and the profession does not formally exclude these students, but it is a deeply uncomfortable process.

Extracurricular Activities and the 'Well-Rounded Personality'

It is important to remember the numbers of potential applicants that each firm deals with in the recruitment process. Thus in 2009, there were 13,803 law graduates (excluding many part-time and joint-honours programmes), 9,337 students enrolled on the LPC, and just 5809 traineeships registered – a 7.8 per cent fall on the previous year (Cole 2009: 37). The firms in the study, reported having to deal with '300', '1,500' or '2,000' applications, and, as they review yet another straight-A student on course for a 2(i), struggle to remember that 'these kids have worked hard for their qualifications' (Interview 8, Female HR, 19 partner regional commercial).

Thus, firms look for 'the X factor ... [the applicant] must have, maybe artistic, sporty or whatever, but something that just makes them a little bit more interesting' (Interview 8). It is an indefinable something that marks them out as 'having an effect on things and people' (Interview 6, Female Graduate Recruitment, Magic Circle). This X factor (see Morley 2007) highlights the tension that Collier (2005: 69) identifies in the firms' informal requirements for applicants to demonstrate both conformity and individuality (Smith 2006). Moreover, while the X factor is presented as bias-free, in practice 'outsider' students will experience differential access to the activities which enable students to demonstrate the X factor in a way that is readily recognizable to the firms. Thus one firm reported that they ask about 'hobbies and interests – we are looking for a blend of solo and team activities – sports, moots, clubs' (Interview 9, Male Graduate Recruitment, National Multi-departmental). Another firm suggested that 'it could be anything; sport, JCR, social clubs, politics or whatever, as long as there's a spark shown' adding that a 'burning ambition to *whitewater raft on the Amazon*' could be a legitimate reason why an applicant had not undertaken work experience (emphasis added) (Interview 11, Male Partner, Magic Circle). Other interviewees highlighted societies at university, participation in mooting, client interviewing and so on. Fundamentally, there should be breadth in terms of the experiences cited:

> You're looking for roundedness, as well ..., so say they were a member of the choir, and they bring all their experiences from that one experience. You'd want them to be really coming at it from work experience, extracurricular and academic studies. (Interview 10, Female Graduate Recruitment, Large Corporate)

Firms see university as an ideal opportunity for students to engage in a range of extracurricular activities which would enable them to demonstrate their well-rounded personality. Moreover, Manderson and Turner suggest that, whether through Law Societies, mooting, Inns of Court dining or careers advice, extracurricular contact with the legal profession can 'provide an opportunity for students to practise, develop and get used to exercising all those skills of social capital that Bourdieu tells us will be essential components in their future career' (2006: 653). It helps students develop instinctive understandings of how to successfully pass within the field. Whereas the full-time law degree provides a wide variety of these opportunities, part-time law students are much less likely to be afforded such opportunities. Nearly 66 per cent of the sample had not participated in any extracurricular activities, with women less likely than men to have taken part – 70 per cent of women rather than 58 per cent of men not participating – which perhaps reflects the divisions of labour in the public and private sphere set out in Carole Pateman's 'sexual contract' (1988: 131).

Increasingly, the issues that inhibited part-time law students from engaging in a wide range of recognizable extracurricular activities also face full-time students. However, the extent to which students are confronted with these challenges varies considerably. Thus, in the Work Experience study, more of the post-1992 students sampled were likely to work, and more were likely to do more work. In contrast, 53 per cent of the pre-92 students did not do any paid work during term-time. 50 per cent of the post-92 students worked more than 11 hours per week, and 10 per cent of the entire post-92 sample worked 21–25 hours per week – very close to full-time paid employment. Moreover, as highlighted above, many of these students are also likely to be attending Universities with less regular contacts with the recruiting profession – certainly in the ways outlined by Manderson and Turner (2006).

All firms were open to a story being told about different types of activities:

> it might be that somebody's had a Saturday job, or even in some cases a full-time job, since their teenage years, and those can provide fantastic examples as well ... it doesn't really matter what the example is, it's actually how well you can extract the skills and what you've gained from that example. (Interview 2, Female Graduate Recruitment, Magic Circle)

However, many non-traditional students are unlikely to realize that they can tell such a story, let alone how they can go about doing so. As the same interviewee conceded: 'we've always encouraged, and will continue to do, a strong degree of self-selection in our applications'. Without support, many of those not following an inevitable pathway into the profession will self-select out of the recruitment process in the face of the mixed and nuanced messages from firms. This is also apparent in the case of informal work experience.

The Importance of Informal Work Experience

In the Work Experience study firm survey, 'previous legal work experience' was typically ranked as the second or third most important criteria in the recruiters' assessment of students for participation on the Formal Vacation Schemes. Its significance is underlined by the following students, interviewed as part of a focus group during the Work Experience project:

Something that was fairly consistent between those of us who got that experience and those who didn't, were the ones who had informal work experience. It was very, very important. In every interview, it was one of the first questions they asked. (Female, Pre-92, TC National multi-departmental)

I would say from the informal work experience that it is decisive on the application form ... But when the application form has five slots to note down your work experience ... it looks like you've got a lot on your form ... it's important but more as a box-ticking exercise. (Male, Pre-92, TC, Large Corporate)

Of the 17 students, across the two institutions, who had secured Formal Vacation Schemes by the time of the November of their final year, all had previously undertaken informal work experience in a range of firms.

The firms said that previous informal work experience signals to them that the applicant has thought seriously about their career: 'work experience can demonstrate their commitment to this profession' (Interview 2, Female Graduate Recruitment, Magic Circle). Thus, it is part of the picture of who firms expect to see. They may consider other applicants, but they expect to see a candidate who has undertaken 'at least three forms of work experience – for instance, I'd encourage them to approach a High Street Firm, or maybe volunteer at Law Centre, or ask around friends and family and to see if they can get some experience' (Interview 5, Female Graduate Recruitment, National Multi-departmental). Thus:

Having some kind of experience is certainly an aid ..., to show that you are knowledgeable about the law, you are committed, you have found out about it, you have come to us and you have taken a rational decision ... someone, who has no experience, isn't necessarily in the outer darkness but it doesn't really show that they are sufficiently clued up, sufficiently committed to the role, to the job ... I think the point is that we would expect people to have had, at least, some experience ... So if, I interview someone who hasn't work experience, then on my list of questions is, 'Why not?'. (Interview 11, Male Partner, Magic Circle)

Critically, the answer to the question 'Why not?' is linked to the expectation that students would have friends and family through which they could secure legal work experience. Students in the Work Experience study with connections to the profession through either family or friends were twice as likely to have secured work experience at an early stage (year 10/11) than those without such connections. Overall, students were more likely to have had work experience than not, except those students whose fathers worked in 'routine and semi-routine occupations'.[16] In her analysis of North American Law and Business Schools, Schleef identifies

---

16   The occupational categorization followed that used by the Office for National Statistics (www.ons.gov.uk/about-statistics/classifications/current/ns-sec/cats-and-classes [accessed: 6 February 2011]).

the inevitability, or 'default' nature of participation in professional education among privileged middle-class students (2006: 200). Brown also highlights what he describes as 'parentocracy', where the 'education [or professional opportunities] a child receives ... conform[s] to the wealth and wishes of the parents, rather than the abilities and efforts of pupils' (1990: 65). Informal work experience appears to be part of a pattern of successful professional engagement and educational achievement among the students surveyed. Given that only 8 per cent of the second-year sample had ever been refused informal work experience,[17] the importance of knowing when, how and who to ask is clear:

> By pure chance and luck I knew one of the practice managers through one of the local theatre groups. At the start I did a couple of days at the end of sixth form, just shadowing different people. (Female, Pre-92, TC, National Multi-departmental)

> I started ... looking at ways of getting work experience in sixth form because I had a law teacher who one day, said 'yes, legal work experience, very important'. I didn't know why it was, but I thought it was something productive that I could be doing. ... I had a bit of a boost and fortune at the very foundations of my career. (Male, Pre-92, TC, Large Corporate)

The sample of 600 firms conducted with the support of the Law Society reveals that 76.7 per cent of 26–80 partner firms and nearly 90 per cent of all 81+ partner firms offer both informal and formal (the vacation schemes) work experience. The firms we interviewed recognized that informal work experience took place (even within their own organization), and that this was often arranged through pre-existing contacts enjoyed by the students:

> Let me give you my quote: 'the firm does not offer any schemes outside of the formal process.' Do partners individually do it? Yes they do. Is it frustrating? Yes it is. ... individual partners will do what they want ... . Because they don't read the policy, don't care about the policy, or because there's either a client relationship or a family relationship, and they don't want to say no. ... [And if you're saying no to a potential or current client ...] It could have implications. (Interview 10, Female Graduate Recruitment, Large Corporate)[18]

---

17 In terms of the reasons students gave for not having undertaken it, the most common was 'Didn't know how to arrange it', and the Post-92 students were *twice as likely* as the pre-1992 students to give this as their reason. 'Didn't think of it' and 'Too nervous' to apply were also responses which the post-92 students were more likely to record.

18 See further Braithwaite on other differences between the HR team and the partnership on diversity issues (2010: 45).

The reality though I think is that although some (whether the parents, child or school) work quite hard to actually do it properly, there's a fair degree of 'my daddy knows so and so and he can get you in somewhere.' (Interview 11, Male Partner, Magic Circle)

While recruiters might be concerned if this appeared to be a student's only form of experience, and were prepared to probe students in these circumstances as to how it had been arranged, firms were happy to see these practices as a natural part of the firm's client development strategy. Although they were clear that such contacts would not lead to a training contract or even a place on a Formal Vacation Scheme within their firm, it was seen as entirely natural for students to take advantage of the opportunities with which they were presented:

Again it's down to initiative, why not if you can? (Interview 15, Female Partner, Large Corporate)

I do think that they've got to exploit every contact that they've got ... because they'll have to exploit those networks once they become qualified, when they go out and market themselves ... So the sooner they learn that hard lesson, probably the better. (Interview 8, Female HR, 19 partner, Regional Commercial)[19]

Part-time law students face particular problems in securing the kind of work experience anticipated by the firms. Over half the respondents had never undertaken such activities. The main reasons why most part-time law students had not arranged legal work experience were 'Couldn't afford to volunteer' (30.6 per cent) and 'Didn't have time' (27.8 per cent). The possibility of access to the legal profession offered by flexible part-time programmes is of reduced value to students whose existing responsibilities mean that they are unable to demonstrate their 'commitment' to the profession by volunteering their time to work on a placement:

They have got all these books on mini-pupillages but if you have got a full-time job, how the hell are you going to be able to get that experience, to be able to put it on your CV? ... they are going to look at your CV and say 'they haven't done this, they haven't done that, they haven't done the other'. (Female, 5B)

One of the barriers is when you are working full-time. You are encouraged as a law student to do summer placements at the end of your second year and all that kind of thing. I can't do that. I don't have that opportunity. (Female, 4A)

---

19   See further Hanlon (1999) and Anderson-Gough, Grey and Robson (2006) on the importance of networking in contemporary professional services.

In contrast, 55.4 per cent of the full-time students in the Work Experience study did have some form of legal work experience. It should be noted that there were, once again, striking institutional differences, with only 45.9 per cent of the post-92 students having had work experience compared to 64.6 per cent of the pre-92 students. However, the situation is, in fact, likely to be even worse for the part-time law students given that 52.6 per cent of those who felt that they *had* legal work experience, gained it in typically more tangential ways, for example through work as a security guard in a court or as a social worker appearing as a witness in a case. Morley suggests employers' preferences for graduates whose normativity is signalled in part by their conventional educational trajectory entails discounting or devaluing work experience, obtained for such instrumental reasons (2007: 201). The recruiters did stress that they recognized the challenges involved in securing conventional legal work experience without contacts, and again some were open to a story being told about the absence of work experience. However, such a candidate remains a departure from who they expect to see, which suggests greater difficulties for those non-traditional students whose participation in higher education and then the legal profession appears far from inevitable.

Walking the Walk, Talking the Talk – 'Fitting in' on a Vacation Scheme

Morgan argues that work is a 'major source of identity' (1992: 96) and Muzio, Faulconbridge and Cook (2010) note the importance of training in professional services in reinforcing organizational cultures. The assessed, competitive Formal Vacation Scheme within a law firm is an intense crucible within which the normative professional identity required for comfortable entry into the legal profession is both forged and subjected to scrutiny. While most students, responding to the Work Experience study in their second year, had a good understanding of the role and purpose of the Formal Vacation Scheme, 24.4 per cent still thought that 'General Mentoring/Providing Insight into the profession' formed part of firms' motivations for offering the Formal Schemes. There were statistically significant associations between this lack of understanding and 'no legal work experience' and attendance at a post-92 institution. This is important, given that previous informal work experience appears to be a marker of other engagements with the firms' expectations, in addition to providing a direct opportunity through which entrants may develop their understanding of the profession's requirements.

Work Recruiters run their Formal Vacation Schemes as mini-training contracts. They attempt to provide a realistic (although also attractive)[20] experience – after all, the placement is also used to compete with rival firms for the best students. However, it is also clear that the Formal Vacation Schemes are a central part of the recruitment process and the students are being continually assessed in both

---

20   See Ginsburg and Wolf (2004) on the importance of this dimension for US law firms.

formal and informal ways, with current trainees and partners feeding into the final decision-making process:

> The vacation scheme really does give us the opportunity to see people over an extended period of time and therefore to assess them. (Interview 9, Male Graduate Recruitment, National Multi-departmental)

> If you're exposed to that for a week or two, you get a pretty good snapshot of a person's personality that you wouldn't get in an hour's interview. (Interview 16, Male Partner, Large Corporate)

It is economically rational for the firms to use the placement as an extended interview, an opportunity to 'get a feel for the students', given that, as Ginsburg and Wolf note in the North American context, firms acknowledge that interviews themselves reveal little (2004: 940).

The firms looked for people who will 'fit' comfortably within the firm and engage effectively with clients. They expected students to demonstrate 'enthusiasm', 'common sense' and 'ability to interact', and, despite the diversity of firm types, all echoed the summary provided by this recruiter:

> We're really looking for people who are happy to get involved – the more involved they are, the stronger their report will be. It's about finding people who want to be part of the firm and who show that they want to be part of it, and all its activities, including the extracurricular ones. We're looking for people who get excited about what we do. (Interview 9, Male Graduate Recruitment, National Multi-departmental)

They were also clear that they were assessing the 'real' personality of the candidate and expressed scepticism about the ability of candidates to sustain an inauthentic identity:

> Quite often you see people and within seconds you think 'god, they're good, they could be really good, I think they'll go through'. And then by the end of the day, they were at the bottom of the list, they are 'over your dead body'. They can't be somebody else for the whole day. (Interview 10, Female Graduate Recruitment, Large Corporate)

'Outsider' students, uncertain as to what is expected of them, may struggle to perform '*extra* identity work … entail[ing] a high level of risk' which sees their authenticity challenged (Carbado and Gulati 2000: 1262). Fitting in, however, often requires a difficult and nuanced approach. While one recruiter recalled having to advise a failed applicant that she had to 'think about being a bit more assertive and clear' (Interview 12, Female Gradate Recruitment, Large Corporate), another stressed that rejected candidates would be those who 'tread on their colleagues, don't listen ... it's "god, shut up!"' (Interview 10).

Appearance and image was also important to firms in assessing an applicant's capacity to fit. Thus, one firm asks its trainees to score the applicants

> on their appearance, time-keeping, presentation – and they give good, bad, poor. You know we had a guy on work experience who came in carpet slippers one day! So he won't score very highly on appearance. (Interview 8, Female HR, 19 partner regional commercial)

Other firms' examples of what they looked for in dress included no 'tongue bars', no 'short skirts' and for the men to be 'clean shaven and wear black shoes not brown'. On one level, it could be argued that these expectations are part of the disciplining role of dress (Collier 2005: 60). However, the process of adjustment in dress for which the recruiters look, also confirms the processes of identify transformation that take place within these workplaces. What is being sought is the reflexive habitus described by Sweetman (2003):

> It's self-awareness really ... . They now need to have the mentality of imagining you're now a city lawyer. Imagine what that looks like and feels like. Because that's part of the transition I think from student life ... . It's absolutely critical that there's that perception that you're a safe pair of hands, that you're sensible, that you have a good personality. A lot of it is mental as much as anything. And the hairstyle and shoes is part of that. (Interview 16, Male Partner, Large Corporate)

Thus, appearance and dress is used to assess the extent to which applicants understand what is required of them in a professional environment and possess an intuitive and 'practical mastery ... of their situation' (Robbins 1991: 1).

The firms' expectations are sensible. They need people to look the part of, for example, the 'city lawyer' to reinforce client confidence, and they also need lawyers who are sufficiently attuned to their environment to make the appropriate adjustments. The difficulty is that many non-traditional entrants may be what Sweetman describes as 'reflexivity losers' (2003: 544), whose field position inhibits the development of the required habitual reflexivity. In particular, earlier and frequent exposure to informal periods of work experience will undoubtedly help students in developing this understanding, and clearly it will be easier for those with longer term engagement in professional classes (Schleef 2006: 23–4). Thus, Anderson-Gough, Grey and Robson argue that individuals without access to the sites in which they learn 'how things work' in professional environments face later marginalization in their careers (2006: 239). Students in the Work Experience study reported that many of the prospective applicants had been rehearsing the role of city lawyer for some time:

A few people already sort of knew each other and they were all strutting and joking about the squash ladder and all the rest of it. Very much moulding themselves into the City boy attitude already. (Male, pre-92, TC, Large Corporate)

A lot of people felt they were lawyers, and some of the other vac schemers, if we went for lunch, did strut around London and speak to bar staff and waitresses as if they were qualified lawyers. (Male, pre-92, TC, Magic Circle)

For students without the benefit of this prior conditioning, the discomfort was reinforced, not necessarily by the firms directly, but from other 'vac schemers' and trainees. This was often on class and gendered bases, with loaded questions about 'What do your parents do?' (Male, Pre-92, TC, Magic Circle), or speeches to the firm from current trainees which expressed, 'thanks to the Grad Recruitment team for this year's intake – the girls are looking really hot' (Male, pre-92, TC, Large Corporate).

As indicated above, the Vacation Scheme was designed as a realistic introduction to all aspects of the firm, including the immersive time commitments demanded of lawyers, particularly in the corporate sector (Seron and Ferris 1995). Thus, with echoes of the ways in which Sommerlad and Sanderson (1998) demonstrate that the neutral partnership criterion of 'commitment' was gendered as male, the notion of 'enthusiasm' also carries particular behavioural expectations in terms of the commitment shown to the firm as a total institution. Goffman defines 'a total institution ... as a place of residence and work where a large number of like-situated individuals cut off from the wider society for an appreciable period of time together lead an enclosed formally administered round of life' (1968: 11), and there is evidence that large law firms are structured along similar lines with on-site gyms, laundrettes and restaurants sold as part of the lifestyle (Collier 2005: 67). The firms were clear that applicants should demonstrate enthusiasm

by not running out the door at 5.30!...We don't expect people to be here for a long time, but not to leave when something's not finished or not to tell anyone why it's not finished and leave. (Interview 12, Female Graduate Recruitment, Large Corporate)

While the firms acknowledged that caring commitments could prevent a student from being able to seize all of these opportunities, it was also clear that such a student deviated from their normative expectations. 47.2 per cent of Part-time Law Students had caring commitments,[21] and for many of them the work/life image presented by the profession, was not a welcoming one:

---

21 While there is no direct comparison with the full-time cohort, just 3 per cent of these students had children, and 66 per cent lived either on their own or with friends. Obviously these students may have other caring responsibilities, but the profile is very different.

> I would be very worried. If I'm going up for a job interview with a 21 or 22 year old, that 22 year old is probably single, hasn't got children or isn't even thinking about children for a long time. So they might potentially see me as someone who's about to have children or run off if my children are sick. (Female, 5B)

> You hear that when you get a job at a law firm, you'd be expected to do 70 hours a week .... I've been there and I've done that and I'm not interested in doing it anymore. You know, is there a job out there for me to do a normal [week's work]? You know because I have a life outside the job now. [All: murmurs of agreement] ... . (Female, 4A)

The law firm's image as a 'total institution' demanding immersive enthusiasm from its entrants, also appears to be an uncomfortable one for many outsider students and appears to contribute to the patterns of cultural reproduction which reinforce social closure.

Play   Socializing is another prominent aspect of firm culture, to which students were exposed during the vacation scheme. Whenever the issue was raised either by the interviewers or interviewees, it provoked knowing laughs. Younger (mainly HR) professionals 'love it', and older partners wryly acknowledged the nature of the events, which meant that 'my days of social activities are long gone!' Sommerlad notes the 'laddish, drinky culture' within the corporate sector (2002: 225). Firms were aware of these concerns (particularly in terms of the exclusionary nature of alcohol-focused activities for those from particular religious and cultural backgrounds) and had introduced other activities, including pro-bono sessions, quizzes or bowling. There were also reports of 'incidents' at various firms, for example:

> someone who got so sloshed they turned up in reception at 7 o'clock for next morning, having not being able to find their way back to their accommodation ... He reeked of alcohol and to this day we don't know what happened to him [that night]. (Interview 6, Female Graduate Recruitment, Magic Circle)

Firms are, no doubt, keen to limit their exposure to such incidents, not least because of the spectre of 'Roll on Friday'.[22]

The recruiters saw the socializing as a means by which the applicants could talk to trainees about the reality of their work in an uninhibited setting. However, it was also seen as an exposure to the realities of the professional setting and formed an assessment of how readily the applicants understood what was expected of them, often by the very trainees with whom they were bonding:

---

22   A website dedicated to showing the reality of life in corporate legal practice. Its discussion boards are not for the faint-hearted (http://www.rollonfriday.com [accessed: 23 January 2011]).

Sometimes they don't realize that when they're out socially with the trainees, the trainees will have a view on people who are about to possibly enter the firm, and people who are just so arrogant or perhaps lacking in judgment, trainees will pass comment back, to say 'I think you should know this.' ... They are keen to make sure that those coming in, the next generation, are the right people. (Interview 10, Female Graduate Recruitment, Large Corporate)

Such surveillance of the informal space challenges those who do not instinctively understand the rules of the game (Fowler 1997: 18). However, the firms emphasize that those applicants 'who've been too heavy on the alcohol and not behaved professionally ... [were not] appreciating they're actually employed by us when they're with us' (Interview 1, Female Graduate Recruitment, Magic Circle). As two interviewees made clear, behaving professionally during the social activities is part of the transition in which the applicants are engaged in and being assessed upon:

If you go out for a drinks evening with clients, it's not the same as going for a drinks evening with your mates, necessarily. ... And it's that understanding. Where do you draw the line? Because you could be quite chummy with clients, to the point where you would go for a bottle of wine but there are boundaries there, and it's that understanding of where the boundaries are. (Interview 16, Male Partner, Large Corporate)

So social nights during the work placement should mean that you can still turn up at 9.30 the next morning and stay all day and still be able to do what's asked of you, even if you are, slightly under the weather, and that's fine. But it is all about learning ..., you can still drink the same amount, but actually the next morning you've got to make sure you're still in the office, on time. (Interview 15, Female Partner, Large Corporate)

And performing at the same level. (Interview 16, Male Partner, Large Corporate).

What is striking from this exchange is not only the suggestion that alcohol continues to lubricate the interpersonal relationships on both vacation schemes and later in practice, but that entrants to the profession need to understand the unspoken boundaries about how to behave in these settings.

In order to be able to convincingly demonstrate the appropriate professional identity to successfully secure entry to the legal profession, it is important to understand the rules of the game, given that 'our job is a bit of a game ... if you can play the game, that's actually quite good' (Interview 16, Male Partner, Large Corporate). Again, there is a strong, and justifiable, economic rationality to all of this. As this partner suggests, this is a key feature of practice and the firms need to recruit people who can successfully operate in this environment. Yet in terms of the reinforcement of exclusionary barriers within the profession, the problem remains that many non-traditional students lack the appropriate habitus – the durable ways of 'speaking, walking and thereby of feeling and thinking' required to enact the field (Bourdieu 1990: 70). They are products of their backgrounds and histories (Bourdieu 1990: 56). As this partner acknowledged: 'it's not ingrained, there's not an automatic mechanism for a lot of people' (Interview 16). Whether by virtue of social, family and educational history, or through the lack of university exposure to the sorts of activities that Manderson and Turner identify as being critical to developing this understanding (2006: 653), the range of possibilities for these students at the edge of legal education and the profession are severely constrained.

The Successful Students – Making it from the Edge?

The data discussed above highlights the ways in which entry to the legal profession is deeply uncomfortable for many non-traditional students. The legal profession has made great strides, generally, in addressing these and related diversity issues (Braithwaite 2010), not least in their engagements with school-age children from more deprived socio-economic backgrounds (http://www.pathwaystolaw.org/ [accessed: 24 January 2011]). However, problems remain.

Nineteen of the part-time law student respondents had secured training contracts. However, all of them, with one exception, already worked within a law firm in an administrative/fee-earning capacity, typically as legal secretaries. Moreover, these individuals (mainly younger[23] women) appear to have received support and encouragement to progress, which militates against the broader challenges they face in part-time legal education (Francis and McDonald 2009). One respondent said:

> [My law firm is] brilliant. They pay my fees and give me time off. I am just about able to take it on, manage everything, my work and have a social life. (Female, 6B)

Some 35.7 per cent of those working in the legal sector, compared to 16.7 per cent of the others, said their employer was 'very supportive'. By way of contrast, those who worked in the non-legal sector had far less support from their employers:

> Employers expect me to focus more on the job, don't make any time available and even try to put more work on in the evening. (Male, Resp. 242)

Part-time law students with personal experience of the legal profession have a much greater likelihood of achieving access to the profession.[24]

---

23   Some 56.7 per cent of those in legal employment were aged between 22 and 30.

24   It would, however, be interesting to trace the career trajectories of those moving from a subordinate role in legal practice (Francis 2006: 488 and, generally, Chapter 4).

The success rate of students surveyed in their third year, as part of the Work Experience study, was even bleaker, although it should be noted that this survey was undertaken during a particularly challenging recruitment cycle (McPartland 2009a). Just four students had securing training contracts, and only 17 in total had secured formal vacation schemes. A total of 15 of the 17 were based in the pre-92 institution, all had previous informal work experience, and all but two had tariff points above 320 points (usually ABB) and most were well in excess of this.

The data from the two studies suggests that the profession is more comfortable to access by either those that it literally recognizes (as in the case of the successful part-time law students employed by law firms) or those who have followed a recognizable pathway. Evidence from other studies also suggests that recruitment processes favour the familiar and the similar (Falkenberg 1990, Chen and Bargh 1997) and, in the case of the elite corporate firms, of the 'class cachet conferred by Oxbridge and elite public schools' (Galanter and Roberts 2008: 168). US law firms also appear to demonstrate a preference for 'insiders' (Carbado and Gulati 2003) and candidates who 'fit' (Ginsburg and Wolf 2004: 917). Critically, however, the recognizable pathway is one that, for some students, seems to have been established from a very early stage, a product of their background and history:

> It's something that almost pervasive ... a lot of those whose parents and families are from the South East and all work in the City, and there's all these assumptions about 'of course, I am going to work in the City'. (Male, Pre-92, TC, Large Corporate)

Certainly, there will always be exceptions and non-traditional students are able to demonstrate agency in challenging the properties of the field (Bourdieu and Wacquant 1992: 133). Some firms recognize a 'heroic narrative'. For example:

> [bringing] up a young child, doing a law degree in parallel, and presumably earning some money somewhere, there's a story in there ... it's challenging people to come up with something like that, ... you're not automatically discounted. (Interview 16, Male Partner, Large Corporate)

While the firms' openness to a story being told is to be welcomed (and disseminated to students), such a narrative leaves little space for someone whose family and educational background was not necessarily so severe but still provided little by way of insight, encouragement and support for entry into the legal profession. Moreover, those without such support may additionally fail to realize there is scope to tell such a story.

Moreover, the exercise of agency required to work against habitus and engage in a successful mobility project can be an uncomfortable one, generating tensions and dissonance with pre-existing family and workplace identities (Costello 2005, Sommerlad 2007). The Part-time Law Students provide stark evidence of the lack of support given by those who perceive themselves as being left behind, whether they are employers, co-workers, or even family and friends:

> [My] Manager thinks I'm not dedicated to my present job and has got the hump – making me work Christmas Day this year. (Female, Resp. 162)

> [S]ome think it's pointless, beyond me. (Male, Resp. 129)

> [They] couldn't imagine a character such as myself practising law. (Male, Resp. 70)[25]

Such tensions operate not only as another barrier to be overcome, but as further confirmation of their 'outsider' status in legal education. One (non-white) corporate lawyer discussed the experiences his black colleague had recounted:

> The peer pressure he faced on achieving academic success and joining what is perceived to be the establishment was very strong. He was saying he was physically intimated by the people who were saying to him 'you're not of us' and 'you've betrayed us'. (Interview 13, Lawyer, Magic Circle)

Another dimension of the difficulties faced by these 'heroes' is illustrated by the discomfort experienced by black lawyers unable to access the old-boy networks that sustain their white colleagues' careers (Granfield and Koenig 2003: 515).

Conclusion

Despite the opportunities for emergent models of legal professionalism (and new actors within such models) generated by a field in flux, the case-studies discussed above confirm the continued prevalence of exclusionary structures within the legal profession (Cook, Faulconbridge and Muzio 2010). It is not the case that the collective profession exerts formal exclusionary strategies, such as bars on women or non-UK nationals (Abel 1988, Witz 1992), rather that the embedded practices of the field render it uncomfortable for 'outsiders'. Fundamentally, the importance of ostensibly neutral requirements imposed by the dominant recruiting sector of the profession, and the significance of a normative identity or pathway, continue to reinforce existing patterns of closure. Thus, for example, while formally the 37.6 per cent of the part-time law student sample aged between 31 and 40 have every opportunity to secure access to the profession, the reality is that among the elite recruiters, 'most of them are young people. We don't have an age bar, but

---

25   Reay, David and Ball note similar concerns from older entrants to Higher Education (2005: 265).

90 per cent of the trainees we recruit are going to be university undergraduates' (Interview 6, Female Graduate Recruitment, Magic Circle).

Many of the factors which constrain the choices for non-traditional entrants to the legal profession result from prior social conditions, over which the legal profession has manifestly little direct control – 'to my mind, by the time we're recruiting people, it's too late' (Interview 6). However, these social conditions generate the habitus which constrains non-traditional applicants in their ability to engage in professional advancement or challenge institutional logics (Lounsbury 2002: 255). At the same time, these conditions may also shape the practices and behaviours of the recruiting profession, in that it appears to find it difficult to recognize merit presented in any form other than those on the normative pathway or who can demonstrate the heroic narrative. While the most elite actors would possess the ability to challenge such logics, given that 'existing institutional arrangements' appear to favour these firms,[26] they lack the willingness or incentive to do so (Battilana 2006: 661–2).

The relationship between collective professions and educational institutions was central to Larson's analysis (1977: 44–5). Despite the fracturing (and fractious nature (Cownie and Cocks 2009)) of this relationship within England and Wales, there remains a connection. First, the data suggests that both legal education and the profession continue to insist on an immersive, somewhat open-ended commitment, which works against non-traditional students (see particularly the case of part-time law students). Secondly, there is a significant (but variable) graduate capital sought among prospective entrants. Given the relatively narrow nature of the normative pathway to entry into the legal profession, it may be a cause for concern that hollow (or insufficiently nuanced) promises of participation in the profession are being held out by legal education providers. This issue seems, again, particularly acute in the case of part-time law students (Francis and McDonald 2009).

The importance of 'graduateness' and of not deviating from a recognizable pathway appears even more important in the context of legal executives discussed in the next chapter. The Legal Services Board, driven by its statutory objective to 'encourage an independent, strong, diverse and effective legal profession', has taken a lead on diversity issues generally and may disrupt some of these structuring conditions. Further change may follow the 'root and branch' review of legal education planned by the regulators (BSB 2010). The Chair of the LSB, David Edmonds, is also clear that social mobility should feature in the review (2010b: 20). However, the experience of women in the legal profession (Sommerlad and Sanderson 1998, Webley and Duff 2007) suggests that the legacy of exclusion is long, and that models of normative lawyers remain powerful forces of cultural reproduction. Even if the legal profession may no longer collectively control the production of the producers (Abel 2003), patterns of social closure remain

---

26 See, generally, Galanter and Roberts (2008) on the success story of the English Magic Circle.

(Sommerlad et al. 2010). The next chapter explores the professional project of legal executives and their attempt to disrupt the structuring properties of the field from the edge of law.

Chapter 4

Legal Executives: Chasing Shadows or the Third Branch of the Profession?

I was told 'Oh, yes, you'll be more marketable' [as a legal executive] ... but ... my experience was that as a legal executive you're not really valued, you're not really recognized by your own colleagues or indeed the public.

(Female Legal Executive, Large Corporate)

Introduction

Legal executives are fully qualified lawyers and hold positions of responsibility in every sphere of legal practice within England and Wales, from large corporate law firms to local authorities. They have made enormous strides in their professional project since 1998 and have pushed at the open doors of governments keen to drive down costs and open up competition within the legal and related services market.[1] Despite this, legal executives remain marginalized at the edge of law. The diversity of their background, the constraining properties of a traditional legal professionalism and the use of their employers'/superordinate profession's knowledge base confirms their subordinate jurisdictional position and inhibits the capacity for the development of divergent models of legal professionalism.

This chapter draws on archive material which dates from the establishment of ILEX in 1963 and its predecessor, the Solicitors' Managing Clerks Association, in 1892.[2] Interviews with leaders of ILEX and the Law Society were conducted during a critical period in both professions' history during the passage of the Access to Justice Act 1999 (which granted increased rights to legal executives). Further data is drawn from a workplace study within which 25 legal executives were interviewed about their experiences in practice (Francis 2006) and augmented by policy documents, legislative material and the trade press identified between 2005 and 2010. After clarifying the role and work of legal executives,

---

1   Mark Bishop, ILEX president 2008–09, reported that the Government viewed ILEX as 'Teacher's Pet' in the context of the diversity and fair access to the professions agenda (Bishop 2009b). See also Burleigh (2010) on the ILEX route fitting clearly within the Access to the Professions agenda.

2   This material is referenced as fully as possible. However the archives are not fully catalogued and, when studied by the author, were housed in a travelling trunk in the basement of ILEX's headquarters at Kempston Manor.

this chapter considers the subordination of ILEX to the Law Society, before it explores the reality of the workplace experience for legal executives and highlights the gendered disadvantages faced by the growing numbers of women legal executives. The workplace study, in particular, draws out the ways in which both formal strategies of occupational closure and systems of cultural reproduction constrain the professional project of legal executives. It argues that, in a similar way to the experience of women in other professions (Manley 1995, Fowler and Wilson 2004), the gendered disadvantage experienced by women legal executives has negative consequences not only for those individuals, but potentially for the profession at large. Moreover, the ideological and practical constructions of the legal executive pathway as a deviant professional qualification suggest the broader relevance of the patterns of closure identified in Chapter 3.

The Role, Work and Field Position of Legal Executives

ILEX oversees the education and regulation of legal executives and represents their interests.[3] Only Fellows of ILEX are entitled to call themselves legal executives, with Fellowship attained after two sets of examinations and a qualifying period of employment (http://www.ilex.org.uk/about_legal_executives. aspx [accessed: 25 January 2011]). However, in reality many non-qualified fee-earners within solicitors' firms (such as paralegals) describe themselves as legal executives, thereby devaluing the achievement and professional status of legal executives. This has been a recurrent problem for ILEX, and is compounded by similar inexactitude from the Benson Commission (1979: 407, para. 31.7) and Lord Irvine (Hansard 1999: 1178) among others. Although legal executives failed in their drive to secure statutory protection for the title 'legal executive',[4] they are fully qualified lawyers employed within law firms, government departments and in private companies. Although they have specialized early in their careers, in most practice settings their work is similar to solicitors' and they possess a level of autonomy comparable with other employed lawyers. Within private practice they work as fee-earners, with their work charged to clients and thus contribute directly to the income of the firm. The qualification can also be used as a pathway to become a solicitor, with 147 legal executives transferring in 2008 (Cole 2009: 48). Although the title is not legally protected, it brings rights that are unavailable

---

3   Following s.30 Legal Services Act 2007 and the requirement for Approved Regulators to separate their regulatory and representative functions, ILEX has established its independent regulation arm – ILEX Professional Standards (IPS) (http://www.ilex.org. uk/ips/ips_home.aspx [accessed 25 January 2011]).

4   The Government, for example, declined to support Lord Kingsland's amendment to the Access to Justice Act 1999 which attempted to make misuse of the title 'legal executive' a criminal offence (Hansard 1999: 1175–8).

to un-qualified paralegals,[5] and will be the basis for further rights if ILEX is successful in its applications to the LSB to award rights to conduct probate and litigation (ILEX 2010a). The Legal Service Act 2007 permits legal executives (as lawyers) to take up positions as partners within a Legal Disciplinary Practice.[6] At the same time legal executives continue to attempt to extend their rights of audience and other professional responsibilities (Burleigh 2010) and to develop their recognition within other jurisdictions (ILEX 2003: 7).

However, 'the only truly important and uniform criterion for distinguishing professions from other occupations is the fact of autonomy – a position of legitimate control over work' (Freidson 1970: 82). Legal executives have been inhibited in reaching this goal due to, amongst other reasons, their employed status. They have no exclusive claim to expert knowledge (Abbott 1988). They cannot become partners in a solicitors' practice[7] unless that firm reconstitutes itself as a Legal Disciplinary Practice, and although their professional body has some disciplinary functions, the regulation of their professional conduct is primarily through the disciplinary mechanisms of their solicitor employers – the Law Society's Solicitors' Disciplinary Tribunal under s.43 Solicitors Act 1974.[8] It is their employer, their solicitor principal, who is ultimately responsible for the conduct of their files.[9]

It is, nevertheless, important to distinguish legal executives from paralegals. The paralegal primarily assists the fee-earning work of the lawyers – a role which combines legal research and writing with secretarial tasks (Pierce 1995: 31–3). Many of the paralegals that Pierce interviewed had no formal training and had developed their role from an administrative one. It was seen by attorneys as a 'dead-end job' (1995: 35). Similarly, the less prevalent paralegal within the UK, notwithstanding the aspirations of the Institute of Paralegals (http://www.theiop. org/ [accessed: 25 January 2011]), is typically an LLB or Legal Practice Course graduate seeking to gain legal work experience to enhance their employability

---

5   The Courts and Legal Services Act 1990 enables Fellows to be awarded extended rights of audience (approved by S.I.1077/98). S.40 Access to Justice Act 1999 awards Fellows the right to conduct litigation.

6   S.9A(2)(a) Administration of Justice Act 1985 (as amended by the Schedule 16, Part 2, paragraph 82 Legal Services Act 2007). Nick Hanning from Poole firm RWPS was the first legal executive to be appointed a partner following the changes in the law (McPartland 2009c).

7   Rule 12 of the Solicitors Code of Conduct (as amended 31 March 2009) (http:// www.sra.org.uk/solicitors/code-of-conduct/rule12.page [accessed: 25 January 2011].

8   See, for example, Anthony David Saunders *Application 9009/2004* (http://www. lawgazette.co.uk/gazette-in-practice/law-reports/solicitors-disciplinary-tribunal-21 [accessed: 25 January 2011]).

9   'Acting with the authority of his principal', determined the validity of advice given by a legal executive in *Barclays Bank Plc v. Coleman and another* [2000] 1 All ER 385.

as a trainee solicitor.[10] Legal executives are in contrast, fully qualified lawyers, engaged in fee-earning work.

The LSA 2007 may disrupt the jurisdictional settlements of solicitors and legal executives (Abbott 1988: 91). However, I argue in this chapter that the field location of legal executives reduces the ability of the profession to successfully disrupt prevailing institutional logics (Lounsbury 2002: 255). Professionalism remains a powerful disciplining discourse (Fournier 1999), particularly for marginal actors. Legal executives are likely to remain a semi-profession (Etzioni 1969).

Institutional Subordination to Approved Regulator

A strong professional association is central to the successful professionalization of an occupation (Larson 1977: 69–77, Lounsbury 2002: 256). In focusing upon the relationships between ILEX and the Law Society, it is possible to identify the underlying limitations of the collective project of legal executives. Crucially, throughout the history of ILEX, up to and including the present day, the relationships between the two organizations have been characterized by the Law Society's power over ILEX and its predecessor, the Solicitors' Managing Clerks' Association (SMCA), despite little evidence of formal links between the two bodies. The employer/employee relationship in the workplace underscores this hegemony.

The First 100 Years: 'with the support and co-operation of the Law Society'[11]

The original impetus for the creation of the SMCA in 1892 came from the managing clerks themselves, concerned about the possible loss of their rights of audience (Murray 1950: 112). Yet the powerful influence of the Law Society dominated the early history of the organization. Although there were few formal links between the SMCA and the Law Society, broader more nebulous influences, or 'mimetic processes' (Dimaggio and Powell 1991) illustrate the true power relationship between the two organizations. The early managing clerks looked to the Law Society for a model of a professional association, and furthermore the needs of the Law Society (and their employers) were central to the strategies of the SMCA. The power of the Law Society and of the solicitors' profession at the time was clear

---

10   ILEX has attempted to broaden its appeal, by inviting such graduates to join automatically as Graduate Members (http://www.ilex.org.uk/membership/membership_grades_and_fees.aspx [accessed: 25 January 2011]). They would need only to complete five years of Qualifying Employment, before they were entitled to qualify as Fellows. This confirms the increasingly (and for ILEX dangerously) blurred lines between solicitors and legal executives and illustrates the key point that the cognitive base of legal executives is (part of) the knowledge base of the superordinate profession (see further below).

11   (http://www.ilex.org.uk/about_ilex.aspx [accessed: 25 January 2011]).

(Sugarman 1996: 98), and was a defining feature of the organizing logics of the field. As the aspirant occupational group, ILEX was poorly positioned to articulate any model of professional advancement that differed from that legitimated by the elite professional group (Greenwood, Suddaby and Hinings 2002).

The initial rallying letter urged managing clerks to meet because it would be 'in our own interests and those of our principals' (cited in Murray 1950: 112). In setting out the objects of the SMCA, the chair of the first meeting of the putative SMCA was clear that, although:

> ... it was necessary that they should have a recognised Association to protect and advance their interests, but it must not be supposed in suggesting this that they were to descend to the level of (cries of Oh!) trade unionism. (cited in Murray 1950: 112)

As Larson notes, subordinate (technician) groups generally are disinclined to associate and act together as trade unions because of a continued deference to professional ideology (1977: 234). Managing clerks were no different. Such a deferential focus does not lend itself to an aggressive campaign of growth and recruitment, and by 1897, the membership had only reached 300 and continued to rise only very slowly throughout the first half of the twentieth century (Johnstone and Hopson 1967: 404). Although the Law Society and the SMCA had established an education scheme in the late 1940s, both associations soon acknowledged that this scheme was attracting insufficient numbers of managing clerks. Consequently, throughout the 1950s, discussions were held in an effort to establish a replacement qualification scheme for managing clerks.

It is important to note that it was the Law Society that initially invited proposals to deal with the shortage of managing clerks – a staff recruitment problem for solicitors. Following the SMCA's response, the Law Society indicated that it was not prepared to examine the issue further. The SMCA council, however, decided to press on and formulate their own revised proposals, 'designed to secure for managing clerks recognition of their calling as a profession' (SMCA 1956: 132). Although there was, therefore, a certain amount of shared interest in the negotiations leading to the creation of ILEX in 1963, the differing objectives between the SMCA and the Law Society were clear. The Law Society's principal objective behind the creation of ILEX was simply 'to encourage recruitment to the unadmitted ranks of the profession' (Law Society's Gazette 1962a: 26). However, SMCA leaders saw the new qualification scheme as a key strategy in their drive for professionalization. Just as Larson identified market and status gain as inseparable and mutually supportive (1977: 66), the SMCA was clear about the dual aims it wanted the new scheme to achieve: 'the Law Society (as representing solicitor employers) accepting Managing Clerks as professional men with a definite status and assuming that those [managing clerks] participating in the scheme would receive some tangible benefits' (SMCA 1956: 132).

While the SMCA was clearly trying to build up the professional status of legal executives, this was only an incidental objective of the Law Society. The fundamental sticking point was 'tangible benefits'. The Law Society was reluctant to concede any more than the minimum necessary to meet its members' staffing requirements. Conversely, the SMCA were, in the words of the then President, seeking to establish 'a separate profession for Managing Clerks ... carrying with it guaranteed benefits' (Elliot 1956).

The scheme that eventually established ILEX bears striking similarity to the first proposals of the Law Society which the SMCA had earlier rejected for failing to guarantee 'tangible benefits'. The plans provided that there should be three grades, Student, Associate and Fellow, with those qualifying for the higher grades entitled to use some sort of distinguishing letters. The focus was on the educational qualifications to be obtained rather than material benefits to be attached to the existing managing clerks. Indeed, one of those existing managing clerks writes in a letter to the *Solicitors' Journal*:

> To offer them [managing clerks] an official status of a lower grade practitioner in the subject or subjects in which for years they have been working as competently as solicitors is not to be reckoned a compliment ... the qualification of legal executive will provide no more real or better stepping stone to advancement in the profession than now exists (Solicitors Journal 1962: 132).

The powerful influence of the Law Society dictated the terms upon which ILEX was instituted. The Law Society provided £2,000[12] to support the establishment of ILEX and its Council resolved that 'the Solicitors' Managing Clerks Association be invited to take immediate action to inaugurate the Institute' (Law Society 1961). This is not the story of a professionalizing occupation which made a jurisdictional attack on an established profession. ILEX was founded with the full support and agreement of the Law Society in full control of its professional jurisdiction. ILEX merely represents the subordinate profession within the task area (Abbott 1988: 69).

The SMCA's acquiescence in the Law Society's dominance of their affairs is underlined by the arrangements for Law Society representation within the constitution of ILEX. The SMCA had been advised that it was unlawful for a Law Society/ILEX committee to be established with power to control alterations to the ILEX constitution. However, the SMCA still offered (or felt compelled to offer) the Law Society significant influence over its activities. It was minuted in the Council of the Law Society that:

> the Solicitors' Managing Clerks' Association were, however, proposing that a joint advisory Committee could be set up with the power to veto any proposal for

---

12   Worth approximately £33,880 in 2011 (http://www.thisismoney.co.uk/historic-inflation-calculator [accessed: 24 January 2011].

change in the memorandum and Articles of the Institute and with the intention that no such change would be made in matters affecting the scheme of education and training and qualification of Legal Executives without the approval of the Advisory Committee. (Law Society 1962)

Furthermore, although a proposal that the Law Society should be represented on the Disciplinary Committee of ILEX had been vetoed by the Board of Trade, 'the Association were prepared to provide in their By-laws for a member of the Council of the Law Society to sit with the Disciplinary Committee as an Assessor'. Unsurprisingly, the Law Society council approved these arrangements. As one solicitor, cited by Johnstone and Hopson put it: 'We do not want responsibility for the Institute, only enough of a veto that they do not do anything foolish' (1967: 407). ILEX failed in its application to the Privy Council for a Royal Charter in the 1960s and 1970s, primarily because it was unable to demonstrate that it was an independent, autonomous and self-regulating profession.

ILEX was anxious to reassure the Law Society that its members did not represent a threat to solicitors. Instead, they presented themselves as 'a profession within a profession' (ILEX 1976a). Thus the proposals that ILEX put forward to the Benson Commission (established to examine the structure and organization of the legal profession) were not, therefore, particularly radical. They were limited to advocating that the status of Fellows should be recognized through higher salaries and greater rights of audience and that solicitors should be required to assist (financially) in the education of members of ILEX (Benson 1979: 410, para. 31.20). Furthermore, not only were they not radical but ILEX appeared, in advocating closer association with decisions taken on professional matters within the Law Society, to see the connections with the Law Society as an integral part of its development.

Although ILEX explicitly denied the spectre of independent practice by its membership (ILEX/The Law Society 1979), it was a possibility that continued to concern the Law Society. The Benson Commission echoed the traditional concerns of the legal profession in limiting the extent to which status would be accorded to legal executives. Although the Benson Commission recognized that many of ILEX's proposals were desirable in practice (for example, that more people should be encouraged to pursue their education up to the level of Fellowship), it did not recommend that there should be compulsion on solicitors to give day release or pay either increased salaries or profit share (1979: 412–13). Furthermore, the Commission refused to accept a number of ILEX's proposals, for example in respect of extended rights of audience (1979: 415, para. 31.38).

The starting point of the Benson Commission's approach to ILEX's claims for enhanced status was that 'there are effectively only two branches of the profession, solicitors and barristers ... [and] we consider that the creation of additional branches of the profession would be contrary to the public interest' (1979: 411, para. 31.22).[13] Once more the subordination of ILEX to the Law Society, and of legal executives to their employing solicitors, was fundamental to the Benson Commission's failure to accept ILEX's claims for professional status:

> all its members are subject to supervision by solicitors, who are answerable to their own governing body in respect of the conduct of all work done in their firms including work performed by legal executives. The Institute cannot, therefore operate in the same way as an independent professional body and exercise the same degree of exclusive control over its members. (1979: 415, para. 31.39)

The Law Society's influence was clearly pervasive and powerful throughout the Benson Commission's deliberations regarding legal executives. The Commission effectively left any change that was to occur to the discretion of the Law Society and recommended that 'the onus for developing these arrangements rests mainly with the Law Society' (1979: 416, para. 31.42). Indeed, one of its central recommendations was that there should be the development of formal arrangements between the Law Society and ILEX – perhaps to clarify and confirm the informal power that the Commission had already identified.

Following the disappointments of the Benson Commission, ILEX refocused its energies on strengthening 'paraprofessional competence' (Johnstone and Flood 1982: 187) rather than continuing the project of raising its professional status. The 1980s and 1990s saw ILEX build its commercial strength with the purchase of new premises in Bedford and the establishment of companies to deliver and administer courses for non-qualified staff in legal practice. Yet during the 1990s there were considerable difficulties within ILEX as council members and salaried staff attempted to reconcile the tension between commercial and professional pressures.

Institutional Logics and the Impact of the Legal Services Act (1998–2010)

The 'mimetic processes' which saw ILEX/SMCA aspire towards the Law Society as the model of a professional association continued to influence the organization's strategies in the years between 1998 and 2010. In reasserting its stagnated professional project, ILEX broadly pursued 'prospector' strategies and sought to identify new opportunities for its membership and attempt to recruit new members. However, it combined this strategy with many of the value systems of the older professions, which are more commonly identified with a 'conserver' approach. Under such an approach, an association relies on exclusive claims of knowledge

---

13   It is interesting to contrast this approach with that first articulated by the Office of Fair Trading and later enacted by the Legal Services Act 2007. In this post-professional environment (Kritzer 1999), the profession's claims are no longer accepted by state and it is the free market not the professionally controlled market for professional services which the state believes to be in the public interest (DCA 2005).

and reiterates the boundaries between the profession, other professionals and the laity (Laffin 1998: 219). In the past, ILEX's professional project failed because it did not possess the necessary specific resource elements (Larson 1977: 208). However, the Legal Services Act 2007 generates new rights for legal executives with the possibilities of more to come.

Lounsbury argues that 'status claims such as those related to professionalization projects will be more likely to occur during periods of institutional transformation, than during periods characterized by relative stability when logics are firmly established' (2002: 258). However, arguably, such claims are easier in the context of the emergent occupational groups in the financial services markets that Lounsbury discusses, than in the case of legal executives. As long-standing subordinate actors within the field, legal executives may find it harder to resist the structuring properties of the institutional logics. In contrast to Abbott's assertion that changes in workplace status predate those recognized in the public and legal arenas (1988: 66–8), legal executives have found their status claims more readily accepted in the formal legal and policy arenas than they have in the workplace (Wilensky 1964: 142).

The reassertion of a prospecting strategy to enhance the professional standing of the occupation was initially a passively grateful acceptance of the Labour Government's agenda during the passage of the Access to Justice Act 1999:

> At the moment it seems as though all the prizes are dropping onto our feet. ... So yeah, we may well be the puppet of the Labour Government at the moment, but whilst it's suiting us to travel along and it's opening up opportunities for our members, then fine. (Interview 4, ILEX Council Member)

> We have been fortunate that we have a government that wants to extend rights beyond solicitors. So that's worked very well really. ... But we haven't made strategic choices. (Interview 9, ILEX Council Member)

In the light of this, and particularly led by the appointment of a new Secretary General from the Law Society in late summer 1998 (The Lawyer 1998a), ILEX did start to articulate a much clearer prospecting strategy.

It is instructive, however, to look to the data from 1999 to highlight the ways in which the shadow of the Law Society cast itself over ILEX's discussions over whether to prospect for further rights or to conserve their current, unexpected, gains. The 'historically constructed repertoire of "legitimate" or "permissible" professional responses' (Nelson and Trubek 1992a: 22), dictate that the debate is framed in terms of the Law Society's responses. Even those on the ILEX council who advocated a prospecting strategy struggled to articulate how far that prospecting strategy should and could be pushed against the continuing power of the Law Society. These two council members highlight the divergent views within the ILEX council:

> Well it's difficult really. I think what we've got to do is not push ahead too quickly ... but make sure that somehow the Law Society is aware of what we are doing. But if they see that we are [taking business from solicitors] I think that would be a real problem. (Interview 9, ILEX Council Member)

> I'm of the camp that says that we should get along and do all this because it's a good opportunity. But some people have said 'oh no, we can't ... it's too dangerous'. Someone piped up and said 'Well, the Institute didn't do very much for its members 15 years ago when the Licensed Conveyancers came along ... when that side of the monopoly was broken...'. And this council member was saying that we don't want to miss the boat again. Now we've been offered these opportunities on a plate, of breaking the Law Society's monopoly, we don't want to miss that opportunity again. (Interview 6, ILEX Council Member)

This focus on the Law Society constrained the institutional entrepreneurship of ILEX. While ILEX could respond to opportunities created by state interventions, its capacity to articulate field-changing reformulations of its members' professional identity and work was limited. Similarly Liaschenko and Peter identify the unrelenting focus of nursing upon an idealized conception of an autonomous (medical) profession, as a key constraint upon its aspirations (2004: 491). Crucially, it prevents an organization like ILEX from engaging in the jurisdictional boundary bridging that Greenwood and Suddaby (2006: 37) suggest is critical in enabling institutional entrepreneurship. The subordinate profession of legal executives remains marginalized at the edge of law.

In contrast, the Law Society council members and policy officers were far less preoccupied with ILEX, either as a threat or even as an issue to take into account. The power imbalance in the relationship between the two professional bodies is well illustrated by the following statement:

> I think it's quite amusing actually because we have this joint committee with ILEX ... which is very much ILEX saying 'What are you up to?', wanting information on what the Law Society is doing. They all seem to come across as being terribly chippy. And I don't think they need to be ... They are still fighting for status and position and authority ... They seem almost paranoid. (Interview N, Law Society Council Member)

The differences between the two councils in terms of their strategic concerns were acute, and powerfully confirm the Law Society's domination of ILEX. The ILEX council members' concerns were: 'How will the Law Society affect the possibility of further rights for our membership?' and so on. In sharp contrast, the Law Society interviewees were more wide-ranging, speaking in broader terms about issues such as fragmentation, globalization and the growth of information technology.

This is not to suggest that Law Society council members are better able to think strategically than ILEX council members. The activities of the superordinate (employer) profession are the *necessary* focus of an auxiliary (employee) profession locked into the cognitive base of its lead profession (and employers). However the inability to develop a strategic focus makes it very difficult for them ever to launch a professional project independently of their lead profession (particularly one that has enjoyed century-long hegemonic control). This is the central contradiction behind the professionalization efforts of an auxiliary (employee) profession under *traditional* professionalism. Throughout the history of the Institute, ILEX council members explicitly and implicitly deferred to the Law Society. Its position was a potential constraint on their aspirations, while paradoxically also served as the yardstick against which to measure their own professionalization.

Yet the changes brought in by the Legal Services Act and the establishment of the Legal Services Board as the over-arching regulator with the power to approve Front-line Regulators, is a major disturbance to the institutional logics of the field (Lounsbury 2002: 255) which shape patterns of behaviour between solicitors and legal executives. There was a growing sense of optimism and of bullishness among Council members in the late 1990s:

> I tell people now that ILEX is the third arm of the law like the AA.[14] We're a force to be reckoned with ... . We are an independent body. We've got to work with the other agencies and that includes the Law Society and the Bar. We're there in our own right as it were. (Interview 7, ILEX, Council Member)

However, this has been surpassed by the increasingly legitimate claims that ILEX is able to make today. ILEX makes public assertions about the equality of its standing as the third branch of the legal profession. As Diane Burleigh made clear during the passage of the Legal Services Bill, 'the world is changing and recognizing that we shouldn't be governed by labels but rather by whoever is the right person for the job' (cited by Robins 2007). ILEX's formal status as an Approved Regulator is a powerful marker of this standing in ways which go beyond even the most optimistic council members in 1999 and which the Benson Commission of the 1970s or indeed the warm words of the Labour Government of the late 1990s (Irvine 1998) were unable to bestow.

Perhaps the most profound change comes from the strategic shift in focus that ILEX has had to make from the Law Society to the LSB as a result of the changes brought in by the Legal Services Act 2007. Thus, in applying for rights to grant its members Approved Probate Practitioner status or rights to conduct litigation in the civil courts, the ILEX Professional Standard Board must frame its application against the regulatory objectives contained within the LSA and set out

---

14   The AA is a large breakdown recovery provider within the UK. In the 1990s it ran an advertising campaign in which it described itself as the 'Fourth Emergency Service'. This is what the interviewee is referring to here.

its qualification processes in detail, in much the same as either the SRA or the Bar Standards Board are required to do in their applications to the Board (http://www. legalservicesboard.org.uk/what_we_do/regulation/applications.htm [accessed: 25 January 2011]). This is a more profound change than simply replacing the Privy Council with the LSB as the audience to which the claims of professionalism need to be made.

The LSB's statutory position as the super-regulator of legal services and, the related re-constitution of the regulatory authorities of the Law Society and the Bar Council, is a significant disruption of established patterns of behaviour. The LSB, particularly at the outset, has required focussed engagement from all approved regulators. In this environment, the long-established Joint Consultative Committee of the Law Society and ILEX no longer exists. The professional bodies work together on shared concerns, but there appears to be real evidence of a loosening of the institutional ties that have shaped the relationship between the Law Society and ILEX.

Thus, the new rights to conduct litigation and to carry out probate as a reserved activity represent an attempt by ILEX to secure rights for its members under the statutory regulatory regime overseen by the LSB, which will increase the practical worth of the ILEX qualification. While the legal executive qualification remains unprotected in law,[15] the fact that, if successful, only Fellows of ILEX (and graduate Members in some circumstances) may hold rights to conduct probate, civil litigation, hold rights of audience, assume judicial office and become partners in Legal Disciplinary Practices, adds real weight to the qualification. This potentially enhances its attractiveness as a career in its own right[16] and, in effect, enables ILEX to engage in closure strategies of accreditation in ways not previously possible (Witz 1992).

However, problems remain in terms of the institutional recognition of ILEX that indicate the resilience of the structural limitations of its professional project. The Government consistently resisted calls for an offence of the misuse of the title 'legal executive' to be created under the Legal Services Act 2007 and, later in the same year, within the Criminal Justice and Immigration Bill. As the Conservative spokesperson on Justice, David Burrowes, noted, 'legal executives constitute the only established professional group that does not have statutory protection' (Hansard 2007: 781–2). In reviewing an otherwise successful year as President, Mark Bishop recalled that 'it would almost have been a perfect meeting if Lord Neuberger [appointed to report on the legal professions' approach on diversity] had actually heard of ILEX' (Bishop 2009b).

---

15   In contrast to the protection of the criminal law afforded to solicitors under ss.20-1 Solicitors Act 1974.

16   This may also address some of the sustained issues of membership apathy and antipathy, which saw some members describe active ILEX members as a 'weird social group' (Francis 2002: 13, 2006: 489), and saw precisely zero members respond to the IPS consultation on the new Code of Conduct (LSB 2010c).

Moreover, some legal journalists appear less than well informed about the status and qualifications of legal executives. Clare Dyer, writing in the *Guardian* about the Government's plans to expand the pool from which judicial applicants are drawn, described legal executives as 'non-lawyers' and Frances Gibb in *The Times* dealt with the story along similar lines (The Legal Executive 2005a, 2005b). It is also interesting to note that ILEX's consultation on its new Code of Conduct, sent out widely to all stakeholders and members, received only five responses. The only ones external to ILEX as an organization, being the CPS and Office of the Legal Services Ombudsman (ILEX/IPS 2010: 49), which was a matter of some concern to the Legal Services Board when they approved the revisions to the Code of Conduct (LSB 2010c: 2–4). ILEX/IPS is still not on the radar of most stakeholders in the legal and related services landscape.

Despite the considerable gains that ILEX has made, there remain doubts as to the extent to which ILEX is on a par with the Law Society and the Bar, any more than you would dial '999' to reach the AA. The continued prominence of the historic support and beneficence of the Law Society on ILEX's website, 'ILEX was founded in 1892 and became a company limited by guarantee in 1963 with the support and co-operation of the Law Society' (http://www.ilex.org.uk/about_ilex. aspx [accessed: 25 January 2011]), also curiously undercuts what is otherwise rhetoric of contemporary parity.

While the leadership of ILEX appears alive to the changing professional landscape, there is recognition that the new opportunities within alternative business structures will remain premised upon traditional understandings about the costs of legal executives as against the more expensive solicitors, with a broader range of expertise:

> I would hate to say our members would undertake a specific role and do it more cheaply than solicitors. They might, but it depends on how that firm is structured. ... But there will be a requirement for a specialist lawyer also, and the legal executive would fit that job very well; elsewhere there might be the requirement for greater breadth which would fit the solicitor model. (Burleigh cited in Robins 2007)

At a time when there is considerable uncertainty about law firm structures amidst the new regulatory environment – the cheaper, specialist legal executive may bring them dangerously into competition with other models of commoditized legal services including out-sourcing and off-shore (Susskind 2008). Equally, the suggestion that legal executives will be well placed to take up job opportunities within new entrants to the legal services market (Burleigh cited in Robins 2007), such as the Co-op (Rothwell 2010a), appears to make a virtue of the employed experience of the subordinate position. It may bring rewards for individual legal executives, but does little to enhance the status claims of the profession.

Overall, however, the picture is of an organization emerging from the shadows, with a renewed sense of purpose – in particular with a re-emphasis of the long-thwarted professional project. A certain loosening of the institutional logics which have consistently limited the aspirations of the profession of legal executives is also apparent. The strategic focus of ILEX is now far less oriented towards the Law Society,[17] but towards the influential new actor, the LSB. This perhaps adds credence to the argument that the solicitors' profession is losing control of its exclusive jurisdiction. However, individual legal executives continue to experience subordination and disadvantage within firms and other settings. The status and market claims that legal executives are able to make in the workplace seems, in contrast to Abbott's analysis, to trail the success that has occurred within the legal and public arenas (1988: 66–8).

Disadvantage in the Workplace: Knowledge, Employment and the Gendered Dimensions of the Second-class Status of Legal Executives

Legal executives have made huge strides in their professional project since the mid 1990s. The formal rights which have been secured include the possibility of partnership within a Legal Disciplinary Practice, the opportunity to embark on the first rung of the judicial ladder as a district judge,[18] and rights of audience in family and civil courts. In practice, the legal executives interviewed reported that they undertook comparable work to solicitors, headed up departments, are treated as quasi partners, supervise trainee solicitors and generally operate with what they described as 90 per cent autonomy, with little control exercised by supervising solicitors.

However, those with the most complete autonomy worked in the smallest firms with the least hierarchical structures. In contrast, the autonomy of women in large, more bureaucratic organizations experienced considerably more limitations on their professional autonomy (Pringle 1989: 90). This reinforces the importance of context in fully understanding the position of women lawyers (Sommerlad 2003: 217). Within the largest firms, a relatively small number of equity partners are supported by vast numbers of assistant solicitors and legal executives (Cole 2009: 6). Sommerlad notes that these 'frequently transient proletarian roles' are likely to be filled by women (2002: 217) and legal executives *generally* are more likely to be women. Moreover, those legal executives interviewed, working in larger firms, who did wield something closer to full autonomy were men.[19] Women

---

17   Although, interestingly, the LSB was prepared to tolerate the under-developed regulatory structure of IPS as low risk, as ILEX members were still subject to regulatory oversight by the SRA (LSB: 2010c : 2).

18   On his appointment as the first Legal Executive Judge (and perhaps slightly caught up in the moment), Ian Ashley Smith declared 'there is now no limit to what Legal Executives can achieve within the legal profession' (ILEX 2010b).

19   'Davies Arnold Cooper takes back legal executive to head up department' (The Lawyer 2000a: 3). This legal executive was a man.

legal executives reported 'people checking up on you' and 'being overseen more' within the bureaucratic structures of the largest commercial firms.

The problems facing legal executives are also acknowledged by the ILEX President (2008–09); 'the biggest barrier that many members will have to overcome comes from within the profession itself' (Bishop 2009a). Johnstone and Flood explicitly identify the position of managing clerks/legal executives within the post-war class structure of the United Kingdom (1982: 187). The historical reluctance of solicitors to accept the repeated claims for enhanced professional status and a somewhat patronizing attitude towards ILEX from the outset are clear in the following letter:

> I hope I do not sound patronising when I say that managing clerks have their limitations. In nothing is this more evident than in their choice of a new name for themselves. It is deplorable enough that they should thus invite ridicule; it is much worse that you, Sir, in all apparent solemnity should endorse this assumption of a title as meaningless as it is unnecessary, and as silly as status symbols generally are (Solicitors Journal 1963: 590, see also Law Society's Gazette 1962: 165).

The employer/employee relationship in the workplace saw the Benson Commission leave it to solicitors to recognize the ILEX qualification on a voluntary and individual basis (Benson, 1979: 412, para. 31.31). Without any national-level recognition, ILEX found it very difficult to carve out a clearly defined niche for the Fellows of the Institute, and although Fellowship has gained increasing value, the qualification is still largely dependent upon solicitors, as employers, to give it status by making it a prerequisite to employment. This has never happened on a large scale (Sidaway and Punt 1997: 15, 31). ILEX has never been able to exert market control for the services of its members. While the new rights may increase the importance of the qualification, this will still depend on either firms (whether traditional law, LDP or ABS) judging that the efficiencies of the firm are best secured by employing a legal executive with such additional rights. If such an entity can more profitably deliver its services without the need for such legal executives, then the qualification will remain under-valued.

Second-class Status and Gendered Disadvantage

Lively suggests that the subordinate status of paralegals is reinforced by their 'invisibility or interruptability' (2000: 46). Similarly the 'othering' of legal executives is a key way in which the hierarchies of legal practice are maintained. These perceptions of being 'second class' and of being looked down upon by colleagues were reinforced by the more tangible disparities of pay between solicitors and legal executives and the types of work allocated to legal executives, with the more interesting files reserved for solicitors. The reinforcement of their second class status was also seen when 'snubbed' by 'sneering barristers', and other professionals (The Legal Executive 1999). The disparity in status is also reflected in the Costs Guideline for Summary Assessment which indicates that only solicitors (and not legal executives with equivalent post-qualification experience) are justified in making a Grade A costs claim (HMCS 2010). It is also interesting to note that legal executives are not included in the 'Qualified Lawyers Transfer Scheme Regulations, only barristers (http://www.sra.org.uk/solicitors/qlts/recognised-jurisdictions.page [accessed: 25 January 2011). Fellows have to apply for exemptions from the academic stage of the qualification process for solicitors, in similar ways to graduates without a fully exempting Qualifying Law Degree (SRA 2010: 17).

Acute disadvantage in the workplace is felt by all legal executives. However women legal executives appear to experience a distinct form of disadvantage, which entrenches their position at the edge of law. This marginal position in the field restricts their ability to challenge the institutional logics which confirm their continuing subordination (Battilana 2006: 660). Just under half of the women interviewed acknowledged that there were problems for all women within legal practice (Hagan and Kay 1995, Thornton 1996). They had observed problems faced by women lawyers seeking promotion and could reflect upon personal experience of a profession still heavily imbued with a masculine ethos (Sommerlad 2002). However, women legal executives appear to experience a distinct disadvantage within legal practice. This intersectional disadvantage differs from that experienced by women solicitors and is different to that experienced by male legal executives (Crenshaw 1989/1993). In addition to the failure of the public and the wider legal profession to recognize their qualification and expertise, they reported being seen as secretaries, typically a role within legal practice gendered as female.

> If you say you're a legal executive, they always mishear you and think you're a legal secretary, especially if you're a female. And I'm not one of those women's libber type people, but they do, they instantly think you're a secretary. If they hear the word legal executive,… they think it's just a posh name for legal secretary, especially being a woman. If I answer the phone at the office, perhaps pick up a call [of a male colleague], they instantly assume you're a secretary because you picked up someone else's call. … If [male trainee legal executive] picked up the phone, they'd probably think he was my boss [laughs]… (Female, medium-sized regional firm).

> People are still thinking it's less than a solicitor. I think that people don't really know who legal executives are really. I'm talking about the man in the street. If I say 'I'm a legal executive,' people say 'oh, you're a secretary' (Female, local authority).

Lower levels of pay than their male colleagues were also a concern for the women legal executives (Sidaway and Punt 1997: 26).

All the women interviewed readily identified the legal executive route as a 'woman's profession', both descriptively and normatively in terms of it being more 'natural', 'suitable' or acceptable' for a woman than a man. This was attributed partly to the pathway allowing legal executives to 'earn while they learn' ('easiest route… if you have a family') and that the pool of entrants is largely from the ranks of administrative or secretarial staff, which are still mainly women within legal practice.

While it was natural for women to be legal executives, the women interviewed felt it was unnatural for men to be legal executives.[20] Older males, who had been managing clerks, were seen as 'dinosaurs' and 'not really belonging to the way in which legal practice operates' today. It was seen as more natural for younger men to get out quick; to qualify as solicitors. Otherwise they ran the risk of being seen as 'failed solicitors' or marked out as having 'a chip on their shoulder' because *just* being a legal executive wasn't 'sufficiently' prestigious or high-earning for them.

> I think the females are a lot more [pause], women are a lot more *acceptable* [as legal executives] (Female, Large Corporate).

> Why [are there] more women legal executives? Because it's not high enough status for a man! [laughs].… I think that a man would automatically, if he was going into law, he wouldn't think of being a legal executive unless he'd come around to it by some other route (Female, medium-sized regional firm).

Although women are seen as natural legal executives, they suffer a double marginalization, reinforcing their atypical status as deviant lawyers. In contrast, men are seen as deviant/un-natural legal executives, yet may experience less direct subordination either by colleagues or clients. They are assumed to be 'lawyers' much more readily – on the first glance, they look like lawyers. For both, however, and intersecting with the other issues below, these deficiencies in their 'lawyer DNA', add to the construction of an unstable and 'edgy' professional identity.

Class and the 'Deviancy' of the ILEX Qualification

The instability of the professional identity held by legal executives is an important dimension of the conceptualization of the legal executive route as a deviant pathway to law. A key aspect of this is that nearly all of the legal executives interviewed described how they 'fell into the profession'. They lacked the commitment and aspiration that could form a stable basis for a professional identity (Friedson 1992: 223, and see also Chapter 3). In contrast, the four men and women who *planned* a career as a legal executive were more settled in their professional identity. Of those only one, a woman, had planned her career from the outset as a school

---

20   Williams notes similar issues for male nurses (1989: 105).

leaver. These were the few who experienced a reduced dissonance between their 'experienced' and 'expected' professional identity (Costello 2005).

Nearly 80 per cent of legal executives interviewed came from lower socio-economic backgrounds or generally complicated personal situations. The men and women described coming to the profession from variously, 'difficult circumstances at the time', of 'having left school at 16 and drifted into awful jobs, got married and had a baby at 20 [when] childcare was poor', of 'having left college and did silly things as you do when you're nineteen' … and then being 'on my own with a child', putting it down to 'parents' financial situation' or not 'being that great academically. law … wasn't an option because solicitors were middle class kids who'd gone to university and I was from a working class crap comprehensive school' or 'couldn't face the thought of having to quit work and have no money coming in and study at university.' Arguably, this background contributes to the perception of legal executives as being part of a less prestigious profession, given the continuing importance of a variable graduate capital (Webb 1999: 232), and, more broadly the role of class in limiting access to the legal profession (Nicolson 2005: 213).

While generally proud of what they had achieved and forthright about their capacity to do the job as well as, if not better than, any solicitor, most were adamant that if circumstances had been better, then they would have preferred to have qualified as a solicitor, believing 'it's not a natural course to be a legal executive'. Of these, all but three were women. Thus, going to university and studying for the professional qualification was not an expectation when they were the age of a typical entrant to university, in contrast to the 'inevitability' experienced by those from middle class backgrounds (Schleef 2006, Reay, David and Ball 2005). Or conversely, their circumstances now, meant that further study to qualify as a solicitor was impractical. One of the underlying reasons why the legal executives would have preferred to have qualified as a solicitor, or in fact intended to qualify, was the constant undermining of their professional identity. Over half of those interviewed about their workplace experiences were clear that they would not advise anyone to do the ILEX route. These tensions about their professional identity and their concern about their role in practice, leads to guilt about 'being embarrassed because I'm *only* a legal executive' and about wishing to qualify as a solicitor because it would detract from their achievements as a legal executive. This anxiety over their professional identity leads many of them to be extremely hesitant about describing themselves as a legal executive.

> You just go under the proviso of solicitor…. And then you feel like a fraud. But at the same time, if you've done it year in and year out, you can pass yourself off as a solicitor. … You're not saying 'I'm a solicitor,' you're just not saying that you're not (Female, large regional firm).

> I never put my Fellowship certificate up on the wall… I wasn't holding out that I was a solicitor. I just never put them up… They assume that you are [a

solicitor]... the one thing I say when I am questioned about it is 'Yeah, well...'
(Male, medium-sized regional firm).

Arguably the continuing subordination of legal executives and the profound status anxiety felt by all interviewed is reinforced by the hybrid nature of the legal executive qualification. As a qualification in its own right and as a stage on the route to the dominant profession, Fellowship can be seen as a deviant or unnatural professional status. It confirms that the holder lacks the 'cultural capital' allowing access to the solicitors' profession via the 'normal' route, of university, law school and then training contract. Thus despite performing equivalent work to solicitors, the continued emphasis of their second class status through this sense of deviancy undermines the stability of their professional identity. As Marriott, Sexton and Staley noted of social workers, a 'major correlate of position satisfaction was the professional respect received from other disciplines and not the specific tasks performed' (1994). Legal executives are denied this respect.

In the 2000s, the Labour Government stressed the importance of increased participation in higher education as means of raising the skills base within the workforce, in part to make the UK more competitive in a global marketplace (BIS 2009). There was also an emphasis upon widening participation within Universities in order to ensure that access to the professions is as fair as possible (Milburn 2009: 80–97). In this context, the non-graduate nature of ILEX's membership can be read as a further marker of the ways in which legal executives lack the necessary social and cultural capital required to successfully negotiate the field of legal practice. Although the trade press highlights the flexibility of the qualification, more pejoratively they also re-emphasize that it is the 'easy' or non-graduate route to the profession (McPartland 2009b). ILEX has given increasing prominence to its Graduate Diploma entry route in an effort to attract those who possess Qualifying Law Degree and/or Legal Practice Course qualifications.[21] In part, this is a strategic response to attract frustrated law graduates unable to secure a training contract (Chellel 2009, McPartland 2009a). However, it can also be seen as an attempt to raise the status of the occupation, by increasing its appeal to those who possess a longer-term commitment to the legal profession.

However, ILEX's wooing of these potential new recruits undermines the status and achievements of its traditional membership and belies the politically expedient virtue it seeks to make about the 'diverse' and 'open' route to the profession it offers (Burleigh 2010, ILEX 2009). Thus, Graduate Members (but not other Members) will receive the same rights as Fellows if the Probate application is successful (ILEX 2010a: 4). Moreover, its attraction of these entrants through various post-92 providers (for example, Thames Valley University), ignores the pronounced stratification of the HE sector, particular within Law (Webb 1999: 232) in which such 'bronze' institutions are rendered 'inauthentic' learning spaces (Archer 2007:

---

21   http://www.ilex.org.uk/study/student_information/exemptions/qualifying_law_degree.aspx [accessed: 25 January 2011].

641, Morley 2007). These associations combine to confirm the marginality or deviancy of the pathway. The 'normal' or 'acceptable' route to the legal profession is not through the ILEX pathway, but through attendance at a well-recognised university law school, before securing a training contract with a leading law firm (see Chapter 3).

> I don't think the qualification is valued very much, quite frankly, in the real world. [You] get a certificate, but you don't actually know what you're getting until you get into the real market, and you see what's what... I mean I've had people say to me, you know, 'I want to be a legal executive', ... and in my experience, I have to be honest with you, I've said to them...don't. Just get your degree. If you want to be a solicitor...get your degree and go down that route instead (Female legal executive, Large Corporate).

The employment relationship between solicitors and legal executives has been crucial to the subordinate status that legal executives have faced. Thus, while increasingly numbers of solicitors are employed (Cole 2009: 15) and now legal executives have the possibility of becoming partners within Legal Disciplinary Practices, historically, at least all legal executives were employed all of the time. However, a far more profound (and continuing) limitation upon the professional project of legal executives has been the use of their employer's knowledge base. Legal executives do not possess a distinctive knowledge base from which to base a professional status independent of their superordinate profession – and historic employers (Abbott 1988: 178).

Expert Knowledge and Subordinate Jurisdiction

Nursing operates within the field of medicine, under the ultimate control of doctors. However, from its earliest origins, nursing has attempted to create its own distinct discourse and has indeed secured 'relative autonomy' in its work, certainly when compared to legal executives. Witz notes that one of the reasons why nursing became a female professional project (together with the widespread exclusion of women from medicine), was the establishment of a discourse of nursing, based upon essentially 'feminine qualities' (1992: 142). However, the discourse of nursing developed, incorporating theoretical ideas about patient care and treatment, distinct from the knowledge base nurses share with doctors. It is argued, drawing on the importance that both Larson (1977: 40–9) and Abbott (1988: 40–56) place on a standardized cognitive base, that this has allowed nurses considerable autonomy over aspects, at least, of their work.

In contrast, legal executives have not been able to develop their own distinct knowledge base. ILEX members (indeed non-members, such as paralegals, outdoor clerks and so on) work exclusively within the discourse of law constructed by their employers. Thus for example, the 'academic stages of the ILEX lawyer qualification' permits some exemptions from the academic stage of the Law

Society's qualification process (SRA 2010a: 17). The ILEX modules on the Law of Contract or Crime are, of course, the Foundations of Legal Knowledge required of entrants to the solicitors' profession (JASB 2002b). Moreover, in their claims for increased professional status, legal executives interviewed asserted that they were doing the 'work of a solicitor'.

Abbott argues that 'knowledge is the currency of competition' for work jurisdictions (1988: 98). An attacking move by an occupation would demonstrate that some task within a jurisdiction (for example within legal services) was more applicable to the attackers' cognitive base (Abbott 1988: 98). Legal executives have never claimed that they possess a distinctly different cognitive base that is better suited to the resolution of a task within the legal services jurisdiction. Indeed such a claim cannot be made, because legal executives share the cognitive base of solicitors, or rather are permitted to use aspects of the solicitors' cognitive base. In this, they have a similar relationship to that between the professional engineering institutions and their auxiliary, technician occupational group (Laffin 1990). Legal executives were employed by solicitors and so used the solicitor's professional knowledge base. It is their use of their employers' knowledge base that is at the root of legal executives' failure to develop their own shared distinct knowledge base or a strong collective identity.[22]

While legal executives collectively hold a subordinate jurisdiction which is reinforced by the use of the knowledge base of solicitors, the marginal position also restricts the capacity of individual legal executives to challenge accepted practices within their firm or wider professional environment. Sweetman (2003) argues that we are increasingly required to act as 'reflexive entrepreneurs', thinking in creative and strategic ways to advance our position in society. He suggests that 'reflexivity losers are those whose location in the field prevents them from developing this habitual reflexivity' (2006: 544). Similarly Battilana argues that an individual's position within an organization will be critical in shaping their ability to challenge structural forces (2006: 660). Legal executives have typically qualified into a firm, often from a subordinate position of being either a very young trainee legal executive or a female member of the administrative staff. They were often encouraged and supported within that firm and thus, their professional horizons are likely to be shaped and constrained within relatively narrow points of reference. As one council member noted,

> I am thankful for education and paying for food through Legal Executives. But on the other hand I wouldn't have been able to have done that if of course the persons hadn't been around, i.e. solicitors of the Law Society, to give me employment (Interview 8, ILEX Council Member).

---

22   Licensed Conveyancers arguably share a cognitive base with solicitors, and yet could be seen to have enjoyed greater dependence. However, they benefitted from state intervention under the Administration of Justice Act 1985 (see further discussion Francis 2002: 19). Legal executives' recent successes have similarly arisen from state intervention.

A further dimension of the pathway to qualification are the limited opportunities that legal executives have had to engage in the sorts of activities that Anderson-Gough, Grey and Robson (2006) suggest are needed to develop the identity of the 'networked professional.' These activities have always been important for professional advancement within law and often were constructed in ways which made it more difficult for women to demonstrate their abilities (Sommerlad and Sanderson 1998). Anderson-Gough, Grey and Robson suggest that many of these activities begin at University or professional school and continue informally through various training and career stages (2006: 243). Moreover, they argue that those unable to learn the 'tacit' lessons of 'how things work' tend to be marginal within firms and have the least promising career prospects (2006: 239). Legal executives, who are already challenged by being looked down upon within the profession, may struggle to secure access to the sites which enable this networked identity to develop.

Conclusion

The strides that legal executives have made throughout their history, but particularly in the years since 1998, have been remarkable. By many measures, ILEX can claim parity with the Law Society and the Bar Council in ways which would not have been countenanced in years past. The institution appears stronger and more self-assured than at any time in its history. It is important too not to ignore the success stories of individual legal executives, both the headline grabbing ones heading up departments in large City firms, but also the quieter stories of women and men who have transcended their class and educational backgrounds.

Yet, it is these successes that cut to the core of the unstable professional identity. These people have secured significant personal achievements against the odds. However, their pride is tinged with the disappointment that despite their qualification as a legal professional they face being patronized, badly paid and frequently forgotten. Women legal executives in particular experience an uncomfortable identity dissonance in their professional lives. As the profession becomes not only gendered as one for women (part-time route, 'secretaries' and so on), but numerically feminised as well (http://www.ilex.org.uk/about_ilex/ equality_and_diversity/membership_diversity.aspx [accessed: 25 January 2011), this may have further implications for the profession as it seeks to enhance its public visibility (Davies 1995: 162).

At the heart of the marginal position of legal executives at the edge of law are the contradictory and paradoxical claims deriving from the use of the knowledge base of solicitors. On one level it confirms that they hold only a subordinate professional jurisdiction. On another level their claims that the work they actually do is the same as that of solicitors has to be taken seriously.

I have complete conduct of my files. ... That's because I've been at it for so long. ... There's very little I don't know about family law. You will see with other legal executives that is usually the case. ... I can't see that there is any difference because solicitors in this firm and legal executives get paid on performance. ... That they are solicitors is no badge of quality (Female legal executive, small rural firm).

The claims that legal executives make about the level at which they operate, and the type of work that they perform, echo ILEX's claims of parity as one of three recognised routes to becoming a qualified lawyer.

ILEX has consistently adopted 'dual closure strategies'; it has challenged the demarcation of the dominant group (solicitors) and invoked exclusionary and closure strategies of its own to support its professional project (Witz 1992: 48). For years ILEX has struggled to place Fellowship in a position where it can be seen as worthwhile qualification in its own right. All too often in the past, potential recruits have not seen any point in qualifying as a Fellow or, if they have done, have seen it only as a stepping stone to qualification as a solicitor. In trying to differentiate its members from the growing number of un-accredited paralegals in the legal services marketplace, ILEX has pushed for greater professional rights in an attempt to assert workplace equivalence with their employers and to make the ILEX qualification a meaningful one (Abbott 1988: 67). Similarly the professionalizing occupation of homeopaths made claims in relation to their work as measured against the dominant profession of medicine, while at the same time, had to try and distinguish themselves from medicine in order to make a distinctive claim of expertise (Fournier 1999: 289–90). Legal executives face similar problems – recognised in part by their leadership;

'We don't necessarily want our Fellows being associated with this Fat Cat pompous lawyer – this picture people have of barristers and solicitors. ... So I don't want the Fellows associated too closely with other lawyers' (Interview 1, ILEX Directorate).

There remain considerable frustrations at both the workplace and institutional level about the continued marginality of legal executives. However, it is important to note that the strategy of prospecting for further rights as approved regulator has brought real advantages for individual legal executives and is an important way in which greater clarity around the identity of the profession can be established and enforced. This may confirm the ongoing relevance of such registration/closure projects (Witz 1992) where appropriate state support can be secured and may provide a template for other professional projects, such as the one envisaged by the leaders of STEP (Chapter 6). However, it is worth noting that the ILEX qualification is most likely to be the primary/only qualification for legal executives. For STEP members, the qualification is likely to be the secondary qualification –

a new, distinct professional identity becomes much less relevant for them (see further Chapter 6).

Legal executives once again stand at an important crossroads in their professional project. While ILEX, as an institution, occupies greater centrality within the legal services marketplace than ever before, this is undercut by other factors within the legal, public and workplace arenas which confirm the position of legal executives at edge of law. Perhaps most strikingly, although there is an increasing fluidity within expert knowledge, holding a distinct body of expert knowledge remains important to professional claims (Aldridge 1996: 191). In terms of the future of the profession, much will depend on how and when law firms and new entrants to the marketplace start to structure their organizations as either LDPs or ABSs. What will be the ratio of partners to other qualified lawyers (by whichever route), let alone to non-qualified paralegals? On one level, the story of legal executives illustrates the declining power of the solicitors' profession to collectively control its jurisdiction, as state intervention has bestowed new rights upon the subordinate profession. Equally however, the new rights attached to the formal qualification of legal executive, strengthen the collective appeal of that profession and increase the likelihood of individual legal executives to maintain their membership post-qualification and submit to the collective control of the profession with ILEX at its heart (Larson 1977: 69–74). This suggests a complex picture in terms of the importance of collective models of professional advancement within the contemporary legal services marketplace.

On the other hand, the marginality that continues to be experienced by legal executives and by women in particular, points to the continuing resilience of exclusionary patterns of social and cultural reproduction. Moreover, it is likely that the ultimate value of the legal executive qualification will depend as it has always done on the importance it is accorded by employers. The developing picture is one of overlapping models of professional advancement with a strong emphasis on the firm as an organizational entity (Cooper and Robson 2006). Legal executives have pursued classical professionalism (Johnstone and Flood 1982: 187) throughout their history and have found their strategic choices and aspirations shaped by the institutional logics of the legal professional field. The next chapter will consider the case-study of another group operating at the edge of law – cause lawyers. However, these lawyers consciously reject many of the core assumptions of classic professionalism. What is interesting, even in this era of post-professionalism (Kritzer 1999), is the disciplining power that professionalism continues to exert over them (Fournier 1999), just as it has always done for legal executives.

Chapter 5

Legal Aid and Legal Activists: Progressive Lawyering and Mainstream Professionalism

Introduction

The previous two chapters highlight the ways in which powerful structural forces inhibit particular groups of actors (non-traditional entrants to the profession and legal executives) in moving from their marginal positions at the edge of law. In contrast, the lawyers discussed in this chapter have exercised agency in asserting their position at the edge of legal professionalism. In doing so, they have developed an alternative conception of lawyering which draws heavily on political activism and enables them to demonstrate creativity, reflexivity and entrepreneurship not found in the marginal groups discussed in Chapters 3 and 4. This chapter presents a detailed case-study of Pivot Legal Society and compares it to a publicly funded legal service within England Wales which stands at a crossroads. On the one hand, it is threatened by funding cuts and restrictions on delivery models. On the other hand, the voluntary sector is being encouraged to engage with both Conservative and Labour interpretations of a 'Big Society', within which community participation is emphasized (Helm and Stratton 2011).

In this context Pivot Legal Society provides an illuminating case-study. Pivot is a not-for-profit campaigning legal advocacy organization, engaged in strategic legal action for the marginalized residents of the Downtown Eastside District in the Canadian city of Vancouver. Canada operates a mixed legal aid system combining elements of the judicare scheme historically present within England and Wales (Moorhead 1998) with the clinics of the United States, and England and Wales may continue its move to a similarly mixed approach in the future (MoJ 2009). Moreover, the innovation in the Pivot model has emerged despite the severe public spending cuts in Canada which the British Chancellor, George Osborne, appears to have taken as the model for his own deficit reduction plans (McRobie 2010).

Pivot lawyers are marginalized in a number of ways. They lack the resources of elite actors at the edge (Greenwood and Suddaby 2006: 39) and also experience internal stratification within the legal profession, through their association with vulnerable and destitute clients (Abbott 1988: 122–4). They are also geographically removed from the centre of Vancouver legal practice; the *edgy* area in which they work – the original Skid Row – is still 'a pretty wild place'. Although they are physically located within the heart of the community they serve, as 'rich kids ... from the suburbs of Ontario' they are at the edge of the Downtown Eastside in ways which longer established, grass-roots, organizations are not.

However, this case-study highlights the ways in which marginalization does not necessarily entail subordination. Sherer and Lee argue that leading legal clinics, while marginal to mainstream corporate legal practice, are better understood as providing leadership within a sub-field (2002: 116). The educational and personal histories and legal and activist credibility provide Pivot lawyers with the ability as individual actors to affect institutional change (Battilana 2006: 660). These backgrounds, and multiple field positions, also enable the organization to bridge boundaries, which enhances its capacity for institutional entrepreneurship and to challenge accepted practices in the fields of law and activism (Greenwood and Suddaby 2006: 37). Thus, the fringes of legal professionalism are a site for innovation and change not found in the embedded core (Abel 1985: 6).

However, notwithstanding the transgressive nature of much of their activist legal practice, it is important to note the enduring disciplinary ties to Law held by Pivot lawyers and the relative ease with which the Pivot approach is accommodated by organized legal professionalism in Canada. I suggest that this points to a much looser co-existence between emergent models of professionalism (such as activist lawyers) and the organized profession than the uneasy accommodation of cause lawyers discussed by Sarat and Scheingold (2005). I argue throughout this book that this looser, more complex and contingent accommodation of different models of professionalism can also be witnessed in England and Wales. Globalization and historical commonalities mean we share and can learn much from case-studies of North American lawyers. However, the direct applicability of different models of professionalism (such as Pivot's) will be contingent upon the context in which the lawyering is to occur. In discussing the innovative methods of progressive lawyers within England and Wales, I argue that the key context here is that the role of the state in publicly funded legal work is more important in constraining progressive potential than mainstream professionalism.

The Pivot case-study draws on in-depth interviews with the organization's, then, four lawyers conducted during winter 2006/07[1] and a further, five, on-line, questionnaire responses from summer 2008, alongside an analysis of the organization's websites, podcasts, blogs and the more traditional campaign literature. The UK discussion draws on recent research studies and policy documents with illustrative perspectives from a number of progressive lawyers.

---

1   Dr Matthew Weait and I drew up the question schedule together. The interviews were then conducted by Dr Weait during a visit to Vancouver, which was supported by the Government of Canada Faculty Research Programme. They were subsequently transcribed and analysed by me. The data drawn upon in this chapter is part of a broader project with Dr Weait which explores activist legal methods. As explained in Chapter 1, the descriptors accompanying quotations from the interviewees and respondents are extremely limited in this chapter, given the small sample and closed nature of the organization.

The chapter first explores the relationship between publicly funded (and, more radical) legal work to traditional legal professionalism both within the UK and in North America. It highlights the ways in which Pivot lawyers articulate a model of legal professionalism which positions them at the edge of mainstream legal practice in Canada, before it discusses the disciplinary ties which bind them to mainstream legal professionalism. The chapter concludes with a discussion of the marginalized position of progressive legal aid lawyers within England and Wales, which emphasizes the difficulties of putting global lessons into local action.

Cause Lawyers and the Relationship to Core Legal Professionalism

Cause lawyers' '[moral or political] objectives move from the margins to the center of their professional lives' (Sarat and Scheingold 2005: 1), and vary widely in terms of how far from the mainstream they operate (Scheingold and Bloom 1998). Thus, '[p]roceduralist' cause lawyering does not deviate from established professional norms and is 'marked by a belief in the separation of law and politics, and a belief that the legal system is essentially fair and just' (Hilbink 2004: 665). Examples of this approach include lawyers working for the Legal Service Corporation within the United States, typically a local office funded and regulated by federal agency, staffed by salaried lawyers and paralegals to provide legal representation for the poor (Trubek 1996: 416) or lawyers working within mainstream legal aid within the UK (Boon 2001, Sommerlad 2001).

On the other hand, 'Grass-roots' (Hilbink 2004: 681) or 'Critical' cause lawyering (Trubek 1996), which plays a supporting role to existing community or grassroots movements, and is marked by high levels of lawyer–client collaboration and activist engagement, is more explicitly located at the edge of mainstream legal professionalism. In particular, the methods and culture of Critical cause lawyering challenge core conceptions of legal professionalism including the duty to the client (Hilbink 2004: 686, Luban 1988: 317–55). Some highly politicized UK Law Centre lawyers would have fitted this model in the past (Landau 2009), and thus, would be contrasted with mainstream legal aid practitioners.

Scheingold and Sarat highlight the chequered relationship between cause lawyers and the organized Bar of the United States of America (2004: 23–50). This varied from outright hostility to a 'fragile toleration of cause lawyers' (2004: 45), who work for causes that mainstream lawyers are comfortable in supporting (2004: 49). From Larson's perspective, the existence of cause lawyers enables the organized profession to claim its public services ideal (1977: 56–63, Abel 1985: 13). However, notwithstanding this support, Scheingold and Sarat (2004) suggest that the extent to which cause lawyering is embedded within the values of civic professionalism is blunted by the power and size of the largest corporate firms and scepticism as to the extent to which these firms are likely to heed the pronouncements of the American Bar Association (ABA).

The acceptance of cause lawyering by the ABA stems from the political impetus of the New Deal of the 1960s and the creation of the Legal Services Corporation during which young lawyers from the elite Law Schools of North America were attracted to work within the Law for the Poor Programmes (Scheingold and Sarat 2004: 38–40, see Martin 1985 for the Canadian context). The legal aid scheme within the UK was far less radical in its aspirations – essentially a judicare scheme within which legal services were delivered along traditional lines (Moorhead 1998). Goriely argues that the profession's success in co-opting the provision of legal advice to the poor following the publication of the Rushcliffe report (1944), and then again in the 1970s in response to the law centres movement, built on the Law Society's public service rhetoric (1996: 233). Lawyers effectively dictated the terms on which the legal aid scheme was delivered in England and Wales until the Law Society's control of the scheme was ended by the Legal Aid Act 1988. Abel, thus, argues that 'the organized profession typically has sought to control progressive initiatives rather than eliminate them' (1985: 12). While Legal Aid work was a key part of the profession's income and there was a burst of enthusiasm for Law Centres in the 1970s (Robins 2008, Leask 1985), there was little scope for more radical conceptions of lawyering to develop (Goriely 1996). This was exacerbated as highly politicized lawyers within law centres became more dependent on state funding (Robins 2008).

Since the late 1980s, successive Conservative, Labour and now Coalition governments[2] have attempted to restrict the profession's control over the legal aid scheme, improve the co-ordination of services, and, perhaps above all, reduce costs (Abel 2003, Francis 2000). The declining numbers of legal aid lawyers within the UK have found themselves at the edge of mainstream legal professionalism, not because they offer a radically different conception of lawyering – they are, after all, largely proceduralist cause lawyers (Hilbink 2004: 665) – but through the internal stratification of the profession (Carlin 1962, Abbott 1988: 122–4). Their links to their disadvantaged clients, low pay, reduced autonomy and unattractive status mean this is an unappealing sector for prospective students (Norman 2004) and is marginalized by other sectors of the profession (Moorhead 2004, Melville and Laing 2007). While many legal aid lawyers joined the profession with political motivations, their core strategies today are largely survivalist (Sommerlad 2001). The Law Society of England and Wales does make representations on behalf of legal aid solicitors and other organizations working in the area.[3] However, the need to be seen to 'defend legal aid' has as much an internal political dimension as any external political strategy, as the Law Society struggles to assert its relevance across a fragmented profession (Abel 2003, see further Chapter 7).

---

2   An early move by the Coalition Government saw the withdrawal of funding for a scheme designed to subsidize training contracts for legal aid firms (Hirsch 2010).

3   'Defending Legal Aid' (http://www.lawsociety.org.uk/newsandevents/news/majorcampaigns/view=newsarticle.law?CAMPAIGNSID=247074 [accessed: 26 January 2011]).

There has been an increasing emphasis on the role of the not-for-profit sector (Citizens Advice Bureaux (CABx), Law Centres and other agencies employing non-lawyers to deliver legal advice and representation) since the mid 1990s, which accelerated following the establishment of the Community Legal Service under the Access to Justice Act 1999 (Francis 2000). However, the radical potential of these organizations is constrained by their location within the same bureaucratic management structures which are imposed upon solicitors (Sommerlad 2001).

Local Action: The History and Politics of Pivot Legal Society

Vancouver's external profile is of a modern, multicultural, liberal, wealthy city (see West Vancouver in particular). As its Tourism website states, it is a desirable place to live, to visit, to eat in, to shop in and much of the recent economic growth and regeneration is linked to the 2010 Winter Olympics (http://www.tourismvancouver.com/visitors/vancouver/about_vancouver/why_vancouver [accessed: 15 July 2010]). It is also, however, a City whose Downtown Eastside (DTES) is frequently cited as the poorest postcode in Canada, with the highest rates of HIV/AIDS, injection drug use, first nation poverty and homelessness (Kiang 2009). For the residents of this part of Vancouver, the claims of prosperity and inclusivity ring pretty hollow and have done so for quite some time (Hyslop 2010, http://www.pivotlegal.org/dtes.htm [accessed: 26 January 2011]). Pivot's offices are in the heart of this community at 678 East Hastings Street. It was founded by John Richardson in 2000, in response to the problems he observed while walking to work *through* the DTES. In contrast to the criticisms of traditional legal services for the poor (Bridges 1975, Cousins 1994), Pivot is located within and informed by the problems of the client base which it sets out to serve.

Although Pivot has been successful in terms of profile, fundraising and results, the poverty of the area had already given rise to long-standing community grassroots activism. For example, the Downtown Eastside Residents Association (DERA) was formed in 1973 and Vancouver Area Network of Drug Users (VANDU) was co-founded by Ann Livingstone in 1998 (Ripplinger 2007). In contrast to other avowedly activist lawyers (Polikoff 1996), Pivot and its lawyers are not naturally *of* the community, in ways such as DERA and VANDU. Richardson himself spent the early part of his life on the East Coast of Canada in Quebec and Ontario and the other Pivot lawyers interviewed and responding to the questionnaire grew up variously in Alberta, Ontario and Utah in the United States, with just one person growing up in (the extremely affluent West) Vancouver. Thus, the backgrounds of Pivot lawyers meant that they have not faced the same problems of poverty and marginalization experienced by the residents of the Downtown Eastside (Vancouver 2006, British Columbia Health Atlas 2004). Thus, attendance at Law School in North America generally serves as a signifier of an elite position within society (Costello 2004), 'inevitable' for the middle classes (Schleef 2006).[4] Nearly all Pivot lawyers interviewed had either direct connections with the legal profession through their parents, or their family had connections with other professionals. As I argue further below, these multiple field positions may paradoxically 'bestow legitimacy in the eyes of diverse stakeholders and the ability to access dispersed sets of resources' (Battilana 2006: 660).

Richardson sets out Pivot's underlying philosophy and approach as follows:

> By using the law to address marginalization and disenfranchisement, it is possible to address the root causes of inequity rather than just the symptoms. This allows for systemic impacts that ripple through society, affecting many people both now and in the future. (2005: 8)

This positions Pivot closer to the grass-roots activism of groups such as DERA and VANDU than a traditional legal aid clinic (let alone a corporate law firm). Pivot lawyers, thus, spoke of traditional legal aid's 'ossification' (Trubek 1996: 416, Feldman 1995, Bellow and Charn 1995): '[I] felt it was kind of staid and old. There wasn't a lot of energy and [it] had become very bureaucratic, sitting there with a form to see whether someone matched the criteria' (Interview 3). So while Pivot lawyers are not a product of the community, they have brought their legal skills to the service of the community. In doing so, they have developed a model of legal professionalism and an identity as an Activist Lawyer which consciously places them at the edge of law. Abel argues that practitioners at the fringes of mainstream legal professionalism:

> have *sought* [emphasis added] and attained the 'power to change' to an unusual degree. They are less constrained by the state, by the profession and established philanthropy. They are a vital source of new ideas and experimentation in the delivery of legal services. (1985: 6)

The following section will explore the different dimensions of this emergent model of legal professionalism.

Activist Lawyers: At the Edge of Legal Professionalism

'Something to believe in'

In contrast to Wasserstrom's 'amoral cipher' (1975: 5–6), the Pivot lawyers needed something to believe in. They rejected the dominance of corporate Law at Law

---

4   In the words of one of the Pivot lawyers interviewed, 'my parents wanted me to become either a lawyer or a doctor. It turned out I was not going to become a doctor so I decided to become a lawyer … I just didn't have anything better to do' (Interview 1).

School (Scheingold and Sarat 2004: 63, Granfield and Koenig 1992, Manderson and Turner 2006) and failed to see their values or their political and professional motivations reflected in mainstream legal education:

> I hated [Law School]. I believe in Justice, but I must say that I didn't find it [at Law School] … . So many of the classes were not acknowledging what I saw as the economics of justice. You know this whole fairytale that the law is available to people when obviously it's totally driven by finance. (Interview 4) (see also Kennedy 1998)

For many of the Pivot lawyers, their left-wing beliefs and political activism predated their enrolment at Law School. Arguably this sustained them in contributing to more realistic views about the challenges that they would encounter at Law School[5] and, consequently ensured they were less likely to wilt under the ideological pressure they described experiencing there (Costello 2005: 134, Granfield 1994: 54).

The literature on legal ethics frequently references the lawyerly 'strategy of detachment' which enables the lawyer to act in ways that they (or others) would not be able to morally countenance (Oakley and Cocking 2006: 141 and Peppet 2005: 501). Sarat and Scheingold argue that this strategy requires a separation between the personal identity and professional identity of the lawyers (2005: 1).

Thomson identifies the unhappiness amongst those with social justice orientations within corporate legal practice, arising from 'the loss of a sense of fighting for what is right' and notes the tensions involved in exploring the limits of the 'resistance permissible within the setting' (2005: 286–7). Such tensions can lead to these lawyers 'feeling bad' for the 'other side' or ultimately leaving the law (Granfield and Koenig 2003: 512, 523). A repeated theme of the interviews with the Pivot lawyers was that their work had to be meaningful to them and they had to be on the 'right side' (Scheingold and Bloom 1998: 230). It was not possible to detach themselves, as lawyers, from their personal lives. The respondent below highlights the unease that they felt in attempting to detach themselves from the work they performed in corporate legal practice:

> I'm a little disillusioned … In litigation in a big firm I just found that … the person on the other side just didn't have a very good chance. There was like, no chance … We would go up against people and I just didn't feel that we were on the right side of things and I didn't want to do that. It made me feel bad …

In leaving mainstream practice they avoid this tension:

---

5   This certainly seemed true of the Pivot lawyers, with 80 per cent of those responding to the questionnaire agreeing that their expectations of Law School were that 'I wouldn't have much in common with the people I met there.'

what attracted me to Pivot is that I'm working for political causes that I think are right, but I'm still doing law work ... I always felt social justice was working to help marginalized people – working towards the 'right' goals. ... I am optimistic about Law being able to do this, and that's why I left the big firm. (Interview 1)

I need my work to be personally fulfilling ... If I needed to earn money for the greater good, I would still need a practice with some aspect of social justice. (Interview 2)

The difference was that I never thought that I was going to be a big time advocate. I always thought that I was going to be doing advocacy on a smaller scale, not in the macho ..., criminal law way ... Clinics, that sort of thing. (Interview 3)

The personal fulfilment alluded to here, extended not just to the political ends to which their lawyering was directed but the quality of the legal work in which they were engaged. The responsibility with which they were entrusted was also contrasted favourably with that that they were likely to experience in corporate practice (see also Scheingold and Bloom 1998: 227, Kiang 2009).

While, there was strong alignment between the personal and political beliefs in their work, the Pivot lawyers framed their professional identity in a broad range of ways:

Play different roles at different times – when I am representing a client – I am first and foremost their lawyer and have their interests in mind. (Questionnaire 4)

More lawyer than activist ... I have found that there are very specific things which I can do that an activist cannot do. (Questionnaire 2)

Very close to the activist end, my traditional legal work is quite limited. (Questionnaire 1)

I see myself as a lawyer ... I don't think that you can always be representing people if you're an activist ... sometimes you can be conflicted. (Interview 1)

Not only is there variation between the lawyers, but there is also variation in terms of how individuals conceive their role at different times (Scheingold and Bloom 1998: 210). Thus, one interviewee justified the relative lack of consultation with residents of the DTES about aspects of the strategies that Pivot adopted, in the following 'elite' terms (Hilbink 2004: 673):

Ideally [in politics] you're supposed to be articulating the views of your constituents. *But we get to have our own ideas about what's right.* (Interview 4)

This individual generally articulated grassroots/activist oriented methods and approach. Moreover, their underlying philosophy (the DTES provides an 'emotional growth experiment for the residents of Vancouver'), positions them more as a 'movement activist' (Southworth 1998: 500). However, the leadership position adopted at other points (and seen in the quotation above), conflicts with the grass-roots approach (Hilbink 2004: 681–90).

Part of the issue appears to be the fluidity with which these activist lawyers define their identity and the role responsibilities which flow from that identity. As Kostiner argues, 'the same actor' may invoke different approaches to the relationship of law and social change at different times (2003: 358). Pivot lawyers may display the characteristics of Hilbink's ideal types in different moments in the different work that they do. As with a number of the other case-studies explored in this book, the uncertainty in the professional identity may generate greater anxiety for those operating in marginal positions at the edge of law than for elites capable of comfortably gliding between fields and identities.

Institutional Entrepreneurship, New Models of Practice and Strategic Legal Action

Through their location at the edge of the field of practice, Pivot lawyers have been able to engage in the sort of boundary bridging that Greenwood and Suddaby (2006: 37) argue will allow organizational actors to break free from the prevailing institutional logics and develop new forms of practice and new technologies of knowledge (Lounsbury 2002: 255). This boundary bridging is seen in their journeys to, and between, high school activism, elite Law School, corporate legal practice, wealth, privilege, environmental NGOs, grassroots activism, civic professionalism and strategic legal and political leadership. Crucially, they are able to translate different organizational forms and methods into new areas of practice and possess the credibility to affect change (Battilana 2006: 660).

Pivot argues that traditional individualized rights-based litigation can only have partial impact (see also Blomley 2007: 1700). Thus, they position themselves as part of a broader activist movement that engages with Law to affect wider social change. John Richardson, the founder of Pivot articled with the non-profit environmental protection organization Sierra Legal Defence Fund (now known as EcoJustice). This organization brings together lawyers and scientists and has 'campaigns, they have media, reports, strategic litigation,[6] fundraising...' (John Richardson, Interview). Richardson took this model from Sierra Legal Defence Fund and has, with great success and acclaim (Ashoka Foundation 2005) applied it to the DTES. Richardson describes Pivot's work in the following terms:

> Like a lawyer to a client, Pivot uses community research and documentation, through legal affidavits and focus groups, to empower marginalized persons to raise their voice and assert their interests. (Richardson 2005: 8)

---

6 'Court victory forces Canada to report pollution data for mines' (EcoJustice 2009).

While these creative approaches are not without their problems (Southworth 1998: 497), the broader strategic approach and the creative methods that Pivot deploys challenge existing conceptions of the lawyer–client relationship (Boon 2004: 258). They attempt to rethink the lawyer–client relationship, so that they are 'taking instructions from a community, rather than from one client'.

Cain argues that lawyers have always played a creative role for capital (1994: 41–2). She describes them as 'conceptive ideologists', thinking the advancement of their class. This creative role in the production of professional knowledge is recognized by Jamous and Peloille (1970) and, in the context of corporate lawyers' work for elite commercial companies, Powell argues that 'lawyers ... acted as legal entrepreneurs with new products to develop and market' (1993: 448). Cain (1994) was clear that lawyers were not a neutral tool to be easily deployed by the poor. Yet Pivot lawyers (like many other cause lawyers before them) not only seek to work in the cause of those whom capital would view as antithetical, but are innovative in their creative use of legal form (in terms of methods, procedures and instruments) in order to achieve these explicitly socialist ends.

The traditional legal work in which Pivot lawyers engage, involves representing clients arrested by police, presenting cases before housing tribunals and broader strategic litigation, for example, geared towards the protection of sex worker rights or safeguarding tenancy rights.[7] Their political campaigns are equally wide-ranging and involve rock concerts, photography competitions (involving the distribution of cameras to the residents of the DTES to record their lives), outreach to the media, campaigning blogs and so on. David Eby, a former Pivot lawyer and now Executive Director of the British Columbia Civil Liberties Association is a prolific blogger, and uses this outlet to maintain pressure on Vancouver police and City officials, for example through embedding video of police abuses of power.[8] One recent Pivot campaign during the Winter Olympics 2010 saw the erection of red tents throughout the city in order to draw attention to the plight of the homeless during the Games.[9] Other campaigns have both legal and activist dimensions, such as the production and distribution of Rights cards.[10] Perhaps the most fascinating aspect of their work, in terms of what it may tell us about the creative work that cause lawyers may be capable of, is their use of affidavits to gather legally credible evidence for use in their Reports and to identify potential claimants for strategic litigation.

---

7   'Methadone patients protected by tenancy laws, Supreme Court rules' (Pivot 2009).

8   'How law pushes people to the margins, and keeps them there' (http://davideby. blogspot.com/ [accessed: 26 January 2011]). See, for example, http://www.youtube.com/ watch?v=rQ7QlQifwjo&feature=player_embedded [accessed: 26 January 2011].

9   http://redtents.org/news/pivot-and-citywide-housing-coalition-launch-red-tent-campaign [accessed: 29 July 2010].

10   http://www.youtube.com/watch?gl=GB&hl=en-GB&v=hIpnPQpZY1A[accessed: 26 January 2011].

The affidavit is ordinarily used as a way of providing information about matters relevant to a dispute. It involves the statements of facts, in a clear, concise and structured form, without argument, opinion or inference on the part of the witness (*Williams et al. v. British Columbia et al* [2004] BCSC 1374, para: 16). Affidavits are therefore an important means by which factual statements about the reality of claimants' lives can be presented to the courts.[11] Pivot recognized their potential, not simply as an evidence gathering technique, but as an important weapon through which legal techniques can be deployed towards progressive political ends:

> The affidavit programme began about a year in, so the first year [of Pivot] was spent in community meetings. Lawyers, and people from the Downtown Eastside, talking about a variety of issues, about what was wrong with their lives, and tonnes of stuff came up – sex work, drug treatment, and welfare. And people would tell just crazy stories about police misconduct, and they say it in such a blasé, off-hand manner, that you just couldn't think that they'd be lying. ... So based on that, that's when we decided to do something on policing. ... So we do an affidavit campaign. ... the affidavits, create a body of evidence that they can't reject and we'll go forward with that. And I would say definitely, that the affidavits were a tool, to take us to the end, which was change, systemic change of the police force. (Interview 4)

Using their mobile affidavit unit, including laptop, printer, digital camera and generator, the Pivot lawyers take to the street and take the affidavit statements from, for example, drug users, in the clear, structured and concise form which is recognizable as an admissible affidavit statement. The primary end to which the affidavits have been put is as evidence in a series of Reports that Pivot have published, which highlight particular issues in the Downtown Eastside. For example, *To Serve and Protect* (Pivot 2002) addressed police misconduct in the area, *Cracks in the Foundation* (Pivot 2006), explored social housing problems and 'changed the discourse on housing' (Eby 2006), and there were two linked reports on Sex Work. Recent work has focused on child apprehension by public authorities. They are highly political documents directed towards the public authorities in order to achieve systemic change on behalf of the community.

One of the clear strengths of the affidavit campaign is its potential to 'increase people's sense of personal and political power' (Gabel and Harris 1982–3: 376) through enabling the residents of the DTES to tell their story. In placing the marginalized community firmly at the centre of the campaign, Trubek argues there is a genuine transformation of the lawyer–client relationship (1996: 439). The questionnaire respondents saw the most important advantage of the campaign as

---

11 The 'Brandeis Brief' was a pioneering example of social science research being presented to the court as evidence (*Muller v. Oregon* (208 US 412)). The full brief is available here: http://www.law.louisville.edu/library/collections/brandeis/node/235 [accessed: 15 July 2010].

being that 'it was empowering for the individual to tell their story' and, secondly, that it enabled 'voices to be heard'.[12] The affidavit is a legal document. It carries legal legitimacy and, were it practicable for the witness to appear in court to be cross-examined, could be formally admissible in court proceedings. The gathering of affidavits produces a collective and powerful truth about experience, especially when those affidavits focus on one particular issue as experienced by each and every one of those people – 'Affidavits make it very difficult to deny that a particular issue exists' (Interview 2). Pivot's innovative use of legal form in their affidavit campaigns, which bring together legal practice, social science and grassroots activism, reminds us that innovation can occur at the edge (Abel 1985: 6), and that emergent models of legal professionalism may be as much about methods as they are about values.

New Organizational Forms

Greenwood and Suddaby (2006) argue that the boundary bridging elite accountancy firms were able to develop and implement new organizational forms, incorporating multi-disciplinary expertise and transnational structures. The not-for-profit, non-hierarchical structures of Pivot involving lawyers, researchers, fundraisers and community workers (http://www.pivotlegal.org/About/staffprofiles.htm#l sadrehash [accessed: 26 January 2011]), with an emphasis on retreats[13] as part of its staff development programme, which draws community residents onto its management committee (http://www.pivotlegal.org/About/board.htm [accessed: 26 January 2011]), presents a challenging and radical model of how Poverty Law can be delivered. It is, as Trubek observed in other settings, 'a vision of the Activist Lawyer who works collaboratively with clients and colleagues, develops a holistic practice and identifies with a subordinated client group' (1996: 439).

The next phase of Pivot's development is a linked fee-for-service private practice law firm (Pivot LLP) explicitly set up to divert part of its profits back to Pivot Legal Society. The key driver for this development is

> economic power for the organization. … Strategic litigation is a very powerful tool if you can put the muscle behind it. And people don't notice what it can do because it's not really been financed the way it needs to be financed. …

---

12   Political strategies, such as the photography competition, similarly seek to place the marginalized person at the centre of the activities.

13   John Richardson explains why he encourages staff to visit the Hollyhock Educational Retreat Centre 'Ghandi said that "you have to be the change you seek in the world." We all need people and places that support that' (http://www.youtube.com/watch?v=vUdrXIOOpVg [accessed: 27 July 2010]). Hollyhock describes itself as existing to 'inspire, nourish and support people who are making the world better' (http://www.hollyhock.ca/cms/mission.html [accessed: 27 July 2010]). This is not a typical law firm team-building exercise.

We need the full systems of a major law firm. We need dozens of lawyers, we need accounting systems, we need articling students, we need researchers. (Interview 4)

Although the progressive approach to a work/life balance to which the firm aspires was attractive to its lawyers (Kiang 2009), this model also carries the potential to resolve some of the tensions of the Activist/ Lawyer identity. How effectively this is managed will be interesting to monitor. In the UK, a separation of publicly funded case-workers within CABx from the rest of the organization which was more holistically focused on client empowerment and social policy work was not without its problems. Many believed it betrayed the organization's roots in establishing formal demarcations between lay and legal advisors (Francis 2000: 67–72). While the separation may enable the tensions in the Activist/Lawyer identity to be managed more formally, there were some anxieties about the future:

> There will be tensions with the LLP because we will have to bill, although the profits come back [to Pivot Legal Society]. But what files do you take in order to get money? ... There may be commercial pressures. It's hard to say, because of the transition to the LLP [how long I'll stay]. (Interview 3)

The commercial pressures anticipated, in particular by one of the Pivot lawyers (by instinct an activist, but following the establishment of the LLP, being clear that, 'when I am representing a client, I am first and foremost their lawyer and have *their* interests in mind') are well evidenced in existing literature (Scheingold and Bloom 1998: 231, Trubek 1996: 432).

At the Edge of Activism

It is also worth remembering that their background and experiences means that Pivot lawyers are, at the same time, outsiders within the Downtown Eastside. They are distanced from the community which they represent by geographical origin, class background, and even through their status as lawyers. This disjuncture manifests itself in their dealings with other organizations, suspicious of these 'outsiders', particularly in the context of a competitive funding environment for grassroots advocacy within the DTES:

> I had a really interesting call from one of the [housing] organizations down here ... I was brand new and I thought everyone was going to be psyched that we were doing this report. ... And he said 'you're so middle class, you don't know what's going on down here, you don't know the first thing, your report's gonna cause more harm than good. Why didn't you talk to us before you put in the grant application? What were you thinking? It'll be a disaster. You're a jerk (in so many words).' (Interview 2)

Thus, in order to win the trust of sceptical activists, Pivot lawyers consciously had to disassociate themselves from other lawyers. In order for them to gain currency as activists, they had to attempt to construct a lawyer identity that differed from what the community had previously experienced. As Abel has suggested, '[political] organizing is hard, demanding work for which legal credentials may be a disqualification rather than a prerequisite' (1985: 8). In one interviewee's words:

> I don't really care about staying professional [in terms of adherence to formal Codes of Conduct etc.]. It's more important that I engage with [our client groups] … I mean it's going to take time. It's just that you have to be there and people have to realise that they can trust you and realise that you're there for the same reason and you can work on these issues together and you can be relied upon … I know that right away people will tell me really bad experiences that they've had before [with lawyers]. (Interview 3)

In such circumstances, therefore, particularly among these educated and reflective individuals, there is discomfort in how they reconcile the Activist and the Lawyer aspects of their professional identity. The following section will explore the prevailing power of the institutional logics of legal field, and the ways in which Law continues to structure the practice of these lawyers at the edge.

Organized Legal Professionalism, Accommodation and Disciplinary Ties

A key argument of this book is the need to recognize the emergence of new models of professionalism which operate alongside, and not necessarily in opposition to, the traditional collective model of professional advancement. What is striking from the Pivot case-study is not only the evidence of support and engagement for the work of Pivot from the organized profession (Sarat and Scheingold 2005), but the way in which the structuring properties of legal professionalism continue to shape and inform the Pivot lawyers' work (Fournier 1999). Part of the story may be one of acceptance and toleration by the core profession of transgressive outliers because, for example, it enables the public service claim to be outsourced and be realized by an identifiable branch of the profession (Sarat and Scheingold 2005, Larson 1977: 51). However, I argue that this should also be seen as part of a complex and contingent legal professionalism. Thus, the existence of a divergent model of professionalism, such as cause lawyering, may be contingent upon state pressures or the autonomies of other actors (Webb 2004: 84), rather than on whether it supports a traditional collective mobility project (Bańkowski and Mungham 1976: 68). The complex picture sees Pivot lawyers operate at the edge of mainstream legal professionalism and yet remain bound by its disciplinary ties.

Pivot Legal Society secures support from the mainstream legal professionalism in a variety of ways. Private practice lawyers sit on its Board of Directors. Its specific expertise and reputation are also recognized by the professional associations. Thus, for example, the Law Society of British Columbia identified Pivot as an organization it needed to speak to before responding to the Government on specific Law reform issues (Law Society of British Columbia 2004: 8). Similarly Pivot is (with other organizations) flagged up by the Canadian Bar Association as a provider of 'low cost and free legal services' (www.cba.org./ bc/public_media/lawyers/430.aspx [accessed: 26 January 2011]) and its funders include establishment bodies such as the Law Commission of Canada, the Law Foundation of British Columbia, the Canadian Bar Law for the Future Fund and the Minister of Public Safety and Solicitor General of British Columbia (http://www. pivotlegal.org/About/supporters.htm [accessed: 26 January 2011]). It also works with more mainstream (and longer established) legal campaigning organizations including the British Columbia Civil Liberties Association (BCCLA 2007); links that seem set to strengthen following the appointment of former Pivot lawyer, David Eby, as Executive Director of the BCCLA.

It is also striking to note the capital that the Pivot lawyers draw from their legal qualification and identity. Law remains the primary tool that these lawyers turn to and there is legitimacy attached to the Lawyer role. This is both a formal legitimacy, for example through the lawyer's signature on an affidavit, but also the cultural capital of a 'lawyer' presenting the report as opposed to an activist, local politician or indeed even an individual member of the Downtown Eastside making a direct complaint:

> You have a lot of credibility [as a lawyer], the amount of education, people look at you and say 'oh you must be so smart'. (Interview 1)

> Having a lawyer empowers individuals to be less fearful of repercussions if they make a complaint. (Questionnaire 1)

> I've had other judges who do recognise me from our work and clearly see us as a bit of 'white hat' in dealing with whatever the issue, so our applications go a bit more smoothly. I think they look at it and say 'if Pivot is acting for person X, then there's probably some kind of issue here that needs to be given due consideration'. (Interview 2)

Notwithstanding the baggage that being a lawyer can bring in activist circles (Abel 1985: 6), the legal identity was important to the Pivot lawyer and they were able to draw on it to effectively advance their cause (Battilana 2006: 660).

Elite Law Schools and the Power of Professional Socialization

Freidson notes that long-term commitment to a profession is an important way in which the ongoing demands of professionalism are reinforced (1992: 221). Larson (1977) and Kennedy (1998), in different ways, highlight the socialization processes at professional schools. Arguably, this is even more powerful in the

Canadian (rather than UK context) given that students study Law at postgraduate level and are, thus, closer to the profession in a number of ways, given the closer proximity to qualification and the greater overlap between academics and practitioners than within UK legal education (Manderson and Turner 2006: 666). Despite the explicit exercise of agency by Pivot lawyers which rejects mainstream ideologies of Law School and legal practice, the profession of Law continues to exert a powerful disciplinary pull on these lawyers.

Pivot lawyers held a continued attachment to some traditional elite values about the position of legal education and even of traditional sites of practices. It is worth noting that they overwhelmingly chose their particular Law School because of its reputation in terms of prestige and league tables – rather than, for example, a commitment to social justice, or the bursaries that were available. There was acknowledgement of the quality of people at Law School:

> I honestly think some of my classmates are among the brightest I've ever met … it was an excellent Law School. The Professors there are the leading legal minds in Canada and the student body, it's so hard to get in. It's sounds so snobby, but calibre of student there, I've never really encountered [anywhere else]. (Interview 1)

There was also acknowledgement of the importance of training in mainstream settings (see also Granfield and Koenig 1992: 324, Thomson 2005: 284):

> You can't help but internalize part of what they're telling you [at Law School], so … I really felt that I needed professional legal training from lawyers who were doing traditional legal work … that would make me a better lawyer for Pivot when I decided to move over … . But that was a big part of why I went there, to do that small piece of professional development before moving over to do Pivot to do the personal stuff. (Interview 2)

Arguably, norms inculcated or internalized during Law School and the formative years of practice ensured that legal aspects of their professional identity remained prominent even at Pivot. It is clearly a *legal* organization and despite their activist orientations and methods, the Pivot lawyers remained lawyers. This generated significant tensions for them, not least in reconciling their lawyer's commitment to the individual client with their political strategic objectives for the cause. Striking, in nearly all cases, whenever there was a dispute, the legal professional role expectations won through, as the next section will demonstrate.

The Client, the Cause and the Lawyer

One of the recurrent criticisms of cause lawyers concerns their apparent breaches of the core ethical duties of lawyers (Boon 2004: 250). A central dimension of this is, of course, their defining focus on the 'Cause', which carries the potential to distort and undermine their relationship with their individual clients (Scheingold and Bloom 1998: 209) – a core aspect of the ethical duties of lawyers in Canada as it is elsewhere in the Anglo-American world (Canadian Bar Association 2009: 25–48). Boon (2001: 151) notes that this may lead some critics to question whether such lawyers are, in fact, lawyers at all and Scheingold and Sarat are clear that the potential tension between cause and client is a central way in which cause lawyers occupy a contradictory position to the traditional ethical norms of the profession (2004: 7).

Pivot lawyers were profoundly aware of the potential challenges that strategic cause lawyering generated (Southworth 1998: 500).[14] There is, nevertheless, a clear concern among these Activist Lawyers about the damage to the individual that can occur through the broader focus on strategic legal action on behalf of the broader marginalized community. There are two principal ways in which this manifests: the classic lawyerly concern about compromising the individual client for the cause (Simon 1978) and, secondly, a more activist concern about how the community's voice is identified.

None of the Pivot lawyers completing the questionnaire disagreed with the statement: 'working as a Pivot Lawyer the wishes of the client are more important than the broader cause'. It is also worth citing some of the lawyers' thoughts on these issues at some length – not simply because of how they frame the potential problem, but also in terms of how ultimately they, as lawyers, feel they have to resolve the tensions. They are experiencing 'the pull of the profession as a disciplining and domesticating force, policing ... the nature of the advocacy they provide' (Scheingold and Sarat 2004: 18, Fournier 1999: 281).

> When you're bringing forward a case for an illegal eviction against a landlord, but the case represents something much broader, for example the Vancouver housing policy, and the client says 'you know what, I just want to settle ... for $300'. And you say, 'this case is about so much more and is worth so much more money to you', and he's like 'I just need the money right now, I want to give it to my mom or whatever'. Those are the times when that conflict between lawyer and activist are most clear. And this has happened to me. At the end of the day, the client makes the call, but that's when I feel most acutely for the loss of the case that would have represented something great ... You need to win the case, because it's a systemic issue that's affecting a whole class of people. (Interview 2, see also Luban 1988: 320)

This tension is one that is not simply experienced as a loss of an individual case that would have represented something great (Shamir and Chinski 1998: 238–9), but is also seen when the law requires lawyers to frame an individual's story in

---

14   For example: 'Do you defend the system in the hope that people will be interested enough to continue, or do you acknowledge that it's total crap and they probably won't go through it?' (Interview 2).

such a way so to undermine the broader political cause the lawyer is attempting to advance. As Hilbink neatly summarises: do they 'save the client, regardless of the political' (2004: 686)?

> In refugee law, you have to make arguments that are not [helpful to the broader cause]. For instance, I did a lot of cases where women had suffered violence and you were arguing for refugee status on the basis of gender persecution. And the whole thing around that is you kind of have to show the woman in a very victimized way.[15] I don't necessarily agree with that ... [But] your role is to get refugee status for *this* person. ... There's a conflict between the individual case and the bigger picture. Immigration stuff is always so unfair, but you have individual clients you have to serve. (Interview 3)

What is notable from the majority of the Pivot lawyers surveyed is that although they recognize and have anxieties about the relationship between the individual client's interests and those of the wider cause or community, ultimately their lawyerly norms provide answers to particular dilemmas. Admittedly, however, there is a formal regulatory dimension – 'it's dangerous. If I was too much of an activist, the Law Society doesn't have a lot of time for that' (Interview 2).

Activist Lawyers and the UK Context

The detailed study of Pivot Legal Society presents an alternative to mainstream legal professionalism. It is explicitly political in its aims, systemic rather than individual in its focus, egalitarian in its organizational form and management processes and seeks to collapse the client/cause distinction in its legal practice. These are lawyers who have decided to locate themselves at the edge; they have chosen to reject the paradigmatic models of legal professionalism to which they have been exposed at Law School (or even earlier (Schleef 2006)) and in previous practice sites. Strikingly their location at the edge has also enabled them to develop new ways of doing Poverty Law, whether it be rethinking the way in which traditional legal tools such as affidavits can be put to progressive ends or reconceiving the private practice, for-profit law firm model as a revenue stream for their Activist Lawyering.

Critically, however, their work is accommodated by the organized profession (Sarat and Scheingold 2005) within British Columbia, and the nature of their practice is still subject to the disciplining discourse of (legal) professionalism (Fournier 1999). Their tool is Law, they are trained as lawyers and notwithstanding

---

15   See also Grabham on clients who had experienced intersectional discrimination and who felt disauthenticated as their experiences were rendered into 'intelligible legal frameworks' (2006: 7). Kennedy also highlights the role of the 'Fragrant Woman' in legal advocacy (1992: 65–70).

their radicalism and activist strategies and orientations, they remain comfortable in proclaiming, 'We're lawyers. We can try selling legal services!' (John Richardson, cited in Kiang 2009).

Although the Anglo-American professions have much in common historically (Larson 1977, Freidson 1994: 16) and arguably still do within a globalized professional services marketplace (Flood 2008, Davis 2010), there are questions as to how broadly applicable this model might be. There are important contextual differences which appear to limit the applicability of this particular model of legal professionalism to England and Wales. Local context remains important notwithstanding these globalizing forces.

Canada is a liberal democracy with generally progressive rights protections (Fredman 2002: 17–18).[16] It is possible to see this political climate giving rise to a broad willingness of the profession to engage with, or at least be tolerant of, progressive endeavours such as the Law Union of Canada (Martin 1985). The funding model for legal aid in Canada sees a split between State and Provincial funding for Criminal and Civil Legal Aid (http://www.justice.gc.ca/eng/pi/pb-dgp/arr-ente/lap-paj.html [accessed: 26 January 2011]). In British Columbia, civil legal aid is administered by the Legal Services Society, and in common with the rest of Canada operates a mixed model of judicare and salaried clinics, and there have been suggestions that the delivery debate paralysed innovation within the legal aid sector (Currie 2000: 317). Park and Lippert (2008) argue that developments in state-funded legal services in Canada have been marked by a shift towards a neo-liberal management agenda, similar to the experiences within England and Wales (Sommerlad 1995, 1999, 2001) including, for example, the introduction of quality audits of community clinics (Zemans 2000). These have been matched by a story familiar to readers within England and Wales, of dramatic cuts in legal aid funding (Brewin and Govender 2010). Trubek (1996), however, argues that innovation can spring from the uncertainties caused by precarious funding models, and it is certainly possible to see Pivot emerging in response to this environment, and taking advantage of funding sources such as the innovative Law Foundation (s.62 (2) Legal Profession Act 1998 (British Columbia)).[17]

There have always been radical lawyers within England and Wales, whose work while explicitly legal, also sought to realize social justice and broader concerns. Unlike, for example, Mr Loophole, Nick Freeman,[18] these lawyers have

---

16   However, Behiels (2010) suggests that Stephen Harper's Premiership indicates a rightwards realignment within Canada.

17   The Foundation is funded by interest accruing from the interest in Law firm client accounts, and supports legal aid, legal education and law reform.

18   Boggan (2006) reports the comments of Nick Freeman, a defence lawyer specializing in motoring offences: 'Morally I can't [square clearing a drink driver on a technicality] but ethically I can … I am a lawyer and my job is to give my clients the best defence I can.'

not attempted to operate with the lawyer's detachment that Wasserstrom sketched out (1975). They see little difference between the political and the professional:

> The fact of the matter is that for me to do the job I have to feel committed, to understand where my client is coming from and why he or she has got there ... throughout, I have attempted to be true to an inner conscience ... Although emotional responses can be very difficult to handle, I believe that to deny them in your working life is as ridiculous as denying them in your personal one. (Mansfield 2009: 214)

Similarly, Saimo Chahal, a partner with Bindmans solicitors in London,[19] has spoken of the importance of using 'law as a tool to promote the rights of the disadvantaged' (BLD 2008) and Gareth Peirce's 'intensity of her dedication to her client's causes' has been noted by profilers, while she herself has spoken of 'the need for instinctive, reactive, imaginative work in criminal defence, responding to a state which has unlimited resources to prosecute' (The Independent 2002). Interestingly, each of these lawyers has received honours and recognition from the legal and political establishment; Mansfield is a QC, Peirce was awarded a CBE (which she later returned) and Chahal won a Law Society Award for Excellence in 2008.[20] Moreover they all operate within traditional practice environments, albeit with engagement and support to more radical enterprises such as Law Centres.

Although Law Centres were conceived of as radical alternatives to traditional legal practice (Robins 2008), the story of publicly funded legal services within the UK has been an increasingly state-controlled model. At the same time, from the late 1980s onwards legal aid eligibility levels have steadily fallen (Moorhead 2004) as part of a state strategy to reduce the overall levels of the legal aid budget (Mackay 1992, Abel 2003). Multiple problems remain for marginal groups seeking access to justice (Mason et al. 2009), but particularly in areas of civil justice (Buck et al. 2005, Pleasance et al. 2008). In keeping with their radical past and (subversive) image of long hair and political posters in the Law Centres of the 1970s, the not-for-profit sector today still offers an alternative model of delivery. There are a far higher proportion of non-lawyers within the not-for-profit sector with a wider range of non-legal and non-traditional qualifications. There are far more women working in this sector (Smith and Tam 2007: 19), and there are also distinctive training needs given the non-legal backgrounds of the advisors (Sommerlad and Sanderson 2009).

---

19   Barclay and Marshall seek to identify a conception of cause lawyering that does not automatically exclude the 'sometimes significant contributions of private practitioners who may make money at the same time that they serve a movement' (2005: 198), and Chahal would seem to fit comfortably within this broader conception of a cause lawyer.

20   Another colleague at the firm, Gwendolen Morgan, was given a commendation at the Awards the following year (http://services.lawsociety.org.uk/events/awards/excellence/winners [accessed: 26 January 2011]).

Strikingly, however, the increasingly reliance by the not-for-profit sector on the contracts with the Legal Services Commission (for example South West London Law Centres receives 68 per cent of its funding from the LSC (Robins 2008)) has generated significant tensions within the organizations as they attempt to maintain their commitments to grass-roots activism, strategic policy oriented work and client empowerment within the structures of what has been characterized as an increasingly managerial and bureaucratic model of legal services delivery (Francis 2000, Robins 2008, Sommerlad 1999, Sommerlad and Sanderson 2009). This model is also applied to the private practice service providers (Sommerlad 2001, Moorhead 2004). However, it is the not-for-profit sector, within which alternative conceptions of legal professionalism had been previously imagined (Leask 1985), where these tensions are most acutely felt. Legal Services Commission rules mean, for example, that:

> From the 1st October [2010], we will be unable to give any advice to anyone who is not eligible for Legal Help. If you are planning to attend our drop in, please make sure that you bring proof of your income and savings (http://www. traffordlawcentre.org.uk [accessed: 7 January 2011]).

This move away from the principles such as 'free at point of entry' was a real concern among CAB volunteers interviewed in 1996–97 (Francis 2000: 71). However, the not-for-profit sector always aspired to more for its communities than simply to provide legal advice and representation. The Law Centre's Federation, in a briefing paper to the incoming Coalition Government (2010–), describe aspects of their work in the following terms:

> We tackle the root causes of poverty and disadvantage through a strategic mix of public legal education, influencing social policy and campaigning for social change [perhaps not so different to Pivot]. (LCF 2010)

This includes, for example, work by South Manchester Law Centre to track issues relating to domestic violence and refugee claims among Pakistani women (Siddiqui, Ismail and Allen 2008) and Southwark Law Centre/Blackfriars Advice Centres' three-year project to reduce evictions by combining outreach, training and policy initiatives (Southwark Law Centre 2007). Steve Cohen, who worked with North Manchester Law Centre until his death in 2009, was described as the 'last Law Centre radical', partly because he remained committed 'to open campaigning and ... a partnership between community campaigns and the legal battle' (Landau 2009).

It is these more radical conceptions of legal work that are seen as most vulnerable to the recent developments. One South Manchester Law Centre Immigration Caseworker, in an interview with the author (July 2010), described the changes in the following terms:

> We used to be quite imaginative [in running cases], [could] explore options, consider campaigns alongside casework, and so on. Now it's like a sausage factory with pressure to close the file because of the payment at the end of the case.

The establishment of Community Legal Advice Centres/Networks in the last years of the Labour Government of the UK (MoJ 2009), envisaged as partnerships with local authorities, are also difficult to reconcile with LCF's stated objectives for a national network of Law Centres (http://www.lawcentres.org.uk/policy/detail/working-with-government/ [accessed: 26 January 2011], Robins 2008). In common with many public sector initiatives, at the time of writing (January 2011), there is considerable uncertainty about these and other future legal aid developments. Following the Comprehensive Spending Review, the Government has signalled further cuts and another major review of legal aid (MoJ 2010). While Prime Minister David Cameron's advocacy of the 'Big Society' (http://www.cabinetoffice.gov.uk/content/big-society-overview [accessed: 7 January 2011]) may hold some potential for more community-based and activist initiatives, all community-based organizations (including Law Centres) face perilous funding scenarios (Butler 2010). South Manchester Law Centre, for example, currently faces closure following drastic cuts from both the City Council and the LSC (http://www.smlc.org.uk/ [accessed: 8 January 2011]).

Notwithstanding the growing gloom in the sector (Robins 2008), it is still possible to identify progressive lawyers being creative in the framing and delivery of legal services provision for the poor. Bindmans LLP, a London law firm with a leading reputation in public law, criminal defence and employment, has taken steps to establish a mini-site (http://www.bindmansg20.com [accessed: 26 January 2011]), specifically to provide information for, and (implicitly) to offer its services to, those caught up in the G20 protests in London 2009.[21] Another initiative emerging from private practice is the Law Shop, which operates in conjunction with Peter Browne Solicitors in Bristol (http://www.lawshopbristol.co.uk/index.html [accessed: 26 January 2011]). This is a service which is designed to equip people with basic information to help them resolve their legal problems themselves. One aspect of the service allows customers to purchase simple and relatively low-cost guides, for example 'Going to Court with a Solicitor (£1.20)' or 'Divorce – Sorting out Money and Property (£1.60)'. Other schemes, which involve lawyers and non-lawyers and attempt to encourage and deepen the understanding of marginalized communities of their rights under Law, are supported and encouraged through the Public Legal Education Network (http://www.plenet.org.uk [accessed: 27 January

---

21   The protests in central London occurred in April 2009 and generated concern about police tactics during the demonstrations. Most seriously, Ian Tomlinson, a newspaper seller on his way home, died after being struck by a police officer on duty (Dodd and Lewis 2010). Other toolkits and rights information for Activists are available via websites such as http://www.activistslegalproject.org.uk [accessed: 26 July 2010].

2011]). 'Lawyers for Young People' is an advice and referral initiative organized by the Children's Society in partnership with social welfare law firms (for their expertise) and large corporate law firms (for their cash), which provides free advice to young people aged between 13 and 19 (www.childrenssociety.org.uk/all_about_us/what_we_do/lfyp/20312.asp [accessed: 26 January 2011]).

It is also possible to identify mainstream private practice social welfare lawyers within the UK, drawing on activist/political strategies, particular through the engagement and use of the media in advancing their legal cases. As Saimo Chahal, a partner at Bindmans LLP, makes clear, these are tools within a progressive lawyer's toolbox to be deployed in the appropriate context and at the appropriate time to advance a client's case:

> I decide when to publicise cases if they are going to be sympathetically and properly reported in the media. I shun media attention when the media's attention is in salacious reporting or when a distorted picture is also going to be painted. (cited in BLD 2008)

Similarly 'radical' lawyers such as Gareth Peirce and Michael Mansfield have used the media to help advance their clients' causes. Books such as *Beyond the Courtroom: A Lawyer's Guide to Campaigning* (Ghose 2005), which give advice on how to draw on the media and lobby law-makers, suggest some accommodation of these strategies by the mainstream, with Ghose winning a Human Rights Lawyer of the year award (British Institute of Human Rights 2010). However, it is also worth noting that this tolerance is not smooth for all, with a number of campaigning and high-profile lawyers having attracted censure and/or investigation by either the courts or the legal professional bodies for their use of such non-legal techniques (Mansfield 2009: 85).[22] Creativity, innovation and the use of non-legal methods and techniques are certainly identifiable among progressive lawyers within the UK. However, the dominant player in social welfare legal services within the UK is the state. In analysing the divergent models of legal professionalism, and drawing on these insights to inform our understanding of the core, we cannot ignore the location of much of the UK's progressive lawyering within state-managed structures. Politically motivated, progressive lawyers and non-lawyer activists, caseworkers and researchers increasingly depend on the state for the funding of their activities. The state, however, directs how these services are delivered. While Law Centres used to deploy 'different ways of challenging

---

22   See Harris (2008) on the contempt charges brought against campaigning Scottish lawyer Aamer Anwar. Although he was cleared, the judgement stated that 'regrettably we do not think that ... [professional] standards were met in this case and the court is entitled to expect better of those who practice before it' (cited in Herald Scotland 2008). See also the professional misconduct charges brought by the Solicitors Regulation Authority against Yvonne Hossack, a campaigning solicitor with a 'tendency to upset people' (The Sentinel 2009).

the Law ... [through] submissions to the Home Office, local MPs, using local press ... there is considerable resistance to that anymore' (SMLC Caseworker). The constraining power of collective legal professionalism may well have diminished, but in the context of social welfare law this has been largely replaced by the constraining power of the neo-liberal state.

Conclusion

Scheingold and Sarat suggest that the differences between cause and conventional lawyering 'drive cause lawyers to, but seldom beyond the profession's boundaries ... the organized legal profession has made a place for cause lawyering – albeit a conditional and precarious one' (2004: 69). This chapter suggests that such radical models of professionalism have a complicated relationship with mainstream professionalism. This is not simply a matter of toleration and accommodation by the organized profession for its own political ends, but also reveals the ongoing connection that cause lawyers have to their disciplinary home.

Jones suggests that

> viewing cause lawyering as 'at odds' with the traditional legal profession may be ignoring the diverse experiences of these lawyers. Not all cause lawyers feel the apparent conflict between their profession and activism because they have defined and created a positive alternative to the traditional profession of law. (2005: 233)

The Pivot Activist/Lawyer model explored in depth in this chapter is, indeed, an example of how lawyers have redefined what lawyering means to them. These lawyers have exerted agency, they have made a choice to position themselves at the edge of law, but in doing so have developed an alternative way in which to conceive of the lawyer's role and methods. This exercise of agency is in stark contrast to the 'inevitable' progression of middle-class North American students into elite Law and Business Schools (Schleef 2006) or, at the other end of the scale in the UK, demoralized publicly funded family lawyers who 'just fell into it' (Melville and Laing 2007). However, it may be that in consciously placing themselves at the 'edge', they close off possibilities for re-imagining what *could be* mainstream lawyering. From the organized profession's perspective, the progressive transformation of lawyering is 'outsourced' to edgy outliers.

The vast majority of legal aid lawyers within the UK are located within the lower reaches of the profession's internal hierarchies (Sommerlad 2001, Moorhead 2004), and grass-roots activists lurch precariously from funding crisis to funding crisis (Robins 2008, LCF 2010). Moreover, both for-profit and not-for-profit sectors remain locked into rigid state structures which constrain their models of delivery (Sommerlad and Sanderson 2009). The Pivot lawyers, who are relatively elite in background, are able to engage in institutional entrepreneurship and challenge existing organizational forms and models of practice. They have been able to exert agency which is unavailable to the marginalized UK groups of legal executives and non-traditional students discussed in the previous two chapters. The subordinated status of these groups means that they find it harder to resist the institutional logics (Bourdieu and Wacquant 1992: 24). Pivot lawyers (and perhaps also some UK proceduralist cause lawyers) have been able to rethink the lawyer role to a much greater extent and with much greater freedom.

The power of Law School socialization and its potential role in reinforcing disciplinary ties was also highlighted in this case-study. Chapters 3 and 4 also consider the power of legal education and the profession to reinforce the message to some non-traditional participants that a career in the profession is 'not for the likes of them'. The enduring powers of disciplinary ties are also explored in Chapters 6 and 7. However, as the arrival of ABSs may enable more people to be involved in the delivery of legal services, without necessarily having to go through these processes of socialization, there may be questions as to the continuing power of legal education as a means of reinforcing the profession's ties to the collective, particularly as more and more training and socialization pressures take place within individual firms (Muzio, Faulconbridge and Cook 2010).

This book argues that a collective model of advancement is less significant than it was in the conditions analysed by Larson and Abel. In the UK however, it is important to remember that a significant dimension of this is as a result of the state's interventions. In the context of social welfare or poverty law, the state has also constrained and managed the ways in which other providers may potentially offer alternative models of delivery. The argument becomes less about the extent to which the power of the collective profession constrains UK cause lawyers and shapes their models of practice, and more about the managerialist imperatives of the state in structuring and organizing public services. Neither the organized profession (Law Society 2010a), nor divergent models of professionalism such as Law Centres (Robins 2008), appear to have much scope to extend the range of services beyond that envisaged by the state.

One of the key themes in this chapter was to highlight the contingency of the Activist/Lawyer identity developed by the Pivot lawyers, who operate at the edge of mainstream legal professionalism. A similar fluidity can be seen in the professional identity of the trusts and estates practitioners located at the edge of law and accountancy. We turn to their story in the next chapter.

Chapter 6
Wealth Professionals: Expert Knowledge at the Intersection of Law and Accountancy

Introduction

This chapter develops the analysis of the complex way in which location within a social field affects the capacity of actors to exert or respond to change. It argues that location at the edge of law can be indicative of agency (and potentially institutional entrepreneurship), or can confirm marginalization and, in the case of some professional actors, both. I draw upon a case-study of the Society for Trusts and Estates Practitioners (STEP) to analyse the complexity of field position and the relationship between institutional entrepreneurship and traditional, collective models of professional advancement.

Trusts and Estates encompasses anything from 'Granny's will' and the administration of her estate to complex trust arrangements which structure the assets of extremely wealthy individuals and families who base much of their lives and fiscal liabilities in sunny off-shore climes.[1] Lawyers working in this area will know Trusts, Probate, Tax and Family Law and will have a good understanding of accounting principles. Other professionals working within Trusts and Estates include accountants, bankers, independent financial advisors, tax advisors and those working with specialist trusts administration and management companies, largely based in the off-shore jurisdictions. STEP has developed since 1991 as the professional association of this disciplinarily and nationally diverse group of professions (just under 800 respondents to the study discussed in this chapter were members of, or subject to, 160 different professional associations and regulators). It now has 16,000 members and regularly engages national governments (including the UK) on issues relevant to its members' interests (STEP 2008a).

Gieryn argues that boundaries between professions are flexible and not fixed (1983: 792). The delivery of professional services has undergone profound change in recent years. Perhaps most fundamentally, expert knowledge itself is changing – fluidity across disciplinary boundaries, fragmentation within professions and of course, the increasingly globalized environment within which businesses and individuals order their lives. STEP has, since its foundation, aspired to a model of a professional organization that is multi-disciplinary and transnational in its membership and strategic orientation. It is, therefore, an ideal case-study through

---

1   These are typically understood to be low-tax jurisdictions, with a disproportionately large financial services sector.

which to explore new organizational forms within the legal and related services marketplace. This chapter explores the extent to which new professions can emerge to take account of the specialization in expert knowledge. After setting out the methodology of the research project and providing background to the organization, I highlight the contradictory field positions occupied by the diverse members and leaders of STEP. I then consider the extent to which a coherent and distinctive body of abstract, expert knowledge in global Trusts and Estate work has emerged. Building from this discussion will be an analysis of the relationship between expert specialized knowledge and professional affiliation and the consequences that this has for STEP's strategic priorities.

I argue in this chapter that STEP is not an example of a new jurisdictional claim on behalf of an emergent, amalgamated profession. It has not successfully yoked the differences that Trusts and Estates lawyers, accountants and bankers share between themselves and against their originating professions (Abbott 1995: 871–2). Rather, it illustrates the complexity of the legal services field and the possibility of a number of models of professional advancement to be invoked at different times. The organizing principles of traditional legal professionalism remain powerful, often with exclusionary effects. However, the analysis of STEP reveals a complex picture within which groups of professionals build (often contingent) alliances with other professionals (Anderson-Gough, Grey and Robson 2006). This suggests a model for making and sustaining claims of expert specialized knowledge separate from, but not in challenge to, the originating discipline of Law.

Methodology and Demographic Profile

This case-study of STEP draws on qualitative and quantitative data, and the research was conducted between June 2008 and September 2009. Interviewees were identified by reference to their role within STEP, and took account of discipline, gender, international location and so on. Eleven interviews in total were conducted, including four from the salaried directorate of STEP, three council members and four branch chairs. A further interview was conducted with a member of the Executive Committee of the Probate Section of the Law Society. The interviews covered the nature of Trusts and Estates Work, the role of the branches within STEP, strategic priorities for STEP and broader challenges facing the Trust and Estates field. Additionally, I conducted an on-line survey, emailed to the then worldwide STEP membership of 13,920 fully qualified Trusts and Estates practitioners and students (3,855). Some 774 completed questionnaires were submitted, giving an overall response rate of 5.56 per cent. Despite the relatively small sample, the demographic statistics demonstrate strong congruence with the overall membership statistics held by STEP.

STEP holds some data on disciplinary background. It reports: Accountancy – 30 per cent, Law – 58.5 per cent and Bankers, Trust Service Providers and others – 10 per cent. The questionnaire respondents are over-represented by those with a background in Banking and Trust Services (28.2 per cent) and under-represented by Accountancy (17.7 per cent) and Law (52.9 per cent). This is of concern, given that the STEP leadership aims to increase STEP's relevance to accountants (both members and non-members). It may be that those with a trusts background engaged more with a STEP-supported questionnaire, because they already feel most engaged to the organization with most relevance to their professional interests – in contrast perhaps, to the more disengaged and hard-to-reach accountants.

Background and History of STEP

Professions have their roots in the mobility and closure projects of the nineteenth century (Larson 1977, Abel 1988). Given that the conditions giving rise to the model of professionalism outlined by Abel and Larson are no longer available to occupations wishing to secure exclusive jurisdictional control of a particular task area (Abel 2003, Kritzer 1999), it is important to note that the emergence of STEP dates from only 1991.

George Tasker, a Senior Trusts Manager in a Big Five accountancy firm, was concerned about the status of Trusts and Estates work in Law and Accountancy – 'the Cinderella discipline' – and, in particular, the consequences of a lack of effective training in the area, in terms of maintaining standards and ensuring succession (Tasker 2010). He identified a need 'for those working in the same field to meet and talk to others about their work', believing that practitioners wanted 'a forum for all those working in the field of Trusts and Estates regardless of their discipline'. STEP was founded as a private limited company and the first annual conference was held in 1992. Even written with the benefit of hindsight, George Tasker's recollections present a relatively cautious picture of practitioners, marginalized within their traditional disciplines, who were keen to meet others working in the same area in an effort to improve knowledge and understanding of and within their field. A marker of how quickly this organization's aspirations have changed is provided by the first of STEP's eight key aims: 'To raise the public profile of Trusts and Estates work as a *profession in its own right*' (emphasis added, http://www.step.org/about_step/steps_aims.aspx [accessed: 26 January 2011]). The shift towards a *profession in its own right* is a critical one and raises key questions about knowledge claims in the field, the capacity of STEP to lead an amalgamated professional project for Trusts and Estates practitioners and, indeed, the relationship of traditional legal professionalism to emergent models of professional advancement.

STEP has a worldwide membership of approximately 16,000 members, in jurisdictions from the USA and Canada to the Middle East and Asia, including Africa, Australia and New Zealand. Its branches are a key dimension of its growth and the primary means by which much of the networking, technical updates and student education takes place. These branches have a considerable degree of autonomy – 'like a franchise' in the words of one interviewee from the Directorate.

It publishes a series of glossy publications, including the flagship *STEP Journal*,[2] which has a heavy emphasis on technical updating and knowledge sharing. In addition to its core education activities which are designed to lead to qualification and membership of STEP, it has increased its commercial CPD activities for people working within Trusts and Estates/Wealth-Structuring. This was seen by the Directorate as a key way in which the profile, profits and presence of the organization could be increased.

Institutional Entrepreneurship from the Edge of Law: The Complexity of STEP's Position within a Field in Flux

In Chapter 2 we highlighted the importance of the organizing properties of 'institutional logics' (Lounsbury 2002: 255). The structuring and constraining properties of these logics mean that it is important for us to consider the ways in which the relative positions of actors within the Trusts and Estates field affect their capacity to resist institutional pressures (Battilana 2006, Greenwood and Suddaby 2006). Careful analysis of location within an organizational field, and the degree to which institutional logics, such as professionalism (Fournier 1999, Suddaby, Gendron and Lam 2009: 410), constrain individual and organizational agency, can enhance our understanding of how and when models of professional advancement (or institutional change) may emerge.

Lounsbury argues that professionalization claims are likely to occur during periods of institutional transformation (2002: 258), and external changes can disrupt settled jurisdictions within the system of the professions (Abbott: 1988: 91). Within the legal and related services market, the processes of transformation since the 1980s (Lee 1992, Hanlon 1999) have been given further momentum by the Legal Services Act 2007 (Flood 2008). In particular, the authorization of Alternative Business Structures from 2011 may indicate a further weakening of these institutional logics. However, the capacity of STEP actors to respond to these changes is not evenly distributed.

Greenwood and Suddaby suggest that field maturity sees increasing stratification or 'dominance hierarchy' (2006: 28, see also Abbott 1988: 134). While Trusts and Estates work is a relatively immature (distinct) field, the fields of Law and Accountancy are mature fields, and are characterized by pronounced differentiation. Those working in the Trusts and Estates areas are often at the bottom of the 'dominance hierarchy'. However, Greenwood and Suddaby argue that institutional entrepreneurship can be found among elite actors, given their ability to transcend boundaries, and draw on the resources of power, influence and capital (2006: 37–9). Similarly, Battilana argues that an individual's ability

---

2   The *STEP Journal* won the 2009 Trade Association Forum Best Practice Award for 'Magazine of the Year' (http://www.stepjournal.org/about_step_journal.aspx [accessed: 26 January 2011]).

to affect change within an organization is shaped by their status and field position (2006: 659–60).

In identifying the field position of STEP and its members we need to first clarify which field we are considering,[3] and second consider whether the organization and its members are similarly positioned. In relation to different actors within STEP we may be variously analysing Law, Accountancy, the Legal and Related Services Market, Banking, Global Trusts and Estates work, or Wealth Structuring Professional Services. Different individuals within STEP occupy different positions within each of these fields.

Greenwood and Suddaby argue that the (as was) Big Five accountancy firms are, by virtue of the size and scale of their practice, able to straddle international and jurisdictional boundaries and seize opportunities for growth in ways which run counter to prevailing institutional logics (2006: 40). Some actors within the STEP world hold this elite status and bridge boundaries through their work in a global field at the edge of legal knowledge. Institutional logics of legal professionalism could be challenged, for example as STEP professionals identify greater differences between themselves and other English lawyers than they do with international bankers and accountants working in Trusts and Estates (Abbott 1995: 868–70). However, many of the founding members of the organization were at the foot of the 'dominance hierarchy' of their originating disciplines and, arguably, private client work in both Law and Accountancy remains something of a 'Cinderella' discipline today. This appears to leave many STEP lawyers (and accountants) on the vertical edge sketched out in Chapter 2 and less able to resist the disciplinary ties of legal professionalism (Fournier 1999).

Trusts and Estates Lawyers and Accountants – Marginal within Their Fields

Few entrants to the legal profession want to join this sector (a core area of concern highlighted in interviews and questionnaires). Thus, 'Conveyancing and Wills' was the least preferred area of practice among surveyed law students, with just 2.4 per cent expressing a desire to work in the area, compared to 43.9 per cent who wished to work in Business and Commercial Affairs (Norman 2004: 32). Student preferences are pragmatic; the largest commercial law firms offer a disproportionate number of traineeships (Cole 2009: 24). This was well recognized within STEP:

> Inevitably the big firms dominate the country's legal training – they don't do that much of this work and also it's not seen as, as glamorous or rewarding as working in other areas of law and accounting. (Interview 7, STEP Directorate)

Even amongst established legal professionals, Trusts and Estates work is not well regarded. Abbott suggests that client differentiation can be an important basis of

---

3   See, for example, Sherer and Lee on the different fields in which lawyers in Clinics or in Corporate Law operate (2002: 116).

stratification (1988: 122). Thus, association with lower-status clients leads to lower status for those professionals who serve them (Carlin 1962). In the legal sphere, the corporation is accorded higher status than the private client, notwithstanding the wealth and power of many of the high-net worth private clients who are served by STEP members. Corporate Law is perceived as exciting and dynamic with high quality work (Collier 2005). Private client work is considered to be altogether more pedestrian, and Trusts and Estates work, in particular, fairly lifeless. Even lawyers working for extremely high-net worth private clients, spoke of the denigrated status they experienced within their own corporate firms. As one interviewee recounted: 'One of my ... partners was saying ... 'Oh [name], all your clients are dead' – well frankly f*** off, they are not, but that was their perception' (Interview 2, Branch Chair).

Abbott argues that another key basis upon which internal stratification occurs is proximity to the core of a profession's knowledge base (1988: 118). Thus, Trusts and Estates lawyers could be seen as peripheral players within the legal profession because the work that they do draws upon knowledge from the fields of Accounting and Trusts Management, thus placing them further away from the core of legal knowledge. Yet, Corporate Law firms themselves do work which moves fluidly between the disciplinary boundaries of Law, Finance, Banking and Management Consultancy (see Chapter 7). Moreover, routine work is carried out within these firms as much as it is within the other sectors of the profession (Abbott 1988: 125). Much of this routine work is, in effect, carried out by para-professionals or more junior lawyers (Muzio and Ackroyd 2005) – the profession differentiated, internally at least, by career (Abbott 1988: 129).

I argue that vertical stratification (and marginalization) is reinforced, not by the use of extraneous knowledge, but by the breadth of Trusts and Estates work itself. In contrast to the increasing specialization within corporate legal practice (Hanlon 1999), and indeed other sectors such as Crime and Personal Injury (Moorhead 2010), Trusts and Estates practitioners insisted upon the breadth of their legal knowledge. Their specialism was their generalism:

> I know plenty of land law and plenty of trust law and I've got a good working knowledge of my corporate law because when somebody dies – I'm studying all the issues. I've been a stockbroker, I've been a hotel manager, a property developer. I've stood in that place and I've had to see what's got to be done ... .
> (Interview 6, Branch Chair)

> As the Law has progressed and practices have become more specialist in their area, I feel that we've been looked on as basically the poor relation ... If you like law as a big subject then you will cover most of it within 'private client'. I think there is more breadth than perhaps some of the other areas. (Interview 3, Probate Section Law Society)

As the comments suggest, the nature of their claim to specialism appears hard to sustain against an elite group of actors redefining core legal knowledge as specialist legal knowledge (Edmonds 2010b: 9). As has been the case in Medicine for decades, greater prestige is attached to the specialist rather than the general practitioner (Freidson 1970: 104); indeed, specialism is the career pathway for those working in hospitals (http://www.nhscareers.nhs.uk/medical. shtml [accessed: 26 January 2011]). Of course, as Gieryn argues, professions have always insisted on the boundaries between what they know and what they don't know (1983: 784–6). However, this move to specialization, and a re-focusing of the profession's knowledge base represents what Moorhead describes as the 'professional paradox' (2010): how is the idea of profession wide competence (Johnson 1972: 55), maintained when specialization is insisted upon (LSC 2010)? The particular challenge for STEP is that although they assert specialism in the Trusts and Estates field, the nature of the work requires them to claim expertise over far broader areas of the traditional discipline than some of the elite actors. It may be that Abbott's notions of 'optimum abstraction' are now being played out within traditional professions as much as they are across a system of interlocking professions (1988: 105). Moreover, what is 'optimum' abstraction may be considerably narrower than in the past.

The large corporate firms dictate where prestige and influence lies. Thus, these firms influence the legal profession's education and qualification routes. Trusts Law remains a foundational subject of the academic stage (JASB 2002b), but Wills and Probate is no longer part of the core of the LPC – there is 'a tilt in training towards the large commercial firms' acknowledged one senior partner within a leading global law firm (see Chapter 3). Private client work is similarly marginalized within Accountancy (Greenwood, Suddaby and Hinings 2002: 64), particularly since the emergence of Management Accounting in the 1950s (Roslender 1992: 135). Lawyers and accountants repeated the refrain that theirs was a 'Cinderella discipline', the 'poor relation', seen as a 'Step-child', 'cast adrift'. This peripheral status was arguably one of the driving motivations to the foundation of STEP and provides much of the continued impetus. Thus, 'the lower group [in Accountancy or Law for example] has to defend its "professional" status and since its superiors will not listen to it, it inevitably seeks new audiences and potentially, too, new alliances' (Abbott 1988: 128). However, as a result of internal stratification within the parent professions, they appear insufficiently positioned to rethink their professional identity, norms and status, in the way that Greenwood and Suddaby (2006) describe Big Five accountancy firms as having achieved. Nevertheless, STEP has made exciting progress since 1991. In many ways this is because the organization itself has been able to engage in boundary bridging, and thus the institutional entrepreneurship, denied to many of its members.

Boundary Bridging, Wealth-Structuring and Institutional Entrepreneurship

In contrast to the marginal and low status of private client Trusts and Estates work, those working off-shore for high-net worth individuals are less obviously marginal players within their respective fields. These actors are more likely to be from a financial or banking background and are more likely to be oriented towards the 'dynamic' wealth-structuring end of the specialism, and are thus less likely to suffer on the basis of client differentiation. They are positioned very differently to traditional on-shore Trusts and Estates lawyers and accountants. While lacking power in terms of numerical weight and corporate ties, they are more likely to engage in institutional entrepreneurship, given their operation across international and disciplinary boundaries (Greenwood and Suddaby 2006: 37–9). The nature of their client base also enables them to build important alliances with other professional groups, government and regulators (Dezalay and Garth 1996).

Lounsbury notes that 'the establishment of a professional association is a specific way in which an occupation can formalize its identity, make claims about its occupational status and participate in a field of governance' (2002: 256, Larson 1977). Yet this same centrality to the professional project may reinforce the institutional logics which inhibit field-changing entrepreneurship. Laffin and Entwistle note that public sector professions have had difficulty rationalizing their professional projects because of the restrictions of Royal Charters, statutory powers and 'an active minority of conservative practitioners'(2000: 216), and Greenwood, Suddaby and Hinings suggest that professional associations are typically seen as agents of reproduction rather than of change (2002: 73, Francis 2004: 342–4).

I argue that STEP is less bound by these institutional logics, precisely because it developed from its inception as a 'boundary bridging' organization (Greenwood and Suddaby 2006: 37) for those originating from Law, Accountancy and Banking who were engaged in Trusts and Estates work. Moreover, particularly with the internationalization of the organization's development and its engagement with new wealth-structuring disciplines from those based in off-shore jurisdictions, the boundary bridging nature of its orientations and expertise has strengthened in the intervening years. This enables STEP to identify new possibilities and markets which are not necessarily visible to those whose choices and patterns of professional behaviour are more deeply shaped by institutional logics (Francis 2002: 14–15, 2004: 342–4). It is also possible to identify a strong institutional entrepreneurship from within the leadership of STEP, who are typically not from the traditional professional disciplines from which the original membership was drawn. Although there are strong and continuing ties to the original profession from those with a Law or Accountancy disciplinary heritage, these ties do not constrain the leadership: 'I'm not a lawyer, not an accountant, knew nothing about wills or trusts and estates, just the fact that I really got intrigued by such an exciting industry' (Interview 8, Directorate).

Moreover, the relatively small size of the Directorate (seven), in fact, enabled a coherent entrepreneurial team to come in and develop their own agenda (see Flood 2007 on the power of the leadership role in developing law firms). They saw an opportunity to develop a fledgling organization – to be there at the outset:

> I got to the point where I ought to show that I could run something rather than just talk about it ... the attraction was that an embryonic body with a number of interesting colleagues ... and a chance to shape it ... It also at that point was a body with branches internationally, but it wasn't a truly global body – there was still an Anglo-Saxon dominance; ... so a chance to pick up the skills from running a growing organization to manage change. That was the attraction. (Interview 7, Directorate)

> You are coming in at what might be a normal level for a 28 year old, but suddenly you find that the organization around you is growing – you're getting promoted entirely just by virtue of the fact that the organization is growing and that is exciting and challenging. (Interview 8, Directorate)

The influence of the salaried officers within STEP should not be underestimated (see also Laffin and Entwistle 2000: 213–14). As one key individual made clear, much of their role involves 'creating an opportunity, a choice architecture, you've chosen the chairman of your ... committee ... you know you can create choices for them to take' (Interview 8, Directorate).

Those on the periphery of the professional field may well be less bound by the properties of the field, as indeed Shils suggests (1975: 10). However, as a result of internal stratification, many Trusts and Estates practitioners appear insufficiently positioned to entirely re-think their professional identity, norms and status in the way that Greenwood, Suddaby and Hinings (2002) describe Big Five accountancy firms as having achieved. The complicating factor when we consider STEP is that its members and leaders occupy different and often conflicting positions. While the origins of the organization were very much at the margins of Law and Accountancy, other features of STEP and the location of its developing, international membership leave it better positioned to challenge institutional structures. On the other hand, as a relatively small organization which represents significant numbers of private client lawyers and accountants who work for low-net worth individuals, there are clearly resource asymmetries which may challenge STEP's ability to fundamentally alter the institutional field.

Expert Knowledge in Trusts and Estates Work

Interdisciplinarity and Professional Knowledge

A standardized body of knowledge provided professionalizing occupations with a legitimate basis for the elite status they claimed and a means by which they could ensure their distinctiveness as against other professionals and the lay-person (Larson 1977, Perkin 1990). The Law Society, for example, took a strong lead in establishing the accepted limits of the discourse of the solicitors' profession and developing what came to be accepted as the profession wide model of legal professionalism (Sugarman 1996: 108). The importance of knowledge is its applicability to the work of which the profession currently has control or would like to move to a position of control (Jamous and Peloille 1970: 116). For example, an attacking move made by a secure profession could show some new task to be 'reducible', in principle, to one of the attackers' already secure jurisdictions (Abbott 1988: 98). Thus, Abbott argues that the accountants, as a profession, were able to stretch their influence and knowledge over long tenuous boundaries at the expense of other professions (1995: 878). However, Greenwood and Suddaby argue that these jurisdictional moves are increasingly made on an organizational, rather than profession-wide basis (2001: 950).

In considering the relationship of expert knowledge to an amalgamated collective professional project of Trusts and Estates professionals, we need to consider how expert knowledge is used by a diverse range of practitioners. It is within organizational settings, within which lawyers may work with tax and trusts specialists, that the similarities in the cognitive bases being drawn upon may become more obvious (Leicht and Fennell 1997: 225). Thus, 'what builds bonds or strains between different professions is common work or common workplaces' (Abbott 1988: 124). Arguably the workplace setting will become even more significant within the new organizational forms permitted under the LSA. For example, financial services deregulation in the United States ended government protection of the financial intermediaries' turf and generated a blending of professional roles across organizational forms. In turn, this led to the establishment of new professional associations to formalize the new profession's identity and make status claims (Lounsbury 2002: 257, see also Abbott 1995: 869). Professionals from a range of environing disciplines already deploy expert knowledge within the Trusts and Estates field. The key issue is the extent to which the realities of the workplace are so stark as to challenge the external coherence of the claims of Law or Accountancy that they still represent a clear and distinct profession reinforced by a single body of knowledge (Abbott 1988: 117–18).

'Trusts and Estates' is, in fact, something of a misnomer given that there is no concept of a 'trust' within some jurisdictions – there are other devices to structure wealth and pass assets through the generations (http://www.step.org/publications/leaflets/trusts_explained.aspx [accessed: 26 January 2011]). Trusts law, of course, remains foundational to the legal profession in England and Wales (at the academic stage at least, JASB 2002b). Although the power of the Corporate Law firms saw the removal of Probate as a compulsory module on the LPC, the minority who are sufficiently interested can still take a module in it.[4]

STEP has, from the outset, delivered education, training and accreditation, and aspired to be the provider of the 'gold standard' qualification in the industry. In terms of the accredited expertise that STEP offers, entry rests on either a Qualified Practitioner route (requiring as little as two years post-qualification, for example, as a solicitor and three short essays in the area of Trusts, Tax, Accounting or International Issues). More challenging are the Diplomas – including ones designed for particular jurisdictions, for example Canada. The STEP Diploma for England and Wales consists of four, three-hour closed-book examinations covering: Administration of Estates, Administration of Trusts, Taxation of Trusts and Estates and Trust and Estate Accounting. Limited exemptions are available and are usually granted on the basis of past exams and experience. There has been some internal debate within STEP about the importance of insisting upon exams as against the less challenging Qualified Practitioner route – framed in terms of expanding the membership on one hand, or maintaining the rigour and high standards of the qualification on the other. Notwithstanding the increasingly organizational focus in professional services training and education (Greenwood and Suddaby 2006: 40), it is striking to note the lead taken here by the professional association to articulate a clear, distinct knowledge base as the foundation for a jurisdictional claim within global Trusts and Estates work.

The Enduring Strength of Core Professional Knowledge

Although the completion of all four papers gives a strong multi-disciplinary knowledge in a range of areas relevant to Trusts and Estates work, in practice the cognitive base of the originating discipline appears strong. Indeed there were concerns expressed within the leadership of the organization that the exams reflected the lawyer dominance of some of the pioneering members within STEP:

> that's also partially because its developed by lawyers ... and they look at things through a glass that unintentionally isn't quite right for the accountant so we need a more comprehensive offering. (Interview 7, Directorate)

Thus, while on the surface the accredited knowledge attempts to provide a multi-disciplinary cognitive base, in practice this reflects the lawyerly dominance of the pioneers. This has subsequently seen the development of a new Diploma for Accounting and Taxation Professionals, designed to 'supplement existing knowledge' with a 'broad legal understanding of the Trusts vehicle'. Although

---

4   The Core Practice areas are now Business Law and Practice, Property Law and Practice and Litigation.

this addresses the perceived gaps in the educational market, it also underlines the enduring strength and appeal of the core professional disciplines (STEP 2010d).

The vast majority of those interviewed were clear that lawyers primarily did law, Independent Financial Advisors (IFAs) did financial planning and trusts administrators administered trusts and so on – 'it's the Law – that's the framework within which I work' (Interview 2, Branch). There was a suggestion that the trusts specialist is 'a multi-disciplinary practitioner' (Interview 9, Council), but, particularly for lawyers and accountants, their broader engagement with expert knowledge beyond the host discipline was simply in terms of knowing when to refer:

> We spread our risk; we take outside legal advice, outside investment advice etc.
> … But that's not to say you have to be completely ignorant of law ... I regard the
> trustee as sitting somewhere in the middle, but taking advice from outside where
> expert advice is needed. (Interview 1, Council).

Networking, Business Development and Sharing Knowledge

In this context, then, the heavy emphasis throughout the questionnaire responses and interviews was of the key role of STEP being primarily one of knowledge sharing, professional networking and an assertion of accredited specialized expertise in traditional disciplines, rather than one of articulating a new distinct body of knowledge (Abbott 1988). Thus, one council member saw the value of the qualification as a means to keep up with international developments, and clearly defined his professional identity as a lawyer. These are the key reasons why people joined and are identified as the key benefits that these practitioners derive from their membership.

While 'defining a specialism' was the most popular reason that STEP members gave for joining the organization (see further below), the second most popular reason, with 60 per cent of respondents, was to 'learn more about trusts and estates work'. Some 85.9 per cent of all respondents identified 'maintaining and developing knowledge' as a benefit of belonging to STEP, with 41 per cent regarding this as the primary benefit:[5]

> [STEP] means somewhere to get information, meeting one's peers and generally
> keeping up to date with what is going on. (Interview 2, Branch Chair)

---

5 Another way in which knowledge is shared in a seemingly open and supportive manner is the STEP on-line discussion forum, within which often quite detailed technical problems are addressed in a mutually-supportive and non-intimidatory environment (http://www.trustsdiscussionforum.co.uk/ [accessed: 26 January 2011]).

I think [STEP] is a networking role for practitioners. I think that's really important, that ultimately helps their job. (Interview 4, Directorate)

Similarly, 73.6 per cent of respondents identified that one of the advantages of branch meetings was the opportunity to learn more about practice developments. With few disciplinary differences, 45.2 per cent of all respondents identified this as the primary advantage of the branch meeting. This strong branch activity (which has been a core feature of STEP's growth - 'that's what STEP does, bring senior people together within the profession' (Interview 1, Council)), appears to be sustained by the fact that STEP members are unlikely to be competitors within the same professional market. Thus, STEP members were more likely to view their primary competitors as being those from within their traditional disciplinary areas – although this was particularly pronounced for lawyers – rather than to identify other STEP members as their primary competitors. Therefore 'people are willing to put things on the table that they wouldn't do in a directly competitive environment' (Interview 7, Directorate). Also:

I think people are quite prepared to share, which is rare in a lot of professions, because I think because we are so specialist, people do share [information]... . Let's say anyone rings me to ask me a question, you don't say 'no'. (Interview 9, Council)

In contrast to the Law Society's experience of dwindling local Law Society activity, with solicitors unwilling to drop in and share gossip with a competitor (Francis 2004: 336), engagement with a STEP branch and sharing knowledge appears to be a way in which businesses can be grown and individual careers enhanced. Thus, all interviewed were clear about the personal benefits that the branch chairs derived from the role:

I suppose from a purely selfish point of view it is an outstanding way of raising my profile in the local community... it isn't altruistic by any stretch of the imagination. I think it is a great way of networking. (Interview 5, Branch Chair)

[People become Chairs] for their own local promotion - it's a prestige for them and raises their profile in the local community. (Interview 4, Directorate)[6]

Anderson-Gough, Grey and Robson argue that such alliance building is central to the construction of the 'Networked Professional' and is an important way in which professionals learn 'the way things work' (2006: 238). This is critical to

---

6   It should be noted that others are keen to stress the altruism – see for example, 'there are a number of young people who phone me up [as Branch Chair] and ask me what do I think about this – and God, I don't think I could ever have phoned up a partner in another law firm, but that's good' (Interview 6, Branch Chair).

the increasingly individual responsibility that actors have to take for their career development (Boltanski and Chiapello 2006: 166), and is perhaps also indicative of more individualized projects to secure market returns and enhance prestige (Hanlon 1999: 156–61 on the 'cult of the individual').[7] As strict jurisdictional boundaries break down, and as professionals are more comfortable working across lines that were historically closely policed (Sugarman 1995a), none of this is odd or unusual. Indeed, it becomes part of the properties of the field – it is how professionals are expected to act. However, Anderson-Gough, Grey and Robson also argue that lower-status actors may struggle to secure access to these sites (2006: 239). STEP's successful intervention to facilitate this access appears to suggest that there may be an ongoing role for collective action in some professional settings (see further Chapters 7 and 8).

Specialist Professionals and Disciplinary Heritage

While there does not appear to be a clearly identifiable knowledge base which is distinct to, and shared by, all worldwide members of STEP, they are clear that they wish to be seen as specialist Trusts and Estates practitioners, albeit within their host discipline. Thus, with no real disciplinary (or other) differences, 63 per cent of respondents identified the fact that STEP offered a 'Qualification that Defined the Specialism' as a reason why they joined – and 31 per cent of all respondents identified this as the primary reason why they joined:

> I see a continual stream of lawyers providing no service – incompetent ... The big thing about STEP for me is can we just get the public to understand that it isn't any old lawyer or any old accountant – they need to be specialists in this area. Otherwise you risk an incompetent service or something going absolutely wrong with the numbers ... I am hoping that the youngsters recognize that they need to be recognised as specialists so they need to have public recognition ... .
> (Interview 6, Branch Chair)

Abbott suggests that 'since a parent profession usually provides specialists with the full protection of professionalism, specialities do not, in general, leave that parent, but develop special education and certification structures within it' (1988: 106). However, as we will explore in the following sections, the extent to which those parental ties remained, varied across the STEP membership.

There was widespread concern that generalists dabbling in the area were doing untold damage to the public, and there was a strong desire to use the STEP qualification and membership as a way of badging their specialism and distinguishing themselves from the Trusts and Estates dabbler. Gieryn similarly

---

7 The interest in the moves of 're-structuring star' Chris Howard, from Linklaters to Freshfields and back again, is an example of the capital attached to key individuals (Hollander 2010b).

highlights the way in which scientists used the 'foil' of non-experts to emphasize the legitimacy of their claims of expertise (1983: 791). STEP has deployed similar tactics in introducing a new Certificate in Will Preparation as the 'gold standard' in the sector (STEP 2010c), alongside publishing research highlighting the 'incompetence and dishonesty of cowboy will-writers' (STEP 2010b).

Yet, even here, disciplinary differences are apparent. While the most common 'Strategic Priority' (identified by 44 per cent of respondents) was to 'promote the qualification to employers', 17.8 per cent of the respondents identified it as *the most important* 'Strategic Priority'. These were far more likely to be those with a Trusts and Estates background or who worked in a bank or trust company. Equally, 59.6 per cent of those with Trusts and Estates background (in contrast to an average of 40 per cent) defined themselves by their specialism and not traditional disciplinary background. Lawyers, on the other hand, were more likely than any other disciplinary grouping to define themselves first by their legal knowledge. This suggests a greater opportunity to promote the STEP qualification in sectors where there is not one clear disciplinary background which dominates the field:

> I don't see that many lawyers and accountants see STEP as being their first choice professional body ... I'm not saying that they don't value STEP..., but I think it's in a secondary, rather than a primary way. (Interview 5, Branch Chair)

Abbott suggests that 'the chief cause for formal division is the presence of other groups – either specialities within other professions or strong outsiders performing the same tasks as the professional specialists' (1988: 106). Arguably in the high-net worth, wealth-structuring end of the market (particularly in off-shore jurisdictions), there is a greater presence of shared work, overlapping knowledge, and 'increasing specialization in the sector' (Resp. 748, economics background, regulator), which enables them to identify the opportunities in amalgamation. As Greenwood and Suddaby argue, 'a network position that bridges fields [in terms of both knowledge and jurisdictions] lessens institutional embeddedness by exposing actors to interinstitutional incompatibilities, increasing their awareness of alternatives' (2006: 38). The lawyers within England and Wales, in contrast, continued to assert the breath of their legal knowledge, albeit applied to the specialist field of Trusts and Estates. At the moment, at least, the 'level of abstraction' required to make the claim of a coherent body of distinctive global wealth-structuring knowledge is not capable of being made coherently by STEP (Abbott 1988: 105). This becomes much more apparent when other dimensions of the nascent jurisdictional claim are examined; not least the aspiration of different parts of the membership to see the creation of a new profession of Wealth-Structuring Professionals.

Trusts and Estates Practitioner to Wealth-Structuring Professional

The following section explores the extent to which STEP is formalizing its jurisdictional claim for control of accredited expertise in global wealth-structuring services. Lounsbury identifies the importance of professional associations in articulating status claims for an emergent profession (2002: 256), and Greenwood, Suddaby and Hinings are also clear as to the vital role that professional associations play in jurisdictional claims (2002: 61). Interestingly, it appears that within the Trusts and Estates field, it is STEP the organization which is articulating the professional project of Trusts and Estates practitioners, in contrast to the increasing focus on firms as the site of professional regulation (SRA 2010b) or as an organizational actor (Cooper and Robson 2006).

Given the absence of a clearly defined knowledge base, there are obviously questions as to the capacity of STEP to serve as the fulcrum of a collective mobility project for an amalgamated profession of Trusts and Estates practitioners (Abbott 1988: 105). Within STEP, however, the emphasis of the organization's aspirations is clear, and can be seen in a recent policy report, introduced in the following terms:

> Thirty-two leading Trusts and Estates Practitioners are ... are decisively preparing for a new professional future where they are actively engaged in global, not just local, tax compliant cross border wealth structuring. (Johnson and Johnstone 2009: 1)

The long-term direction of travel is also signposted in this extract from the Chief Executive's statement within the Annual Review of 2008:

> [STEP] should be first choice for anyone working in the stewardship and structuring of wealth, whether through the Trusts and Estates model of STEP's more traditional jurisdictions or through other inter-generational planning approaches in other parts of the STEP world. (STEP 2008b: 4)

This looks more like a new jurisdictional claim based on amalgamation of cognate professions, than a means of accrediting specialisms within the parent profession (Abbott 1988: 106). As discussed above, the origins of the organization and its salaried leadership (if not the early lawyer pioneers) enable STEP to bridge jurisdictional boundaries in ways not typically seen in professional associations (Greenwood and Suddaby 2006, Francis 2004), and see it well positioned to engage in this institutional entrepreneurship.

However, Abbott warns that such amalgamations often fail because 'distinct professional heritages and tasks prevent a unified cognitive and social structure' (1988: 105). The 160 different professional associations to which 800 respondents belonged, and the emphasis on sufficient knowledge to refer (see also STEP 2010a: 27) rather than a new genuinely distinct knowledge base, signal that 'the required level of abstraction [is likely to lead to] an ineffectual vagueness' (Abbott 1988: 106). There is some enthusiasm for the journey towards the establishment of a distinct profession of Wealth-Structuring Professionals, but this comes from specific sections of the membership, who are currently in the minority.

Those most strongly supporting the wealth-structuring direction of travel are 'non-lawyer' members and leaders of STEP.

> [STEP] is my only qualification and as the years go by there will be more people for which the TEP is their only qualification and that's what we're aiming at … It's trying to project an image of a profession in its own right, which pulls together lawyers, accountants, tax professionals, financial professionals, notaries, bankers, barristers and the odd judge. (Interview 9, Council)

> There's a member in Norfolk doing Granny's will [on the one hand] and the member in London who is doing international business in Dubai with rich Americans … . Provincial members like to be called trusts and estates practitioners … they are always seen as lawyers, accountants…, whereas the international members whether in London or Hong Kong or in the Caribbean have no problem with being called as wealth-structurers … . I think we are preferably suited to be the Wealth Management Body. (Interview 8, Directorate)

In terms of the broader membership, in their responses to questions such as 'How would you describe yourself?', 'Is there are a distinct profession of TEPs?', 'What are the strategic priorities of the organization?' and so on, Trusts Specialists, Independent Financial Advisors and Bankers were the strongest supporters of such a jurisdictional claim. Thus, for example, those with a Trusts background were more likely than others to indicate that they felt that Trusts and Estates was a new profession (adjusted residual value of 3.6).[8] Those with a Financial Services background were far more likely, than any other disciplinary background to describe themselves as Wealth Professionals (40 per cent of them, with adjusted residual of 6.9). The respondents with a Trusts and Estates background were those who indicated that they had most in common with Trusts and Estates Professionals worldwide (Abbott's shared sites of difference, 1995: 869). Lawyers, in contrast, were more likely than any other disciplinary background to highlight firm-specific affiliations or connections with Trusts and Estate Practitioners *nationally*. Those with a Trusts and Estates background were also three times more likely than any other category to say that the most important strategic priority for STEP was to ensure the emergence of a clearly recognizable wealth professional. A linked variable, which was in fact the strongest variable for a number of questions, was the on-shore/off-shore divide.

---

8   See discussion on methodology in Chapter 1.

Lawyers and Law, Accountants and Accountancy

There was a very strong connection (measured through responses to different questions) to their originating profession and (and association) from lawyers and accountants. Thus, accountants were six times more likely to say that they had more in common with their own discipline, than any of the professional sub-groups within the STEP membership. Equally, lawyers (with an adjusted residual of 7.2), were more likely than any other professional grouping within STEP to state that 'I am a lawyer (or accountant, IFA and so on) first, and a Trusts and Estates specialist second.' As one (non-lawyer) branch chair noted:

> I think generally speaking, the lawyers and accountants look up and down their straight lines much more than they do towards STEP. I think it's a fact. ... if there was a Law Society Probate Section going on, on the same night as a STEP meeting, the lawyers would go to the Law Society meeting in preference to the STEP meeting. (Interview 5, Branch Chair)

This was a little surprising given that lawyers and accountants saw themselves towards the bottom of the internal stratification of their own professions (see above). Moreover, in the case of Accountancy, responses elsewhere in the questionnaire confirmed their historical ease with describing themselves as specialists in tax, for example, rather than generalist accountants. Suddaby, Gendron and Lam also note the complexity of accountants' ties to their host profession (2009: 424).

The engagement with, and support for, the Law Society from many UK solicitors was also surprising, given their location with that professional field – 'we get put rather to the bottom of the pile which I think is a great shame actually' (Interview 3, Probate Section) – and the general disdain in which most solicitors seem to hold the Law Society – 'the Law Society is the world's worst trade union – gets in the way I think ... I can never see what it does' (Interview 2, Branch Chair, see also Francis 2004). Workplace is a key variable affecting the strength of that connection to the originating profession (Abbott 1988: 124, Suddaby, Gendron and Lam 2009: 424). For example, lawyers in law firms were overwhelmingly more likely to describe themselves as lawyers (83.9 per cent of responses), than any particular specialism. If they worked in a trust company they were more likely to describe themselves as Trusts Specialists (38.3 per cent), than lawyers (31.9 per cent). Accountants in law firms were most likely to describe themselves as Trusts Specialists (77.8 per cent); yet in trust companies they were most likely to describe themselves as accountants (40 per cent). The fluidity of the professional identities generated by these workplaces and variable connections to the parent discipline is well summarized by the following comments from the members of the Directorate: 'the particular characteristic of STEP I draw attention to just is, *herding cats…* whether jurisdictionally or in different sort of [professional] subsets' (Interview 7: Directorate). And:

I think it's representing lots of professionals from different disciplinary backgrounds and I mean it's not just common law jurisdictions. ... I think it's quite a bit of melting pot – you can't say it's just the trusts and estates profession because some jurisdictions don't like trusts, some don't do estate planning, some of them are common law, some are civil law, ... so yeah kind of loads of different people coming from different directions... Even writing a STEP description has become difficult ... to make it broad enough to encompass everybody's needs and wants. (Interview 4, Directorate)

While there is a continuing connection to the historical professions from lawyers and accountants, these practitioners are not necessarily going to their traditional professions for accreditation of their specialist expertise (or indeed for many of their other members' services – technical updates and so on). There was also broader scepticism as to the regulatory competence of the traditional professions (see also Suddaby, Gendron and Lam 2009: 424, Flood 2010, Chapter 7). The establishment of the Probate Section in 1997 does, however, appear to have been broadly well received by solicitors within England and Wales. While this represents an effort by the Law Society to respond to differentiated concerns within its membership, it appears to have been set up more by committed individuals responding to their marginalization, rather than a co-ordinated strategy from the professional association.

However, the Probate Section is simply a representative section, supporting solicitors who work in the field of Probate and Trusts (although the section has relaunched as the 'Private Client' section). The Law Society has shown renewed and active interest in accredited expertise, but Moorhead notes that such schemes always face the problem of not upsetting the generalists and consequently never set the standards particularly high (2010: 252). Despite the Law Society's interest in accreditation, the Probate Section was against such moves in its area, as 'we feel [that what] we've already done is a very good professional qualification to get us as far as being a solicitor ... we don't want our members to feel that they've got to be jumping through further hoops' (Interview 3, Probate Section).

In order to advance their interests, STEP members said it is they themselves (43.1 per cent of respondents) or STEP who take the lead (37.8 per cent of respondents), with no disciplinary or other differences. In terms of demonstrating their brand of specialized general expertise to employers, government and the public, it is again STEP that they draw upon – whose standards, in terms of the examination route at least, appear significantly more stringent than most schemes discussed by Moorhead (2010: 252). The continuing connection therefore appears to be based around their core identity or status as a professional. This remains despite the strong networking bonds they share with environing professionals.

Abbott refers to a 'parent discipline' (1988: 106), and Jacob is clear that notions of 'kinship' can be broadly conceived beyond biological ties, to encompass forms of 'bureaucracy, materiality or spirituality' (2009: 98). The nature of the disciplinary pull of Law, in particular, appears to have an affective and instinctive element, suggesting interconnectivity redolent of kinship. Law Schools have been identified as powerful sites of socialization (Granfield and Koenig 1992, Manderson and Turner 2006), as indeed have professional service firms (Anderson-Gough, Grey and Robson, 2000). However, a further dimension of the kinship ties to law may be the long-standing commitment to the profession that lawyers have demonstrated (Freidson 1992: 223). Is it harder to breach such ties of kinship when a marginal position within the field may reinforce the institutional logics?

Future Directions and Continuing Tensions

STEP has made rapid progress since its inception. However, both the internal tensions explored above and the external environment framed, in part, by the Legal Services Act 2007, raise important questions as to the future direction and priorities of the organization. Thus, an aspect of any amalgamated professional project might involve consideration as to whether it would wish to become an Approved Regulator under the LSA. ILEX, for example, has made an application to the LSB for rights to award its members Approved Probate Practitioner status (ILEX 2010a). STEP is not in a position to do this, either in organizational terms (a point the leadership was keen to stress), but also, probably as importantly, on the basis of its relationship with its members. The critical point is that STEP is effectively a secondary or overlapping qualification, whereas the ILEX qualification is a primary, or intermediate, qualification.

The position of private client lawyers within STEP raises challenging questions when exploring the extent to which emergent models of professional advancement can operate in parallel to our traditional understandings of legal professionalism. In many ways these private client lawyers in different jurisdictions (but perhaps, particularly within England and Wales) find themselves at the edge of their traditional professional disciplines. As Abbott (1988) has identified in other professional settings, they have sought out environing professionals working within the same field to build alliances and assert their specialist knowledge in Trusts and Estates work. Yet this challenge is undercut by a sense that many of them see themselves as the last bastions of a traditional legal professionalism (Franklin and Lee 2007), under siege by the commercialized professionalism within Corporate Law firms (Hanlon 1999). They assert that they do mainstream law, and it is others who have moved away from that. They are faced with an additional problem in that the organization which developed to support their claims of expertise in the field of Trusts and Estates has evolved in a way with which many of them are distinctly uncomfortable. This additionally highlights the overlapping and contradictory ways in which claims to professional status and share of the market for professional services are made. To put it crudely, there may have been an element of English private client lawyers who felt ignored by their legal partners and began to flirt with environing professionals in Accountancy and Trusts Management. However, it is one thing to flirt with someone, quite another to go all the way and formally amalgamate. It is this direction of travel about which the lawyers, in particular, are expressing serious reservations.

There are, therefore, real questions for STEP about its direction of travel and its capacity to bring an extremely fragmented membership along with it. A clear measure of the extent of this fragmentation can be seen when analysing the responses of the membership to some general questions about the strategic priorities of the organization and the challenges facing the Trusts and Estates field. Lawyers were generally concerned about the threats of de-regulation and increased competition particularly from unregulated will-writers and for some within the UK, the advent of so-called 'Tesco Law'.[9] Those working in Trust Companies, on the other hand, were more concerned about over-regulation and a sense of feeling embattled by Governments around the world. The international dimension of on-shore versus off-shore jurisdictions was frequently cited as a fault line – '[there's a need] to ensure that no split arises between the so called offshore bodies and mainland groups. We stay as "One"' (Resp. 180, Off-shore Lawyer) – and repeatedly came through as the key variable in the analysis of the questionnaire. Thus, on-shore STEP members were three times as likely to be concerned about issues of de-regulation and unqualified practitioners. Off-shore STEP members were four times as likely to be concerned about over-regulation, and 2.4 times as likely to highlight Government antipathy to their work as an issue (see also Johnson and Johnstone 2009). One said: 'Increased regulation makes effective running of private banks harder' (Resp. 018, Trusts Planning and Management); another:

> The offshore attacks from countries such as the UK and USA that see the likes of the CI + IoM [Channel Islands and Isle of Man] as havens for 'dirty money'.
> (Resp. 243, Trusts Planning and Management)

These are different professionals, with different priorities and different clients to the majority of the current STEP membership. As one interviewee neatly summarized:

> it's going to be an interesting challenge particularly when the off-shore or non-UK part of it becomes predominant in terms of decision-making ... and [show] a rather different vision than now, then that's going to be interesting. (Interview 2, Branch)

The possible development of an amalgamated profession is set out by a member of the Directorate:

---

9   Ss. 71–111 Legal Services Act 2007. See Rothwell (2010a) on the Co-op's move into the field.

> At the moment there's a lot of uncertainty about it, but I think it should be a Wealth Management Body because that's the kind of people I meet all the time and that's the dynamic end of the business ... we should also take on a wider role in terms of defending wealth-structuring and wealth management – we should be liaising much more closely with the investment managers in private banks. (Interview 8, Directorate)

The lawyers and accountants (who still comprise the bulk of the membership) with strong disciplinary heritages and task areas, are unlikely to see this as 'historically inevitable' (Greenwood, Suddaby and Hinings 2002: 70). As one interviewee said:

> My perception is that the majority are lawyers[10] and they tend to be very introvert in their approach ... The parochial England and Wales members have been saying – 'we ought to be spending all our money and concentrating all our resources in England and Wales'. It is a very short term view and an extremely narrow view because if you are a wealth manager – in its broadest sense – and I think that is the market that STEP is really addressing, then those clients are international and global. (Interview 5, Branch)

For numerically dominant English and Welsh lawyers and accountants, STEP membership and qualifications remain a way in which they can demonstrate their specialist expertise within Trusts and Estates without severing their ties entirely with their disciplinary homes. The logical conclusions of the international, off-shore and Wealth-Management orientations implicit in the professional project of STEP are not yet fully shared by all of the membership. Arguably, those on the periphery of a professional field, for example Law or Accountancy, may well be less bound by the properties of the field. However, as a result of the internal stratification, they appear insufficiently positioned to entirely rethink their professional identity, norms and status. Yet, crucially, STEP itself continues to play an important part in their professional advancement as lawyers operating at the edge of the traditional professional field.

Conclusion

This chapter confirms the complexity within the professional field (Webb 2004). Individuals and firms derive different things from different bodies at different times. Their expert knowledge may be demonstrated in some ways by their qualification as a solicitor, their firm letterhead, or perhaps their membership of an organization such as STEP:

---

10   They are – see STEP data and in responses to this questionnaire.

In a market [for professional membership services] ... you keep the batch of services, the provider that best suits you, you'll look for the best accreditation. ... It doesn't mean that [in the future] people will have a clear identity that they are a STEP member and that's it – people will have multiple professional identities – one or other will be more emphasized – primarily all depends on the [issue]. Whichever body, you know, gives you the extra edge is the one you'll opt for. ... That's how we'll create that stronger identity [for STEP] just with that increased value, increased specialisation and giving members more of an edge against their competitors. (Interview 7, Directorate)

This framing of how an amalgamated profession may develop is, admittedly not so removed from the motivations of individual professionals serving their self-interest by working collectively (Larson 1977: 74). However, it is the notion of multiple and overlapping professional models of advancement that represents a development from Larson and Abbott's conceptions of professions with strong organizing associations patrolling jurisdictions and ensuring a clear and distinct professional identity.

Traditional professions such as solicitors are no longer able to exercise exclusive control of the markets within their jurisdictions or to legitimate knowledge (in all its specialized forms), but these professions still retain appeal. They retain a powerful pull as a disciplinary home:

[I am a] Private Client Lawyer... It's the Law – that's the framework I work within. (Interview 2, Branch)

I work in the Off-shore Finance Industry, Trusts are part of what I do. I see ICAEW as my first qualification and discipline and STEP provides additional resources. But it does not stand alone. (Resp. 492, Accountant)

This almost emotional connection may require us to consider the affective domain in greater detail than has hitherto been explored in professionalism literature (Krathwohl, Bloom and Masia 1964).[11] I do not argue that there is a commonly held trait of professional altruism (Carr-Saunders and Wilson 1933), or even refer to the public interest dimensions of legal professionalism stressed by Halliday (1987). Rather, that there may be an instinctive connection to the original disciplinary home – perhaps a product of the long-term commitment of contemporary professionalism (Freidson 1992: 223). The constraining ties of the 'kinship structures' identified by Burrage (1996) when personalist relations were more pronounced within the legal profession, and by Jacob in other settings (2009), are perhaps more influential upon those who are marginal within a social field (Battilana 2006, Greenwood and Suddaby 2006). Of course, there may be

---

11 I am grateful to Julian Webb for raising this issue when an earlier version of this chapter was presented at the SLS Conference 2009.

more instrumental reasons underpinning this connection. As Abbott argues, 'even on the periphery ... pressures against division may be strong particularly within a dominant profession. Retaining the affiliation may confer protection against competitors' (1988: 107). Thus in the case of the solicitors' profession in England and Wales, the Law Society (alongside STEP) has been at the forefront of recent campaigns against unregulated will-writers.[12] I will return to these points in the final chapters.

Obviously this is not clear cut, and the Law Society may have a role, for example, in protecting international and other markets and also in negotiations with Government (Greenwood, Suddaby and Hinings 2002: 68), but this will be on a more contingent basis than in earlier models. In terms of knowledge used and status held, Trusts and Estates lawyers appear at the edge of the legal profession. Yet, in reaching out to foster bonds with neighbouring professionals, however difficult the practicalities of those alliances might be, they offer a model for a more complex claim of expert knowledge separate from, but not in challenge to their core, originating discipline of Law. Interestingly while there was an attempt by some interviewees to articulate something of a common set of values (see also Greenwood, Suddaby and Hinings 2002: 72) which focused on specialism and the soft-skills required in dealing with people facing difficult life-course decisions, it is hard to distinguish these values from a traditional non-STEP solicitor.

In the next chapter we will explore how other actors, alongside organizations like STEP, have responded to the post-Legal Services Act landscape and, thus, contribute to overlapping patterns of individual and collective advancement. At the same time, we will explore how seemingly elite players within legal services, the Law Society and the large corporate firms, may at different times and in different ways, operate at the edge of law.

---

12 'Unregulated will-writers damaging the public' (http://www.probatesection.org.uk/pages/news/item/302 [accessed: 26 January 2011]).

Chapter 7
Collective Professional Projects, Individual Models of Advancement and the Legal Services Act 2007

Introduction

The Legal Services Act 2007 (LSA) has the potential to disrupt jurisdictional settlements, in creating new tasks and in generating new forms of knowledge (Abbott 1988: 192). Moreover, it may enable actors to more readily challenge prevailing institutional logics and establish new organizational forms or patterns of behaviour. In analysing the responses of different actors to the LSA, I argue that elite corporate law firms are edging away from traditional notions of legal professionalism and engaging in institutional entrepreneurship. The new models of professionalism developed by these actors reinforce their positions of privilege (Greenwood and Suddaby 2006: 43), not only within the legal profession's internal hierarchies, but also in terms of their market share and status within global professional services. Yet the position they occupy is a complicated one. It does not appear that a new social entity has emerged (Abbott 1995: 869), which comprises elite law firms (let alone these firms and other professional service firms) as a product of the differences between themselves and the rest of the solicitors' profession.[1] As this chapter argues, they retain too great an influence over the traditional collective profession and an enduring (if somewhat instrumental) connection to the professional core.

Bucher and Strauss caution that the most powerful segments control professional associations (1961: 331). However, although I argue that the strategies deployed by the largest corporate firms indicate a redefinition of aspects of professionalism to support their interests (particularly its regulatory dimensions, Flood 2010), the profession as a whole is not being reconstituted solely in the image of the elite actors. Moreover, there is no outright take-over of the professional association – the elite law firms have their own powerful advocate of their collective interests, in the City of London Law Society (CLLS). Their engagement is partial and contingent, although generally on their terms.

In analysing the position that the Law Society developed prior to the LSA and the changes generated by it, it is possible to identify a traditional professional

---

1   Although this may be contingent upon the profession-wide regulator addressing the pressure for differentiated approaches to regulation (CLLS 2010b).

association, deeply embedded within the field: instinctively 'an agent of reproduction and not change' (Greenwood, Suddaby and Hinings 2002: 73). Nevertheless, the Law Society, and its model of traditional collective professionalism, retains relevance. Through its attempts to advance the interests of less powerful, but numerically significant, smaller firms, through its standing with national and international governments, and its deployment of residual social, cultural and political capital, it has attempted to secure the most favourable outcomes, both for itself as an organization, but for also for the collective profession it continues to represent.

Thus, I suggest that the traditional collective profession-wide model of advancement appears to operate alongside (and contingently with) an increasing emphasis on more individualized models of advancement. Securing control of the professional association to advance professional interests seems less important than in the past. Equally, however, the location at the edge for the elite legal actors appears not to be a one-way journey away from mainstream professionalism, but an orbit occupied in parallel to, and occasionally in concert with, the traditional core. While the large corporate firms cast an undeniable shadow over the profession, theirs is not the only story in the evolution of a contingent legal professionalism.

The timeframe considered in this chapter covers mid-1999 to winter 2010. This addresses a period in which the Law Society emerged from a period of internal restructuring, continued paralysis in terms of how its regulatory and representative roles were reconciled and battles with the government during the passage of the Access to Justice Act 1999 (Abel 2003, Francis 2004). It analyses the responses of different segments of the profession to events leading up to the LSA and the subsequent landscape. The case-study draws on qualitative interviews with the leadership of the Law Society conducted in 1999 which covered broad strategic challenges, understandings of professionalism and so on (Francis 2004) and Minutes of Law Society meetings, Consultation Responses, Briefing Documents, speeches and the trade press between 1999 and 2010. In addition, a selective sample of the websites of firms of various sizes provides illustrative examples of the way in which these actors position their market claims (Flood 1996: 182–9).

This chapter is organized into three main sections. The first analyses the interaction of collective and individual models of legal professionalism in generating a new regulatory settlement for the profession as a whole. The power of the elite corporate law firms is prominent within this account. It next considers the way in which both individual firms and the profession collectively have attempted to manage the competition anticipated following the establishment of the new organizational forms of Legal Disciplinary Practices (LDPs) and ABSs (Alternative Business Structures). Finally, the relationship between traditional collective professional projects and individualized models of advancement, which often cohere around organizations, is explored in the context of expert knowledge and professional education and training. Potential changes in the way in which legal education is delivered (at all stages) and the different bases upon which expert knowledge is claimed and deployed within organizations may further disrupt institutional logics. The importance of a new actor, the Legal Services Board, should also not be underestimated. It may not advance a particular segment of the profession's interests, but it is as intimately involved in the redefinition of contemporary legal professionalism as any other special interest group.

Background to the Legal Services Act

As outlined in Chapter 1, the LSA 2007 introduced a number of key features which further undermine the 'enclave of relative autonomy [from market and state]' within which the legal profession operated (Abel 1989: 321). To recap, the LSB is the oversight regulator, Front-line Regulators including the Law Society are required to separate their representative and regulatory functions, new organizational forms in the shape of ABSs and LDPs are permitted and professional principles are clearly set out in the legislation. The 'licence and mandate' between profession and state (Hughes 1981: 78–80) is now firmly on a statutory footing.

In the years leading to the LSA 2007 the Law Society was, like other classic professional associations, deeply embedded within the institutional logics of traditional professionalism (Laffin 1998: 219). Consequently, it made a considerable journey from an absolute insistence upon self-regulation to a more nuanced approach within which the watchwords became 'involvement', 'proportionality' and 'light-touch regulation'. Nevertheless, it did not make these arguments alone. The other powerful actors, with their eyes firmly on their own interests but overlapping with the Law Society as and when it suited, were the large City firms. They acted both on their own and through the increasingly confident CLLS (Flood 2010). Moreover, state interests dominated and drove the development of the legislation.

It is easy, now, to underestimate just how badly positioned the Law Society was in the period immediately prior to the Office of Fair Trading's 'Competition in the Professions' (2001). Abel highlights the high farce of vitriolic presidential elections and internal Law Society politics in the late 1990s (2003: 407–54). However, the indifference of much of the profession to the drama being played out in Chancery Lane, points to the declining importance of the professional association as the fulcrum of the collective professional project (Francis 2004). Most acute were the tensions the Law Society faced in balancing the competing roles of regulation and representation (Francis 2004: 337–40) and increasing pressure from the state (Abel 2003, Francis: 2004: 340–2).

In contrast, the largest corporate law firms continued their exponential growth (Galanter and Palay 1991, Lee 1992) and challenged traditional conceptions of professionalism in their work (Hanlon 1999) and approach to profession-wide norms of conduct (Lee 1999, Griffiths-Baker 2002). Their size, in the late 1990s, already dwarfed that of the rest of the profession (Cole 2000: 32). Their international work and knowledge had also moved beyond the narrowly legal (Flood 1995, 1996). These features of resource asymmetries and boundary bridging (Greenwood and Suddaby 2006: 36–42) enabled them to challenge the prevailing logics of the field and thus, move towards the edge of mainstream legal professionalism. As Chapter 2 argues, this is not simply another dimension of internal stratification within the profession, but signifies a far looser and more contingent connection to the originating discipline of law. The interaction between this range of actors, including the freshly separated Law Society and Solicitors Regulation Authority will be explored in the next section as the battle over regulation developed not simply between lawyers and state but between lawyers themselves.

LSA 2007 and the Regulation of Legal Services: From Self-Regulation to ... Self-Regulation?

The Regulatory / Representative Split and Oversight by the Legal Services Board

Despite criticisms of self-regulation (M. Davies 1999), during the late 1990s and early 2000s, the Law Society, and its leadership insisted upon the preservation of self-regulation and argued that it was in the profession's and public's interests (Francis 2004: 337, see also Larson 1977: 56 on the role of the 'service ideal' in the professional project). There was, however, a recognition that in order to conserve this position the Law Society would 'need to be a good deal tougher about regulation ... in other words there would be a bit more stick' (Law Society Council Member (L) 1999). Thus, the Society reaffirmed its commitment to self-regulation, but conceded that in order to make good on its desire to be seen 'as a model regulator,' it could no longer be half-hearted about its regulatory role (Law Society 2000a: 4). Thus, the Law Society deployed a conserver approach, characteristic of the classic professions, 'which have few reasons to change and plenty of reasons to resist change' (Laffin 1998: 219).

The Government announced Sir David Clementi's wide-ranging review of regulation in legal services, by declaring that the current regulatory framework was 'outdated, inflexible, over-complex and insufficiently accountable or transparent' (Department of Constitutional Affairs (DCA) 2003: 14). Janet Paraskeva, then Law Society Chief Executive, insisted that 'self-regulation of the legal professions remains the best way of securing the necessary high standards of competence and integrity and the profession's independence from Government interference' (Law Society 2003). This position was increasingly out of step, not only with the state but also with the wider profession (Abel 2003: 407–54). Nelson and Trubek argue that professional ideology is shaped partly as a result of the 'orderly dispositions that actors possess as a result of their historical and social location' within particular arenas of the profession (1992a: 23). As an actor, deeply embedded within the field, the elite professional association is constrained by the institutional logics, and is thus unable to readily anticipate and articulate new patterns of behaviour in the same way that other elite organizational actors are able to do (Greenwood and Suddaby 2006).

Amongst Clementi's recommendations was a proposal that the regulatory and representative functions of the legal professional bodies should be separated (Clementi 2004b: para. 70). The Law Society's response to Clementi's consultation document (Law Society 2004), represented a significant departure from its instinctive insistence upon self-regulation. Thus, it asserted that 'the separation of its regulatory and representative functions is now firmly on [its] agenda' (2004: 7). Pressure from other arenas may affect the construction of professional ideology in different arenas (Nelson and Trubek 1992a: 22–3, Greenwood, Suddaby and Hinings 2002: 70). It seems unlikely that the shifting Law Society position was unrelated to the elite corporate law firms' articulation of an even clearer split between representative and regulatory functions than the Law Society was envisaging at that stage (Allen & Overy 2004: 6). These firms had long been clear that self-regulation did not work for them (Perrin 2000), and their interventions also enabled them to advance the argument that professional regulation should be more responsive to the differentiated needs of their sophisticated corporate clients (Allen & Overy 2004: 7). Despite this pressure, it is also worth noting the areas of convergence between the Law Society and Allen & Overy responses, particularly in relation to asserting the importance of the independence of the profession (Law Society 2004: 16, Allen & Overy: 2004: 2).

Yet it was not just pressure from the elite corporate firms that challenged the Law Society's position. The Law Society also appears to have been influenced by increasingly explicit hints and threats from the Lord Chancellor. Speaking at the Council Meeting of 20 January 2005 which approved the split the Lord Chancellor, Charles Falconer, was clear:

> For your own interest, it is far better that you come up with your own proposals. It's pretty clear what's coming down the track ... provided you meet the [Legal Services] Board's standards, it *should* allow you to retain the ability to regulate your own profession. (emphasis added, cited in Law Society 2005: 35)

The Law Society sought to 'maximise its influence' (Law Society 2005: 26) subject to the constraints of the elite firms and the state, by drawing on residual capital as the voice of the profession (Francis 2004: 346). Its response to the Government's White Paper (DCA 2005) published in the wake of Clementi's Report was a nuanced one (Law Society 2006). Certainly it continued to stress the key issues of concern facing the profession, particularly around the need to maintain the independence of the profession (2006: para 58).[2] However, the call now was for the *involvement* of professionals in their regulation and a concern to limit the powers of the oversight regulator to intervene (2006: para 45). Nevertheless, the framing of this is still premised on rhetoric that Larson (1977: 51) would recognize; 'there are enormous

---

2 The Law Society saw 'the independence of the profession' challenged by a combination of the Legal Services Board's powers and the proposals that the Chair would be appointed by the Secretary of State (2006: 6).

benefits in professionals being substantially involved in their own regulation and that the concept of professionalism has real value for society' (2006: 7).

The Law Society continued to make the calls for regulatory involvement by the profession and for 'proportionate and light touch' oversight by the Legal Services Board in its submissions to the Joint Committee of the Commons and the Lords on the Legal Services Bill (JCLSB 2006: para 162). The Committee heard evidence from a range of interested actors orally, including the CLLS and the Sole Practitioners Group (SPG). The CLLS demonstrated its increasing influence as a powerful actor in its own right, publicly stating that the bill was 'an own goal' and it would 'fight hard' for its position (McIntosh cited in Harris 2006a). However, individual firms, including Freshfields, Clifford Chance and Allen & Overy, also submitted their own responses to ensure that that sector was represented as effectively as possible (Flood 2010). These firms' submissions, while echoing Law Society concerns about the need for any regulation to be proportionate and the powers of intervention to be subject to clear objective tests (JCLSB 2006: para 164 and 165), were also designed to address their specific concerns as 'international (and therefore organizationally complex)' (Allen & Overy cited at JCLSB 2006: para 327) providers of legal services to 'sophisticated consumers' (Allen & Overy 2006).

The final Act reflected many of the profession's concerns. Thus, the Lord Chief Justice would be consulted when the Lord Chancellor makes appointments to the Legal Services Board (Schedule 1, para 1(3)). However, contrary to the Law Society's arguments (2006: para 45), the Act does permit the cancellation of a designation of an Approved Regulator (s.45). The Lord Chancellor, Lord Falconer, reassured the Law Society that 'it would take an earthquake before the Legal Services Board would propose the removal of powers from the Law Society or the Bar Council' (Law Society 2005: 35). However, Fiona Woolf (President of the Law Society, 2006–07) felt it was 'naive in the extreme' to think the LSB would not use its powers (cited in Harris 2006b). David Edmonds, the first Chair of the LSB, was also clear in a speech directly to the Law Society Council that while (in line with s.3(3)(a) LSA 2007) the LSB was a proportionate regulator; 'We're not light-touch ... . It will instead be strictly proportionate – major failure means major prescription, opacity will mean heavy monitoring' (2010a: 4).

Regulation in the Post-LSA World – the Uneasy Separation of the Law Society and the SRA

I would argue that the difficulties that faced the Law Society as it developed arrangements that satisfied s.30 LSA 2007 were shaped by 'the historically constructed repertoire of "legitimate" or "permissible" professional responses' within the arena of the national professional association (Nelson and Trubek 1992a: 22). Thus, as late as 2003 (see above), the Chief Executive of the Law Society insisted upon self-regulation. Although, the Law Society is an Approved Regulator under the LSA (Schedule 4 1(1)), it is required to separate its regulatory and representative functions (s.30 LSA). This led to the creation of initially, the Law Society Regulation Board from January 2006 and then the Solicitors Regulation Authority (SRA) as the regulatory arm of the Law Society from 2007, with the Law Society acting to represent the profession's interests and involve itself in law reform (SRA 2007). The arrangements enabled the Law Society to reassert its representative relevance across a large and fragmented profession and cast itself (in its representative capacity) as the profession's friend and advocate.[3] However, the Law Society appears to have struggled to acknowledge the challenge to the institutional logics by the regulatory arrangements required by the LSA.

One of the main problems appears to have been a lack of understanding as to which body was the Statutory Approved Regulator. This issue was raised in the Regulatory Affairs Board (RAB) of the Law Society[4] meeting of 21 May 2009 when a committee member was concerned that the SRA had described itself as an Approved Regulator at public events, RAB 2009a), and again in June (RAB 2009b: para. 92.6). The issue came to a head over the arrangements for the appointment of the new SRA Chair and Board in the summer of 2009. *The Lawyer* described this as a 'turf war', with the Law Society managing the process, without input from the SRA (McLeod-Roberts 2009a). The SRA raised its concerns in response to the LSB consultation on the s.30 rules, stating that 'it is quite legitimate for representatives of the regulated profession to have a defined role in the appointments process, but never a dominant voice' (SRA 2009a: para 26).

The LSB was unimpressed with the regulatory/representative arrangements and, in a speech to the Law Society Council in 2010, David Edmonds was clear that

> we do need to be sure that there is effective separation of the representative arm from the regulatory arm, and that the regulatory arm has the competence and the resources to run its business effectively. … I am dealing with this at some length, because we asked for the issue to be resolved by 30 April [2010]. … I will say this evening that the LSB now expects agreement in compliance with our internal governance requirements in the next few days. (Edmonds 2010a: 5–6)

And lo, this was done, with the Law Society President (2009–10), in his final column, announcing:

---

3   See, for example, *Terminating retainers: Society Protects Solicitors (25 February 2010)* (http://www.lawsociety.org.uk/newsandevents/news/view=newsarticle. law?NEWSID=426330 [accessed: 29 January 2011]), which details the Law Society's intervention in a case before the Court of Appeal to protect the interests of solicitors. Another example is the following web resource, *Surviving the downturn: resources and some interventions* (http://www.lawsociety.org.uk/newsandevents/news/majorcampaigns/ view=newsarticle.law?CAMPAIGNSID=415651 [accessed 29 January 2011]).

4   This is a separate body to the SRA Board and sees its role as providing the Representative Body's input on Regulation matters.

> A fortnight ago [days after Edmonds' speech] the Society and the SRA formally
> signed a regulatory independence certificate, covering such matters as budget
> approval, provision of support services and oversight of SRA operations. This
> marks a watershed in the relationship between the Society and the SRA and
> bodes well for the future. (Heslett 2010a)

There is little doubt that the LSB is now a significant actor. Lord Hunt in his Law
Society commissioned review of legal services regulation (2009: 48, see further
below) recommended that a neutral corporate Law Society should be established
which would provide strategic oversight and resources to a representative body
and the SRA, an approach which David Edmonds considers 'offered a clear way
forward' (2010a: 5). It would certainly help to address the confusion and lack
of strategic clarity about the role of the Law Society in the longer term. In late
2010, Law Society leadership continued to insist upon the formal position of the
Approved Regulator status enshrined within the legislation (Ames 2010).

Regulating the Edge of the Profession

The following section examines the way in which the elite corporate law firms
challenged the institutional logics of profession-wide regulation post-LSA.
However, the position they adopted is also indicative of their partial (and
contingent) engagement with the traditional collective profession. Their position
at the edge does not appear to presage a new professional entity (Abbott 1995:
869). Moreover, we also see in the Law Society's response a (partially) successful
attempt to accommodate the divergent professionalism of the large corporate firms
within the profession as a whole.

City firms have long had concerns about the Law Society's regulatory role
(The Lawyer 1999b). Thus, for example, the Managing Partner of Osborne Clarke,
Lesley Perrins, criticized the rules on Conflicts of Interest and attacked the Law
Society for being 'lamentably out of touch with reality for the commercial firms [in
offering] hopelessly inappropriate regulation' (Perrin 2000). The appropriateness
of the Conflicts rules had been an issue for some time and epitomized the City
firms' sense that the Law Society simply had no understanding of their needs (The
Lawyer 2000b, Fleming 2003, Lee 1999: 25). The Law Society's vulnerability
to these firms (whose turnover dwarfes its own)[5] and the convenience that the
firms saw in remaining as part of the profession, saw attempts by leading figures
within the Law Society to reach out to the profession. Michael Napier and David
McIntosh in their joint ticket campaign for the Presidency and Vice-Presidency in
2000 (Irwin Mitchell and Davies Arnold Cooper respectively) offered to establish

---

5   The Law Society Annual Report (2009b: 11) lists the annual income as £144.4m. In
contrast, Clifford Chance, Freshfields, Linklaters and Allen & Overy all generated income
in excess of £1billion (Dean 2010b).

a City Forum within the Law Society precisely to head off these criticisms (The Lawyer 2000a).

Post LSA 2007, however, the Corporate Sector grew increasingly exasperated with a regulator for which it had little respect (City Firms Working Group 2008). The Law Society appeared eager to demonstrate to the profession as a whole that it could operate as a powerful advocate in its interests and challenge the profession's favourite bogeyman, the SRA. The Review on Regulation within Legal Services, chaired by Lord Hunt, and a specific review of regulation in the Corporate Sector, chaired by a former senior civil servant at the Ministry of Justice, Nick Smedley, commissioned by the Law Society, reveals the Law Society's effort to redefine a collective representative (and regulatory) role. Paradoxically, it also highlights the power of the large corporate firms in redefining a model of professionalism on their terms and in their interests (Flood 2010).

The Review was announced to Council at its November Meeting (Law Society 2008a), by the Chair of the RAB, Helen Davies (partner with a four partner firm in the South-West of England), who emphasized the need for the Law Society to take a lead as the representative arm of the profession and that

> there were consistent messages coming from the corporate firms who felt that regulation should not be eased but should be more appropriate and proportionate to the type of firm; and who were unsure whether the SRA had the skills to deal with the regulation of corporate firms. (Law Society 2008a: 21)

It is worth noting that there were concerns expressed by the other Council members about the power of the corporate firms. They queried whether a model of dual regulation with lighter touch regulation for the larger corporate firms had already been decided.

The Law Society responded to increasingly strong pressure from the Corporate Sector and bypassed Council to a large degree in appointing Hunt and Smedley without advertising the positions and approving the proposal by email (Law Society 2008a: 29–30, 2008b: 39). The appointments of Smedley and, in particular, Hunt were critical in the Law Society's efforts to maintain profession-wide relevance. Lord Hunt had connections with David McIntosh (Chair of the CLLS) from his support of McIntosh's efforts to establish a City Forum during his campaign to be elected as Law Society Vice-President alongside Michael Napier. At that time, Hunt affirmed the benefits of remaining as part of one profession: 'We are all one profession and we should unite rather than divide' (Hunt, cited in The Lawyer 2000a). Hunt had also been generally receptive to the arguments put forward by the Law Society in his chairing of the Joint Committee on the Draft Legal Services Bill and coincidentally was also a partner of Beachcroft LLP alongside the Law Society Vice-President (2008–09), Robert Heslett (The Lawyer 2009). Social status and the organizational position of key individuals can be in critical in generating institutional change (Battilana 2006: 668). The Law Society faced intense pressure from the largest firms, but it was still able to draw on both formal and informal networks to attempt to deliver a profession-wide outcome (see also Anderson-Gough, Grey and Robson 2006, on the importance of the 'networked professional').

Although the elite law firms threatened a complete split, in fact a profession-wide outcome had benefits for the largest firms, in terms of costs and a level of capital, in belonging to a recognizable independent legal profession, which could be deployed in international markets (CLLS 2007a). The Chair of the RAB acknowledged that it was likely that a separate corporate regulatory unit would be proposed, but stressed that the RAB 'did not consider this was necessarily in the best interest of the profession or the public [and] it was hoped to find a solution to effective regulation under one umbrella' (Law Society 2008b: 39).

Notwithstanding the benefits that the Corporate Sector derived from engagement with the profession as a whole, the CLLS pushed hard in their representations to Smedley:

> Good regulation can only be achieved where the regulators understand the markets in which the regulated firms operate, and the needs of their clients ... .
> City Work Regulators should be a separate division within the SRA or a separate Regulator. (CLLS 2009a: 2)

Smedley was clear, both in the report and in an interview broadcast on the Law Society website with Joshua Rozenberg (a legal journalist) and Chris Perrin (General Counsel of Clifford Chance and Chair of the Professional Rules and Regulation Committee of the CLLS), that, 'there has been an absence of corporate regulation' (Smedley, Perrin and Rozenberg 2009). He proposed new rules for corporate regulation, but additionally there should be a smaller number of 'larger firms who can invest in high-end risk management systems and designated Risk and Compliance Partners' who would be subject to new supervisory arrangements (2009: iv). He also recommended that there should be 'a new Corporate Regulation Group at the SRA, headed by a Group Director, either a very senior and highly experienced lawyer with a corporate and commercial background or, alternatively, someone with very strong regulatory experience in a comparable sector' (2009: vi), operating as a 'quasi-autonomous part of the SRA' (2009: vii) based in London (2009: viii). He urged a response from the SRA within two months and suggested that if the recommendations were not implemented then it was likely that the notion of a separate regulator for the Corporate Sector would become the 'de facto solution' (2009: v) – essentially the line floated by the CLLS.

Chris Perrin welcomed his recommendations, which was later endorsed by the Law Society Regulatory Affairs Board (RAB 2009a: 3), and was happy that the model avoided the separate regulator route, less because of profession-wide solidarity but more because 'it's too complex, it's too expensive, it's too cumbersome' (Perrin in Smedley, Perrin and Rozenberg 2009). The CLLS was bullish about what it had being able to achieve, with its chair David McIntosh, writing unashamedly in its magazine (a far glossier publication than most local Law Society newsletters):

> It is not a co-incidence that so many of Nick Smedley's criticisms of the SRA and his recommendations for improvement reflect our City oriented concerns. We and our members, many of whom met with Nick Smedley individually have put forward the right arguments to him and expressed commonly held concerns regarding the inappropriateness of the SRA's current non-differential approach and a lack of understanding of how commercial practice is conducted by large commercial firms. (McIntosh 2009)

The CLLS, concerned about the equivocation in the SRA's response to Smedley (SRA 2009b: para 29), continued to demonstrate its power and confidence in forceful submissions to the ongoing Hunt Review (CLLS 2009b). However, in attacking the regulatory approach of the SRA, the City firms were not, in fact, out of line with the broader profession. Hunt himself noted that 'only a tiny minority [of submissions] could bring themselves to praise the SRA or its methods in any way' (2009: 64, see also Law Society 2010c). While there was not necessarily a comfortable confluence of interests, nevertheless this provided an accommodating environment within which the CLLS could advance its claims.

In similar ways to the major reports which recommended Multi-Disciplinary Practices (MDPs) to the wider accountancy profession (Greenwood, Suddaby and Hinings (2002: 69), Hunt's final report appealed across the profession. His starting point was that 'I would not like to see this profession divided because I strongly believe in the old maxim about the benefits of standing united' (2009: 4). But then, of course, we (and presumably the Law Society when it appointed him) already knew this, given Hunt's earlier public statements to this effect and his efforts with Napier and McIntosh to re-engage the City firms with the national Law Society (The Lawyer 2000a). Equally telling, was his assertion that 'I firmly believe that professional values and professionalism, suitably invigorated for a modern age, are on the march, not on the wane' (2009: 3). If this was a reconstitution of the institutional logics of the professional field in the interests of the Corporate Sector, then Hunt was doing so in a way which would be both intelligible and acceptable to the wider profession. The appointment of Hunt, as someone with credibility with the large firms alongside public statements in support of profession-wide outcomes, is indicative of the Law Society's residual power as an institutional actor. However, his proposed model, also suggests that the elite corporate firms continued to subscribe to profession-wide solutions, when it was in their interests to do so (Larson 1977: 73–4).

Hunt's solution was that Smedley's recommendation of Authorised Internal Regulation (AIR) is 'so self-evidently[6] appropriate for the best legal firms that it

---

6   See also Greenwood, Suddaby and Hinings on the way in which the development of new organizational forms within accountancy was presented as being 'historically

deserves to be extended far more widely ... potentially *across the entire profession*' [emphasis added] (2009: 5). Indeed this was the solution proposed by the Law Society in its response to Hunt's Interim Call for Evidence (Law Society 2009a: 7). However, the reality of this headline approach of collectivity, a twenty-first century attempt to maintain the façade of homogeneity (Larson 1977: 69–71, Abbott 1988: 106), was that it was 'perfectly sensible to start the ball rolling with the firms identified by Nick Smedley at the vanguard ... they naturally have the most sophisticated internal governance and compliance systems' (Hunt 2009: 5 and Rec. 42, see also PricewaterhouseCoopers (PWC) 2007: 3). Hunt, was clear, however, that the SRA still needed 'to 'tool up' to meet the requirements' of these firms even those with AIR. While he is at pains (post LSA) to clarify that AIR is not self-regulation for a select few under another name, at other points it is proposed that the SRA regulatory levy be 'significantly reduced for *self-regulating* firms' (2009: 75, emphasis added). In order, arguably, to reinforce that this was a review for the whole profession (Hunt 2009: 76), Hunt proposed a number of other recommendations, including different ways in which professionalism might be inculcated within the profession, and a call for further intervention in the undergraduate Law Degree (see further below). Specifically, he also proposed that will-writing (a core part of the private client work largely conducted by smaller firms) be brought under the regulatory net (2009: 81).

The RAB (2009b) recommended to Council that it was in broad support of Hunt's recommendations – indeed the whole profession 'solution', was, of course what it had envisaged a year earlier when it set up the Review (Law Society 2008b: 39). In securing firm-based regulation for the Corporate Sector, Flood argues that 'large firms have won not so much a turf battle but a class war within the profession' (2010: 22). Indeed they have continued to drive home their case that Hunt be fully implemented (CLLS 2010a: para 7). Flood argues that there has been institutional change, driven by the large firms, both individually, through the CLLS and through pressure placed upon the national Law Society. Thus, 'by making the organization the salient unit, [the City firms] shifted away from institutional logics based around notions of public interest and asymmetrical relationships and supplanted them with the logic of the market' (2010: 24). They did this, not by ignoring 'public interest', but redefining it to mean the public interest of large corporations continuing to choose the City as the financial and legal market of choice (CLLS 2007a, CLLS 2010a). It should also be remembered that the notion of the firm as the salient unit for regulation was explicitly signalled by Clementi in the context of LDPs (2004b: 127), and even in critical calls for a contextual approach to legal ethics (Nicolson and Webb 1999: 121). Corporate law firms are clearly elite actors engaged in institutional entrepreneurship (Greenwood and Suddaby 2006). However, they continue to recognize the importance of the collective profession (Greenwood, Suddaby and Hinings 2002, Flood 2010: 23).

---

inevitable' (2002: 70).

New Organizational Forms, Managing Competition and Collective Advancement

Even within the very largest firms with managerial structures and processes, partnership remains the primary governance mechanism (Pinnington and Morris 2003: 97), with lawyers retaining occupational control (Faulconbridge and Muzio 2008). These structures provide the profession with links to its past (Burrage 1996) and across a fragmented marketplace. In broad terms, the new organizational forms permitted under the LSA 2007 (LDPs from March 2009 and ABSs from October 2011) permit a wider range of firms to deliver legal services. This may mean external investment in existing law firms or new models of multi-disciplinary partnerships. The ABS model challenges the profession to think differently about how it organizes and delivers its services (Flood 2008, Mayson 2010a). Thus, ABS firms, in terms of their size, resources and capacity for boundary bridging, may challenge institutional logics in developing new structures, practices and patterns of behaviour. Moreover, the language of competition first pushed by the OFT (2001) and emphasized by the current chair of the LSB (Edmonds 2010a, 2010b) is in marked contrast to the controlled competition that reinforced the collective mobility project of the profession (Abel 1988: 293). The response of the Law Society (as with regulation), suggests an attempt to accommodate these new models of professionalism, in an effort to 'maximise influence'. However, it also highlights the strains it faces in attempting to provide collective leadership and shelter from the harsher winds of competition to different sectors of the profession. While, many of the larger firms are able to shelter lawyers within their walls, the Law Society (and other representational actors) struggle to provide this historic role to the smaller firms (Abel 2003: 477).

Managing the Competition from Alternative Business Structures

Although the Law Society abandoned its opposition to MDPs in 1999 (Law Society 1999), in the debates leading to the LSA 2007 it continued to assert traditional professional values (McVea 2002: 833) and concern for client protections (Law Society 2000c: 15). Thus, in its submission to the Lord Chancellor's Department position paper (LCD 2002), the Law Society reiterated its support of MDPs but also stressed strong traditional values – the 'official story' of professionalism (Nelson and Trubek 1992b). Thus, 'the absolute trust between solicitors' and 'the public's trust in solicitors' were highlighted (2002a: 16) and 'access to justice' concerns about new competitors were emphasized, with their members' livelihoods downplayed as secondary issues.[7]

---

7   See Larson (1977: 56) on the role of the 'service ideal' in a profession's project. Incidentally, these passages did not appear in an earlier version of the Law Society's response, the draft of which was circulated to the membership (2002b). This suggests a need to be seen to be more emphatic in the assertion of these traditional profession-wide values.

The Law Society highlighted issues which spoke to the non-Corporate Sector's concerns in its response to the Government's White Paper (DCA 2005). Thus, it emphasized the regulatory gap in relation to will-writing and raised 'concerns about the potential impact of ABSs on the network of smaller high street firms, which might lead to a loss of accessibility in rural areas' (Law Society 2006: para 104). Notwithstanding the number of solicitors employed by the largest corporate firms and their wider influence (Flood 2010), just over 4,000 of the 10,000 solicitors' practices are Sole Practitioners and a further 5,500 firms are 2–10 partner practices (Cole 2009: 24). These firms account for 45.5 per cent of all solicitors in private practice (Cole 2009: 25) and remain a key constituency of the Law Society. The SPG raised concerns about 'Tesco Law' in 2005 (SOLO 2005) and continued their opposition as the Act received Royal Assent: 'your Committee will continue to look for opportunities to make others aware of the elephant trap which the public and the legal profession are fast approaching' (Sutton 2007: 11). The SPG's denial that ABSs will affect them, while asserting that they were the 'lifeblood of the profession' where its 'true ethos' could be found, suggests a level of anxiety about their place within the profession (Peter Williams cited in SOLO 2001: 3), particularly when they saw the Law Society simply attempting to control the process rather than risk outright objection (Sutton 2007: 10).

Notwithstanding its determination to appeal across the broad collective profession, the Law Society was significantly closer to the position of the large corporate firms than they were the interests of the smaller firms.[8] The Law Society advocated LDPs as a first step, with the MDPs (ABSs) to follow (Law Society 2006). This approach mirrored the arguments of the largest firms (CLLS 2007a, Allen & Overy 2006), who prioritized LDPs as a means to ensure 'that City Firms are able to attract and retain the best non-lawyer professionals and they can compete with other professional advisors' (CLLS 2007a: 3).[9] There was strong confluence of interests between the traditional Law Society and the elite actors, but it is also clear that the professional association provided valuable 'cover' for the firms in being able to more convincingly articulate 'public interest' arguments to the state (Greenwood, Suddaby and Hinings 2002: 68), particularly in the international field (City Firms Working Group 2008). While the elite firms do challenge traditional conceptions of professionalism, the developing picture is more complicated than either outright departure from, or takeover of, the traditional profession.

Post-LSA the Law Society has responded to profession-wide concerns, such as those expressed by the SPG that there should be a 'level playing field' between the new ABS entrants and traditional law firms (Sutton 2009: 21, Sutton 2010). The Law Society's 2010 Election Manifesto highlighted the need for a 'proper level

---

8   The SPG ran the headline 'Law Society is a Waste of Space' in 2001 (SOLO 2001).

9   The confluence of interests between the City solicitors and Law Society owed something to shared interests, but also much to the work of Fiona Woolf CBE, President of the Law Society (2006–07) and Consultant with CMS Cameron McKenna (The Lawyer 2007).

playing field', maintained ongoing pressure to ensure will-writing is regulated and cautioned that work on the ABS model was progressing too quickly (Law Society 2010a: 21). Similar concerns were echoed by the Law Society President (Heslett 2010b) and the Chief Executive confirmed that the Law Society continued to press the case for a 'level playing field' (Law Society 2010c, Chief Executive's Report: 5).

However, the LSB is equally clear that it wishes to see a level playing field in the regulation of ABS and non-ABS entities by Front-line Regulators – thus not imposing more onerous requirements on ABSs (LSB 2010b). Similarly, David Edmonds was clear that ABSs are embedded in the Act and are there for creative and entrepreneurial organizations to take advantage (Edmonds 2010a). As Abel points out, 'the genie of competition is hard to force back into the bottle' (2003: 235). In this context, a range of actors have, nevertheless, attempted to manage the competition, and at times have attempted to deploy collective strategies to shelter those within their walls.

Collective Shelter from Competition

Notwithstanding the competition between large law firms, they have shown themselves capable of recognizing when it is in their mutual interest to pool resources. Other sectors follow a similar pattern. Thus, the Chief Executive of the 5,000 strong Association of Personal Injury Lawyers suggested its members show more enthusiasm for APIL than the Law Society, because 'they know what we're about, what our objectives are and we involve them in what we do' (Kitchener, cited in Ames 2010). Similarly, the Trusts and Estates lawyers, discussed in Chapter 6, look to STEP to accredit their expertise and advance their interests rather than the Law Society.

The smaller firms are far less comfortable or, indeed, able to assert an individual or even a collective claim on behalf of their sector. While the SPG is a significant organization, with over 4,500 members and, alongside the CLLS was permitted to present oral evidence to the Joint Committee on the Legal Services Bill (JCLSB 2006), it nevertheless represents a sector at the foot of the internal stratification of the profession (Abbott 1988: 118). The small firm and High Street sector faces undoubted pressures (Devonald 1994, Jopson 2001) and, notwithstanding the optimism of the Oxera research commissioned by the Law Society (Rothwell 2010b) which suggests limited impact of ABSs for the High Street firms, it seems that the pressure is unlikely to abate post-LSA.[10] Particular problems face those in rural localities (for example succession, Franklin and Lee 2007: 240), those

---

10   Indeed the RAB's Report to the Law Council Meeting of July 2010 notes: 'It is fair to say that not all members of the Regulatory Affairs Board were persuaded that this analysis was likely to prove correct. Members doubted whether it was sound to place much weight on the perhaps over optimistic views of the practitioners Oxera interviewed' (RAB 2010: 1 located in Law Society 2010c: 172). Other recent research suggests High Street firms fear for their future (Baksi 2010a).

who remain in publicly funded work face reduced fees and challenges to their traditional ways of working (Melville and Laing 2007, Moorhead 2004) and Sole Practitioners face recurrent difficulties in relation to Professional Indemnity Insurance payments and remaining on Lenders' panels for conveyancing matters.[11] The pressures which face these firms and their unrealistic expectations of the role that the collective profession could play where recognized by one Council member (themselves from a small firm) in 1999:

> I think a lot of the smaller firms are actually expecting that their hands will be held – 'this appalling thing is happening to me, why isn't the Law Society doing something about it.' They've still got the same issues about competing on a level playing field. I think that they fail to appreciate the limits of what the Law Society can actually do. (Law Society Council Member (N))

As Abel neatly summarizes: 'the [Law] Society was merely a scapegoat, neither responsible for the demise of the good old days nor able to restore them' (2003: 442).

Post-LSA, the Law Society is no longer formally, of course, hamstrung by combining its regulatory and representative functions (Francis 2004: 340). It has, through a variety of campaigns, initiatives and interventions, attempted to provide organizational support for its members' claims of professionalism in the competitive market in which they find themselves. Notwithstanding the large corporate firms' imposition of their model of regulation on the rest of the profession on their terms and in their interests (Flood: 2010: 24), the Law Society has continued to reach out across the entire profession. This is not an argument that the rest of the profession is a sufficiently powerful counterbalance to the large corporate firms. The City elite clearly dominate the profession, but theirs is not the whole story. Thus, for example, it is possible to see the type of work undertaken by smaller (often publicly funded) firms of solicitors feature prominently on campaigns to promote the brand of solicitor. Thus, we have 'accused?' 'homeless?' and 'carer?' rather than, for example, 'engaged in a hostile takeover of an East Asian Energy conglomerate?') (http://www.lawsociety.org.uk/new/documents/2010/a3_poster_ english.pdf [accessed: 29 January 2011]). Other examples can be found in the Law Society's campaigns to ensure that will-writing is brought within the LSA (Law Society 2006, 2010a),[12] and in the judicial review proceedings against the Legal Services Commission (*R (on the application of the Law Society) v. Legal Services*

---

11   See 'Talkback', the SPG discussion forum http://www.spg.uk.com/forum/ viewforum.php?f=1&sid=e40a69a9c07ba9dab26bc6014543cd13 [accessed: 29 January 2011]. While not attracting as much traffic as the STEP forum (albeit having a quarter of the members), this forum also generally indicates a level of supportiveness and engagement said to have been lost from real Law Society branch activity (Francis 2004: 336).

12   Although will-writing was not brought within the regulatory net, it is an area of work that the Legal Services Board continues to monitor (LSB 2010a).

Commission [2010] EWHC 2550 (Admin)). It should also be noted that when the Law Society President Linda Lee (2010–11) with a non-corporate background, announced her Presidential theme of 'Solicitors – adding value, qualified to answer', the 'inclusiveness of the theme was welcomed' (Law Society 2010d: 123). However, the Law Society has also taken significant steps in supporting the work of the largest firms, principally through the activities of its specific international section (http://international.lawsociety.org.uk/?=lshome [accessed: 29 January 2011]) – although the CLLS are also engaged in this work (CLLS 2007c).

Fiona Woolf made clear in an interview with the SPG, that 'the Law Society can only do so much. It cannot buck the market, but it can provide support and minimise the expense of regulation' (cited in Kendrick 2005: 4). This is an accurate description of the limited ability of any segment of the profession, whether core or marginal, elite or small firm to control the increasingly competitive legal and related services market. However, different segments require different types of support and the Law Society cannot always minimize the expense of regulation, despite its best endeavours. The Law Society still attempts to shelter older organizational forms from harsh competitive winds. However, the importance of the wider profession to the Law Society, as an actor in its own right, should not be dismissed. On one level engaging in the cross-profession representative action, builds its own credibility – it is able to demonstrate its relevance to its membership.[13] However, if support was not given to the smaller firms, eventually they may disappear with the work and clients swallowed up by increasingly larger organizational units potentially owned and/or managed by non-lawyers (Mayson 2008). Such large firms with greater resources, political power and capability to operate with AIR may prove an increasingly strong challenge to the Law Society. It is in the Law Society's organizational interests to ensure the survival of a sector which disproportionately relies upon it.

Alternative Business Structures, Professional Scepticism and Enduring Ties to the Legal Profession

ABSs (a 'licensed body' s.71 LSA) will be licensed by a 'licensing authority' (s.73), of which the Law Society (through the SRA) is likely to be among the first. They must deliver a reserved legal activity (s.71(1)),[14] and may be either owned and/or managed by non-lawyers. Notwithstanding this, the ABS must have a Head of Legal Practice (s.91) who must be an authorized person in relation to, at least, one of the licensed activities (Sch 11, para 11(3), and the reserved legal activities need to be delivered by a person who is authorized to deliver that activity (Sch 11 para 16). It is possible to have an ABS wholly owned by non-lawyers – the classic model of 'Tesco Law', or by a multi-disciplinary partnership. ABSs accordingly

---

13   'Law Society seeks to block privilege for non-lawyers' (Dean 2010a).
14   Although see Mayson on the lack of clarity in the legislation (2008: 11).

generate new challenges for the profession – 'the shake-up is coming and it will be huge' (Hodgart 2008, Flood 2008).[15]

Mayson argues that law firms, as a whole, have been slow to see themselves as businesses and have subsequently been on the back foot in the context of these regulatory changes (2010a: 3–4). While there has been criticism, particularly from smaller firms, about the 'quality' of service provided by such new entrants (Sutton 2007, 2009),[16] Mayson stresses the importance of brand reputation to these corporations (2010a: 9). He also suggests that there is considerable interest from external investors, precisely because the reserved legal activities market is a regulated (and thus controlled) market (2008: 16). However, these new entrants may bring new ways of managing and delivery of their services (Mayson 2008: 19). Moreover, as non-lawyers, they will be immune from the processes of socialization that take place within Law Schools (Kennedy 1998), and law firms (Muzio, Faulconbridge and Cook 2010) and subject to a greater diversity of professional and organizational norms and cultures.

Moreover, Susskind argues that when the impact of a globalized economy for professional services[17] is added to the exponentially developing capabilities of information technology, it is possible to envisage an increasingly commoditized approach to the delivery of legal services. Thus, rather than a traditional law firm selling a 'Rolls Royce' product of bespoke legal services, Susskind argues that firms (particularly new entrant firms with less attachment to the traditional way in which lawyers have worked) will start to break down legal services down into smaller component tasks which could then be delivered in a range of ways, for example by outsourcing, sub-contracting, off-shoring or fully computerising the smaller tasks (2008: 47).[18]

There is, admittedly, a mixed message from the profession and commentators as to how quickly and which type of law firms are likely to be affected by ABS models. Rigby and Hancock (2010) canvassed the views of various leading legal

---

15   While this is not an uncommon assessment, it should be noted that Hodgart is a Management Consultant selling services to law firms. Change, and encouraging early adopters, is his business (http://www.huronconsultinggroup.com/about.aspx [accessed: 29 January 2011]).

16   A Law Society Gazette story on the Co-op's plans to enter the market to provide legal services saw one 'anonymous' poster complain that 'The public are largely unaware that the person actually dealing with their file might be 18 year old Jenny with GCSES in English and Maths and IT skills with possibly no knowledge or indeed interest in the law. To her clients are "customers" and as a young adult she will be under a lot of pressure to do as she is told.' ('Tesco law -misleading the public? Submitted by Anonymous on Fri, 23/04/2010 - 09: 19', Rothwell 2010a).

17   See, for example, Lin (2010) on the growing importance of the Chinese sector in Mergers and Acquisitions.

18   It is worth noting that Susskind is also heavily involved in providing consulting services to global professional firms (http://www.susskind.com/consulting.html [accessed: 29 January 2011]).

and management consultancy figures to explore what the reforms could mean for City firms. While, it was felt that the firms on the next tier down from the Magic Circle might benefit from additional injections of capital to fuel their development, external investment was said to be unnecessary for the largest elite City firms. Felicity Banks of the Institute of Chartered Accountants in England and Wales (ICAEW) asserted the association's support of MDPs to the Joint Committee on the LS Bill and argued that when an accountant needed to refer to a solicitor, 'We would like that solicitor to be there in the office ready to hand the client on to' (JCLSB 2006: para. 263). However, as late as 2010, the indications were that while still interested in the possibilities of ABSs, accountants were not significantly advanced in their preparations (LSB ABS Implementation Group 2010). Others, including Chris Perrins, highlight the complexity of setting up an ABS for large international law firms operating in multiple jurisdictions, and Cyrus Mehta at Nabarro points out the loss of control to external investors would be a significant drawback to any partnership considering external investment through the ABS model (cited in Rigby and Hancock 2010: 3). The CLLS remain keen to preserve the 'shared sense of duty ... of a solicitor partnership' (2010b: 10)

The caution shared across the profession may, of course, be a product of measured business decision-making. Thus, the elite law firms, for example, may have the ability to change, but lack the willingness to do so. As incumbents, the status quo rewards them (Battilana 2006: 661–2). The partners have control of the strategic direction of their practice (Faulconbridge and Muzio 2008), they are well rewarded (Galanter and Roberts 2008), and continue to draw in the benefits of their selective engagement with the collective profession: belonging to 'an independent legal profession', for example, supports them in strategies to open up international markets (CLLS 2007a). However, it may also be indicative of the power of the institutional logics of the field in framing even these elite actors' capacity to generate institutional change (Greenwood and Suddaby 2006).

Of course, the degree and pace of change will not be known until after the first ABS is licensed in October 2011, but there are already signs that there may be benefits to firms that are able to recognize that, as Mayson puts it, 'this notion of being professionals – and just professionals – is being replaced' (2010a: 12). Optima Legal Services' rapid growth was funded by a series of loans from the leading outsourcing firm Capita. Although the SRA intervened (given that the arrangements predated the formal licensing of ABSs), it is indicative of the expansion that could be achieved through significant external investment (Dowell 2010). Similarly, the reported profits of the first Law firm to float on the stock exchange – the Australian firm of Slater & Gordon Limited – may also provide an incentive for the development of new business models (Swift 2010).

Specialization, Professional Education and the Accreditation of Expert Knowledge

The relationship between knowledge and education is central to the developing picture of elite actors moving to the edge of law and yet retaining both influence over, and residual ties to, the traditional collective profession. Moreover the capacity of these models of professional advancement to be accommodated by the traditional profession is likely to come under further pressure within the post-LSA environment. The increasing emphasis upon fragmented knowledge which draws on disciplines far removed from the profession's core knowledge, and the tendency of legal multinationals to 'invest heavily in legal education and production of discourse' (Dezalay and Trubek 1994: 430), undermines orthodox understandings about the relationship of the elites (and the marginalized) to expert knowledge and to the sites of professional education and training. The shift from shared professional socialization to organizational culturalization (Muzio, Faulconbridge and Cook 2010, Anderson-Gough, Grey and Robson 2000) also underlines the divergence of the models of contemporary professional advancement. At the same time, however, the disproportionate power that the elite actors hold over entry to the profession (Chapters 1 and 3) casts an influential shadow back over the profession at large.

Education, Training and the Organizational Focus

The gate-keepers to the profession are now the firms which offer training contracts (Savage 2002) and the 'tilt in training towards the largest firms' acknowledged by a Partner in a Magic Circle firm, has seen the establishment of a City LPC (D'Souza 2001). Moreover, Clifford Chance and Linklaters have recently gone further, and established a fast-track (seven-month) LPC for their trainees (McPartland 2010). As a Law Society Salaried Officer interviewed in 1999 reflects, 'it's probable that the High Street firms have lost out because we've dropped Probate as a core subject [on the LPC]'. This seems an increasingly partial conception of the profession's traditional expert knowledge and values. While a steady proportion of trainees do begin their legal careers outside the largest corporate firms (44.7 per cent of traineeships in firms with fewer than 26 partners, Cole 2009: 40), this sector has already cast a shadow: first over their aspirations (see Chapter 3), but later in terms of the development of their professional expertise.

The firms, of course, are also large-scale providers of training for their own employees. As Muzio, Faulconbridge and Cook demonstrate, this sees firm-wide values and training needs prioritized over profession-wide aspirations (2010) – 'the cultural glue that holds [the firm] together' (Greenwood and Suddaby 2006: 40). Firm assessment centres are also productive sites for the development of the 'networked professional' upon which individual and organizational advancement is increasingly premised (Anderson-Gough, Grey and Robson 2006). This challenges the importance of universities as a site for professional socialization and the reinforcement of the collective coherence of the profession. The strong disciplinary connections to Law among the Cause lawyers and Trusts and Estates lawyers, identified within Chapters 5 and 6, may come under pressure if the organizational focus in education and training continues to develop.

Thus, the specialized training delivered within, or on behalf of these firms, is in addition to the common education and training of the profession. Moreover it is directly linked to the skills and expertise which these firms require of their associates (Muzio, Faulconbridge and Cook 2010). The two-tier associate track of elite US law firms within which the work given to 'associates on the training track [to partnership] ... is not drudgery, it is not over-specialized, there is mentoring and the associates do develop relationships with clients' (Wilkins and Gulati 1998: 1676), may also be developing within England and Wales. Thus, for example, Clifford Chance has established global Assessment Centres to help 'senior associates to cultivate the business and commercial skills required for partnership in an elite firm' (Clifford Chance 2010). The arrival of a wider range of professionals in the delivery of legal services following the introduction of ABSs may further disrupt traditional links between professional knowledge and training.[19]

The Law Society has long attempted to control the nature of the undergraduate degree (Cownie and Cocks 2009, JASB 2002a) and reinforce the links between the collective profession and the universities (Larson 1977: 44). Since 2009, there have been growing calls for an increased place for the study of ethics in the undergraduate law curriculum. This idea has its most recent impetus from a Law Society commissioned report by Kim Economides and Justine Rodgers, and has support from the Law Society (Law Society 2010c) and the CLLS (2010a). The CLLS appears to seek broader influence on the Qualifying Law Degree through its insistence that 'the content, quality and level of assessment of QLDs is in urgent need of review' with a new syllabus perhaps involving 'company law' (2010a: 5). It is worth noting that the agenda to exert greater control over the quality assurance of Qualifying Law Degrees is also advanced by the Law Society (2010b: 16). Rather than this being the case of the Law Society following the large firms' agenda, I would argue that this is more likely to be a synchronization of interests which capitalizes on the increasing importance of employer needs in undergraduate education following the Browne Review of Higher Education Funding (2010). This drive may be given further weight by a wide-ranging review into legal education, scheduled to begin in 2011 (BSB 2010) and the arrival of private providers such as BPP and the College of Law into the undergraduate market.

---

19   My thanks to John Flood for discussion of these points.

Accredited Expertise and Individualizing Claims to Market Share

While specialization has always existed to some degree, the increasing specialization in all (not just the corporate) sectors of legal services disrupts the myth of equal professional competence (Johnson 1972: 55), by exposing the reality of the individualized models of advancement and challenging the traditional professional organization to articulate a convincing and coherent response.

One of the ways in which the Law Society has attempted to do this is through the establishment of Accreditation Schemes. These schemes had originally been the responsibility of the SRA, however the Law Society brought these back into the representative side of the organization in 2009. This strategy, in part linked to the 'turf war' between the Law Society and the SRA (see above), is an example of what Moorhead (2010) argues is the professional paradox – recognizing quality and specialization, while maintaining the profession-wide claim of expertise. In bringing the Accreditation Schemes into the representative side of the organizations, the Law Society insisted upon the additional and voluntary nature of the schemes (Moorhead 2010: 252). However, at the same time, it claims that membership of such a scheme is indicative of the 'special recognition of their expertise' (http://www.lawsociety.org.uk/productsandservices/accreditation.page [accessed: 29 January 2011]). It promotes the expertise of the accredited solicitor above that of the generalist. Thus, the Legal Services Commission prioritized 'Advanced Members' of the Law Society's Family Law Accreditation Schemes in its tender criteria (LSC 2010: 3). This provoked ire from many without the contract who questioned whether membership was any 'guarantee of quality' (see, for example, Robertson's online comment on Baksi 2010b) and the judicial review action brought by the Law Society. Only 16 per cent of the entire profession are members of the schemes (http://www.lawsociety.org.uk/productsandservices/ accreditation.page [accessed: 29 January 2009]), which suggests a further dilution of the shared standardized knowledge base across the profession.

Abbott argues that the key determinant in terms of internal stratification within a profession is proximity to the profession's core standardized knowledge base (1988: 118). However, within legal services, it is now harder to define the profession's core standardized knowledge base, let alone determine whether the elite actually use it. Within the large corporate firm, the genuinely creative legal work (Jamous and Peloille 1970, Flood 1991, Powell 1993) is performed by small groups of partners (Muzio and Ackroyd 2005, Faulconbridge and Muzio 2008). Teams of trainees and assistant solicitors perform the relatively routinized or proletarian tasks (Smith 2006, Sommerlad 2002), in which Abbott saw subordinate or lower-status professionals engaged (1988: 125–34). Equally, the knowledge that these elite players within legal services deploy can be conceptualized as a site of difference (Abbott 1995: 866–7) (as between themselves and non-providers of elite global professional services) that these law firms share with management consultancy and accounting firms.

The similarity in terms of language and content in PricewaterhouseCoopers' (Big Four Audit firm) and Freshfields' (Magic Circle Law firm) assertions of their Mergers and Acquisitions expertise is striking:

> We provide a full range of M&A and financial advisory services across all industry sectors, from acquisitions through to raising finance. Wherever you are in the world, we are able to deploy local teams at short notice – teams that combine our deep industry expertise with local knowledge to focus on your deal. For every deal we are able to draw on the full range of PwC services – including due diligence, tax and legal advice. (http://www.pwc.co.uk/eng/services/MandA_advisory.html [accessed: 29 January 2011])

> We have particular expertise in the formation and acquisition of banks and financial institutions, advising on licence requirements, regulatory compliance and the protection of deposits. We can help lower capital costs by optimising bank asset structures and liquidity ... Our M&A clients not only include banks and financial institutions but also many of the large international corporations in the IT and telecoms, media, defence and manufacturing sectors. (http://www.freshfields.com/practices/corporate/ma/index.asp [accessed: 29 January 2011])

Abbott argues that a jurisdictional claim involves the assertion that the abstracted knowledge of a profession is most appropriate to the resolution of a particular task (1988: 59). However, Greenwood and Suddaby argue that 'commodification and colonization [of expert knowledge] appear to be the direct result of the tendency of professional services to be delivered by large complex organizations' (2001: 950). Thus, jurisdictional disputes are not resolved by well-organized and coherent professional associations (Abbott 1988: 106, Sugarman 1995a), but by the global professional firms, with 'firm profit as the primary justification' (Greenwood and Suddaby 2001: 950). Thus, Freshfields is not claiming that the profession's legal knowledge is most appropriate for advising on a particular Merger or Acquisition, rather that, as a 'leader among international law firms' it 'provid[es] business law advice of the highest quality throughout Europe, the Middle East, Asia and the U.S.', with experience on 'some of the most challenging, complex and stimulating transactions in the world' (http://www.freshfields.com/aboutus/ [accessed: 29 January 2011]). The focus is on the *firm*'s market position, expertise and prestige.

Smaller firms, while increasingly adopting web presences of varying degrees of sophistication, are more comfortable in stressing traditional expertise and values across core areas of work (Franklin and Lee 2007, Melville and Laing 2007). Thus, Lewis Rodgers Solicitors (a three lawyer High Street firm in a small town in Cheshire) stress that 'some people find the thought of visiting a solicitor quite frightening so we make every effort to make you feel comfortable' (http://www.lewisrodgers.co.uk [accessed: 29 January 2011]). Similarly, McCarthy Bennett Holland (a four partner High Street firm in Wigan) emphasize that they are 'approachable, talk common sense and have a track record of getting things done' (http://www.wigansolicitors.com [accessed: 29 January 2011]). Even the smallest firms are compelled to think about their market claims. They might make them in ways which stress recognizably legal expertise and more generally demonstrate greater connection to traditional professional values, but even these firms do not rely on the profession-wide claim of competence[20] – their market claim is that they offer the client something different to other law firms.

Conclusion

This chapter highlights the divergent (although at times, complementary) models of legal professionalism in the post-LSA legal services market. The power of elite law firms is clear (Flood 2010). They are able to resolve the paradox of embedded agency through their size, resources and boundary bridging capabilities and engage in institutional entrepreneurship to reinforce their positions of privilege (Greenwood and Suddaby 2006: 43). Yet the picture that emerges is not uniformly of profession-wide dominance and takeover. It is clear that although the largest firms do not appear to need the Law Society there remains an ongoing connection. The core brand of solicitor remains important, and was seen in the position papers of the largest firms (individually and through the CLLS) prior to the LSA and subsequently (CLLS 2010a, 2010b). There still appears to be a role for a collective articulation of legal professionalism, which at times includes the elite law firms, at other times, pointedly safeguards the interests of other less powerful segments. The Law Society and its collective conceptions of legal professionalism are not an irrelevance; it has not been relegated to the vertical edge of law. Thus, it has continued with the strategy of 'managed heterogeneity' (Francis 2004: 345), and has attempted to provide differentiated leadership and support to the various sectors within the solicitors' profession. In part, it has attempted to do this through the Accreditation Schemes discussed above, but it also established more explicit sections for International Work, Junior Lawyers and Private Client solicitors (discussed in Chapter 6).

However, it is no longer the fulcrum of professional advancement. It is not the primary driver of the collective mobility project. Strikingly, while the City firms stated that they did not wish to compete with the Law Society (City Firms Working Group 2008), the announcement that the CLLS is to appoint a Chief Executive as part of its intention 'to create a management and representative model capable

---

20   An interesting new development is http://www.qualitysolicitors.com [accessed: 29 January 2011], essentially a commercially driven web-based advertising/database model. High Street firms can sign up to the Scheme, if they meet the Quality Solicitor 'mark of excellence'. Potential clients can then search the database for their local 'Quality Solicitor'. What is striking is that the law firms who have signed up for the Scheme are not relying upon profession- wide guarantees of competence, but a commercially driven enterprise to enable them to position themselves in the market.

of expanding our services beyond the present as and when needed' (McIntosh 2010), confirms its role as an alternative fulcrum of collective advancement for an individual sector of the wider legal profession. This is a significant 'tooling up' of the CLLS and may presage it positioning itself as an alternative regulator.[21] However, the City firms' location at the edge does not yet presage a complete fracturing with the rest of the legal profession (Abbott 1995). They are too central to the solicitors' profession, in their capacity to re-frame institutional logics, for example on regulation and provide leadership, for example in responding to legislation. Moreover, they draw on the language of traditional professionalism, whether it be the independent legal profession (CLLS 2007a) or the shared sense of duty held by solicitor partners (CLLS 2010b). Small, beleaguered firms may well be considered at the edge, in terms of the internal stratification of the profession (Abbott 1988: 118), but they derive continuing support from the profession as a whole and also show some capacity to deploy more individualized models of advancement, whether through other representative associations or their own firm efforts.

In thinking about the edge of law and the boundaries between things (Abbott 1995) we can identify shared sites of difference, between different groups of actors and organizations. However, this chapter highlights the contingency of much of this sharing. The final chapter will pull together the main arguments and attempt to articulate the importance of contingency, in understanding the complex interaction of these divergent models of legal professionalism.

---

21   Much will depend upon whether the SRA's appointment of Nick Eastwell as 'Chief Advisor to City Firms' will address the demands set out in the Hunt/Smedley Reviews (Hollander 2010a).

Chapter 8

Emergent and Divergent Models of Legal Professionalism: Towards a Contingent Professionalism

Introduction

In order to take account of the fluidity, fragmentation and heterogeneity of the legal profession, a sustained analysis of those individuals and organizations which operate at the edge of law is required. The boundaries of law provide opportunities for institutional entrepreneurship which generate new organizational forms and patterns of behaviour. At the same time, location at the vertical edge indicates subordination within the profession. The case-studies considered in this book present new analysis of original empirical and archival research which explores a series of actors positioned on the different edges of the legal profession in England and Wales, as well as one example from Canada. As such, I hope it represents an additional dimension to studies of the changes facing contemporary legal professionalism. This chapter sets out the main findings and establishes the central themes of the book. These themes are used to signpost the features of a model of contingent professionalism. It concludes with discussion of the policy implications of this and the challenges which face the legal profession.

Main Findings and Central Themes

Chapter 3 drew on the experiences of 'outsider' students recorded during the course of two projects exploring legal education and access to the profession. It highlighted the influence of large corporate law firms in laying down a normative or expected path into the profession and the discomfort faced by those outsider students who have not been able to follow this path. Notwithstanding the weakening of collective control over entry to the legal profession, the embedded practices of the field render it uncomfortable for these students. A key dimension of this is the variability of cultural capital accrued at different university Law Schools. The institution attended not only remains an important marker of class, but also of likely success in securing entry to the profession. The institutional logics appear to shape not only the normative 'route' for students, but also the firms' expectations. The apparent reluctance of these elite actors to challenge the inconsistencies in these logics (Braithwaite 2010) could be ascribed to a desire to reinforce existing positions of privilege (Battilana 2006: 662).

Similar issues emerge in reviewing the limitations of the professional project of legal executives. From their inception as an occupational group, the strategic choices of legal executives have been framed by the institutional logics, which denote them as a semi-profession (Etzioni 1969), holding a subordinate jurisdiction. Their use of the knowledge base of their employers and the continuing importance of graduate capital reinforces this second-class status. Meanwhile, the intersectional disadvantage experienced by women legal executives presents a serious challenge for a profession with an overwhelmingly female membership (particularly at junior levels), in its efforts to occupy a more mainstream and prestigious role in the delivery of legal services. However, the successes that the profession has secured, in terms of further rights and responsibilities, suggest that collective strategies of closure or registration may still have relevance, at least where appropriate levels of state support exist.

Pivot lawyers are based in Vancouver, Canada and, like other cause lawyers, attempt to achieve something more transformative for their community in their practice of law than mainstream UK (or indeed Canadian) legal aid practitioners. Notwithstanding our global interconnectedness, the Pivot study reminds us that local context still matters. Although the Pivot model of 'activist lawyering' cannot be readily applied to the UK, it is a useful illustration of the way in which different actors and organizations engage with Law in order to pursue explicitly progressive political aims. These lawyers demonstrated agency in moving to the edge of mainstream legal professionalism within Canada, they are creative in their use of methods and organizational form and yet, strikingly, also appear bound to Law by a number of disciplinary ties.

The enduring power of disciplinary ties is also evident in the amalgamating professional project of Trusts and Estates Practitioners. There are strong aspirations amongst the leadership of STEP for the creation of a new distinct profession. These aspirations are shared by those within the membership whose area of work is not dominated by a strong existing profession, or whose practice or geographical location enables them to bridge boundaries and thus identify institutional inconsistencies within traditional fields. However, in their use of expert knowledge and assertions of professional identity, lawyers (and accountants) demonstrate strong connections to their parent disciplines, notwithstanding their marginal location within those stratified mature fields.

The complexity and contingency of field location is drawn out further in Chapter 7 which analyses the positioning and strategic arguments of key professional and state actors, in the debates leading to the Legal Services Act 2007, and their responses in the years which have followed. It recognizes the increasing power of elite corporate law firms, acting both individually and collectively through the City of London Law Society (CLLS). This power sees them move towards the edge of the profession in terms of size, knowledge used, organizational form adopted and so on, and thus potentially closer to environing professional groups. However, they concurrently exert influence over the collective solicitors' profession on issues such as education, regulation and recruitment. Moreover, they continue to subscribe to traditional professional values, such as the 'independence of the legal profession', or draw on the Law Society's cachet as the professional association for the whole profession, when it is in their interests to do so, for example in the context of international work. The Law Society, itself, the traditional fulcrum of collective professional advancement, retains a level of influence and seeks to consolidate this influence by reinforcing its whole-profession legitimacy through the support of the non-corporate sector. Alongside this, there remains a great deal of uncertainty about the precise impact of Alternative Business Structures. Even before the first ABSs are licensed from October 2011, individual law firms are already making differentiated claims of expertise in an increasingly competitive marketplace, which challenges traditional understandings of professional-wide competence (Moorhead 2010).

The Importance of Field Location

The case-studies presented in this book emphasize the importance of field location in shaping the capacity of different individuals and organizations to deploy strategies of professionalization or challenge the institutional logics of the field (Lounsbury 2002: 255). These social structures have the capacity to constrain the choices and agency of the actors located within them (Mutch, Delbridge and Ventresca 2006: 622). The framework of the 'edge' has to take account of both internal stratification and those moving away from the core of mainstream legal professionalism in other ways. The diagram at the end of Chapter 2 illustrates not only the different ways in which actors are located at 'the edge', but also the uncertainty of this location for many of them. Thus, in some ways, Pivot lawyers or Trusts and Estates lawyers could be viewed as subordinate players within the traditional legal profession. In others they appear capable of challenging institutional logics and developing new methods, organizational forms and even professional identities. What is clear, however, is that the capacity of marginal players to challenge mainstream values or models of professionalism is more uncertain than Shils' conception of change being generated from the periphery (1975: 10).

What is striking when surveying the contemporary legal services landscape is the resilience of exclusionary patterns of closure (Sommerlad et al. 2010). The capacity of the collective profession to exert control over entry has been in decline for some time (Abel 2003, Francis 2004). However, the experiences of outsider students and legal executives highlight the continuing disadvantage for many on the basis of socio-economic disadvantage. Moreover, while many of the recruitment practices originate from the elite sectors of the profession (who, in some ways, appear to be edging away from the traditional profession), the effect is more widespread. With some sector variations, a normative pathway into the profession has emerged which assumes early and frequent informal work experience, excellent academic performance (particularly from A-level onwards), a well-rounded personality evidenced by a startling array of extracurricular activities and the capacity to 'fit' readily within the professional environment. Legal executives, usually coming from broken or non-traditional educational backgrounds, also struggle to demonstrate they have followed anything other than a deviant pathway. Notwithstanding the expansion of higher education and the increasing diversity of the legal profession throughout the 1990s and 2000s, a relatively narrow pool in terms of socio-economic background continues to dominate, particularly within the elite corporate sectors (Sommerlad et al. 2010). There is concern that the changes to the higher education funding model (Browne 2010) and the forthcoming review of legal education (BSB 2010) may result in a further narrowing of the profession.

Internal stratification is also experienced by other occupational groups who have secured access to the profession. Thus, private client lawyers, working in the Trusts and Estates field, consistently complain of being the 'cinderella' discipline within law, very much the poor relation. Publicly funded lawyers also experience professional marginalization and complain of a lack of status, poor pay and reduced professional autonomy (Sommerlad 2001, Moorhead 2004). High Street and smaller firms in general have also consistently felt threatened, with the survival of their sector in real jeopardy (Franklin and Lee 2007, Jopson 2001). Lacking resources, or the ability to move between fields, these lawyers appear constrained by a traditional professionalism which restricts their ability to articulate alternative patterns of behaviour. Thus, they insist that they are the last bastions of professionalism, contrasting their values with the corporate sector (Franklin and Lee 2007: 241) and casting themselves as the only prophets to foresee the catastrophic challenge to professionalism heralded by the arrival of ABSs (see further Chapter 7). Similarly, the Trusts and Estates lawyers saw their use of a broad-based legal knowledge as true professionalism in contrast to the increasingly specialized use of expertise in the corporate sector. Such groups will generally find it difficult to advance along traditional lines of professional advancement by virtue of their internal subordination and are inhibited from challenging institutional logics by being deeply embedded within the mainstream field of legal professionalism.

Field location also appears to be important in affecting the stability of the professional identity of the actors. The edge of law appears to be an uncomfortable place for many of these individuals and organizations. Carrie Yang Costello invokes the notion of identity dissonance and consonance. She argues that many entrants to professional schools (law and social work in her study) are faced with challenges in reconciling their pre-existing personal identities with the new professional identities that are (often implicitly) expected of them (2005: 117–63). Those for whom the new professional identity represents a profound challenge, for example a working-class Filipina woman going to Law School (2005: 4), experience 'identity dissonance' and face a more uncomfortable time in adapting than, for example, the white, middle-class male (2005: 3). Similar discomfort is identified in the gaps between aspiration and reality for 'outsider' law students and legal executives and, in different ways, in the tensions experienced by the Pivot lawyers as they seek to reconcile their dual identities as lawyers and as activists. Trusts and Estates lawyers also face discomfort and uncertainty in their professional identities, unsure as to the extent to which they are able to reconcile their existing primary disciplinary kinship with a new amalgamating professional project. In contrast, elite actors not experiencing subordination, but nonetheless operating towards the edge of mainstream legal professionalism (for example corporate law firms and the CLLS), experience Bauman's lightness and detachment. They possess the capacity and resources to glide between fields, identities and patterns of behaviour much less problematically (Bauman 2005: 135) – notwithstanding the enduring nature of some disciplinary ties.

The variable way in which I have invoked the framework of 'the edge of law' in this book allows us to consider the influential positions of elite actors within a mature stratified field (Greenwood and Suddaby 2006: 28), who are able to engage in boundary bridging that takes them closer to environing professionals. In the context of law, it is one which the elite corporate law firms seem well placed to occupy. The resource asymmetries between these elite organizations and the rest of the profession (indeed even the professional association), equips the corporate law firms, and their collective voice the CLLS, with the ability to engage in institutional entrepreneurship. The organizational drive to prevent adverse performance and the ability of the firms to bridge jurisdictional and geographical boundaries enables these actors to identify new opportunities and the inconsistencies in the field, which are hidden to those more deeply embedded within the field (Greenwood and Suddaby 2006: 42). Thus, for example, during the course of the Smedley / Hunt Reviews they developed a model of differentiated regulation which challenged existing conceptions of profession-wide regulation (Flood 2010). However, it has not been a simple story of either breakaway or takeover. The developing patterns of professionalism appear more complex than that.

Divergent Models of Legal Professionalism

Notwithstanding the degree and pace of change within the legal services marketplace, one of the central themes of the book is the level of consistency and continuity that has been maintained. Elite law firms continue to exert influence over the profession and develop their own market share (Galanter and Roberts 2008), with lawyers retaining occupational control within the organization (Faulconbridge and Muzio 2008). 'Outsider' entrants to the professions still struggle to secure access (Sommerlad 2007), and the private client (public and privately funded) sector continues to experience marginalization and second-class status (Moorhead 2004). However, it is also possible to identify divergent models of legal professionalism developing on the edges and fringes of law.

Thus, Pivot lawyers in Vancouver exert agency in consciously rejecting the paradigmatic conceptions of mainstream corporate law to which they have been exposed at elite Law School (Manderson and Turner 2006). In doing so, they attempt to articulate a new explicitly political professional identity, that of an Activist Lawyer. This is systemic rather than individual in its focus, egalitarian in its organizational form and seeks to collapse the client/cause distinction. Moreover, the boundary bridging location also enables them to develop creative new methods, whether reframing legal tools, such as affidavits for political ends, or invoking activist tools such as fundraising gigs in law reform campaigns.[1] STEP is also an example of a divergent model of professionalism, in that is multi-disciplinary and cross-jurisdictional. The organization transcends traditional demarcations and yet continues to insist upon the importance of accredited expert knowledge. Moreover, while the organization as a whole is working towards the establishment of 'a profession in its own right' – Abbott's 'thingness' (1995: 870) – it is also relaxed about its members going to a range of professional membership associations at different times for different reasons. Elite corporate law firms operate within the constraints of 'commercialised professionalism' (Hanlon 1999). They bridge geographical borders in their work (Beaverstock 2004), and the boundaries of the expert knowledge upon which they draw are increasingly fluid (Dezalay 1995). They have even been successful in advancing a model of professional regulation which recognizes them as explicitly different to the rest of the profession (Hunt 2009).

However, it is also possible to identify these models of professional advancement being deployed alongside, but not necessarily in opposition to, traditional collective values. The STEP members reported that it was either they themselves or STEP who advanced their professional interests and it was STEP that they drew upon to demonstrate their expertise to government or employers. However, the lawyer membership did this alongside a continuing, almost emotional, connection to the parent discipline. Lawyer is their instinctive and primary professional identity. Although Pivot lawyers recognized and had anxieties about the relationship between the individual clients' interests and those of the wider community, ultimately their lawyer norms provided answers to particular dilemmas, and they secured support and accommodation from mainstream legal professionalism in a number of ways. Moreover, their explicit positioning of themselves at the edge of law arguably fails to disturb assumptions as to what should be the values and ethics of mainstream lawyering.

Elite corporate law firms also demonstrate enduring connections to mainstream legal professionalism. They draw on the rhetoric of the value of an 'independent legal profession' and of the 'shared sense of duty of solicitor partners' when it is their interests to do so. Moreover, they also exert a strong influence over the collective profession on issues such as regulation and education. Suddaby, Gendron and Lam similarly note an ongoing adherence to traditional professional values among elite actors in Accountancy, which appeared to contradict other stances

---

1   While I have been clear that the Pivot case-study is as much about the importance of context as it is about direct applicability, some variations of these activities are found in the UK publicly funded and voluntary sectors.

taken by these actors, for example in relation to profession-wide regulation (2009: 424). However, I argue that the invocation of divergent models of professionalism, alongside traditional collective models, is not necessarily evidence of contradiction and inconsistency. Particularly for those elites capable of boundary bridging, and thus able to 'glide' between the centre and periphery, such apparently contradictory views are entirely predictable given the ease with which they move within and between fields. They are not contradictory, but a product of the multiple field positions that these actors can occupy. Relatedly, it may be that the power of these disciplinary ties has an even more profound effect on more marginal actors. Thus, legal executives have consistently found their strategic choices framed by their strong connection to a traditional conception of legal professionalism (Fournier 1999, Francis 2002). It may be that the constraining properties of kinship are more pronounced for those located at the bottom of the vertical edge (see further above).

However, it is possible to identify a continuing role for the Law Society as the fulcrum of a collective model of professional advancement. The Law Society took a prominent role in seeking to 'maximise its influence' during the passage of the LSA 2007, and premised much of its arguments on traditional, profession-wide rhetoric. It continues to regularly intervene, on explicitly non-corporate issues. It did this most visibly towards the end of 2010 in its judicial review proceedings against the Legal Services Commission which successfully challenged the legality of its family law tendering process. It is far from central, but it does appear to have a continuing role. Similarly, the case-studies of legal executives, and to a lesser degree the Trusts and Estates Practitioners, also indicate that collective models of advancement or closure/registration may continue to have a level of success. Thus ILEX has, in recent years, been able to secure significant increases in the rights and responsibilities for its membership, ensuring that only fully qualified Fellows are entitled to apply for further rights of audience or to conduct litigation. Thus, this distinguishes them in the eyes of the public and employers from unqualified paralegals, who may otherwise have been performing similar work (Witz 1992: 44–50). However, the crucial determinant appears to have been the existence of state support for such a project.

The Role of the State

The central role of the state in legitimizing the professional project is continually emphasized throughout Larson's work, because 'only the state, as the supreme legitimizing and enforcing institution could sanction the modern profession's monopolistic claims of superiority for their commodities' (1977: 15). However, the role of the state in the context of the contemporary English legal profession appears to go far beyond Larson's notion of the professions requiring an affinity with the dominant ideology (1977: 47–9), or Freidson's argument that a successful professional project will share 'some of the established values of the civilisation' (1970: 73). The state in the contemporary legal services marketplace is a powerful actor in its own right. It has not acted simply to sanction the legal profession's claims, but to challenge and limit them (Abel 2003, M. Davies 2010).

Legal executives, for example, consistently failed to make any substantial progress in their professional project, limited as they were by their position as a subordinate profession under the jurisdictional control of solicitors. It was only when the Labour Government (1997–2010) acted to drive down civil justice costs and challenge what it saw as the restrictive practices of solicitors and barristers, that legal executives found themselves as the grateful (and somewhat surprised) recipients of the most far-reaching extension of the rights of legal executives in their history. Similarly the story of the Legal Services Act 2007 is marked by the enthusiastic embrace by the Government of first, the OFT's report on restrictive practices in the profession (Office of Fair Trading 2001), and secondly the Clementi Review (2004b). The responses of the then Lord Chancellor Charles Falconer in a meeting of the Law Society Council reveal the public nature of the implied threats of the government to the profession (whatever else may have been said behind closed doors). Subsequently, the Legal Services Board has acted with the confidence and enthusiasm of a body with statutorily bestowed legitimacy and its officers have been vociferous in making clear to the professional bodies the way in which they would like to see regulation of the sector develop (Edmonds 2010a). The state has increasingly restricted the autonomy of lawyers in publicly funded work (Moorhead 2004), which has also seen restrictions on the progressive potential of the not-for-profit sector (Robins 2008). More recently, the Legal Services Commission has had a powerful (and controversial) role in developing the criteria through which the diminishing public funds for legal aid are administered. All of this signals a much more proactive actor than past models of professionalism seem to envisage.[2]

A new Conservative-led, Coalition Government took office in the UK in May 2010. Many of the policy announcements leading up to and including the Comprehensive Spending Review in October 2010 have indicated a substantial retrenchment of public spending in general, and perhaps more broadly, an ideological rolling back of the state. It remains to be seen how far the momentum of the state as a leading actor in the development of contemporary legal professionalism will be sustained during the course of this Government.

The Fracturing Claims of Expert Knowledge

In contrast to the conceptions of Johnson (1972) and Larson (1977) of a standardized body of expert knowledge that clearly identified the profession in the minds of the wider public, expert knowledge no longer appears to play the same unifying role for the legal profession. In the context of claims to professional expertise more generally, Aldridge argues that 'expertise exists, but is situational. Any mandate or

---

2   Although Paterson does suggest that the state drove a harder bargain than he believes Abel, for example, countenanced (1996: 142).

privileges based upon it must be continually justified and renewed' (1996: 191). Thus, in the increasing complexity of the contemporary professional services market, individual actors and organizations are less likely to rely on traditional markers of expertise such as 'solicitor' or 'barrister'.

The work of elite law firms is fluid and crosses disciplinary boundaries (Dezalay 1995). In many ways these lawyers appear to share more, in terms of their knowledge base, with environing professionals such as accountants than they do their fellow solicitors. Activist lawyers, or even publicly funded family lawyers within the UK, may draw on the skill sets of community and social workers, as much as they do their legal expertise and training (Melville and Laing 2007). Different models of accreditation schemes are also invoked, whether those developed by the traditional professional association (Moorhead 2010) or by organizations such as STEP, in order to more clearly delineate specialist expertise. Arguably, claims to traditional generalist professional knowledge which would support a range of legal work now appear to reinforce the internal stratification of the profession, with actors claiming generalist expertise located in marginal positions at the edge of law (see, for example, the experience of private client lawyers in Chapter 6 and the rural solicitors of South Wales discussed by Franklin and Lee (2007)).

In 2000, the Law Society placed its faith in 'a common regulatory framework' and a 'willingness to sign up to a professional body that commanded respect by virtue of its standing and performance' as the key factors that unify the profession (2000a: 3). In November 2010, David Edmonds, Chair of the LSB, noted that 'maintaining the collective sense of identity across the profession is a key part of incentivising properly professional conduct' (Edmonds 2010b: 18). If profession-wide, abstract legal knowledge is no longer able to play this unifying role, is it possible to identify alternatives which could perform a similar function? Shared submission to a sufficiently attractive regulatory framework may be an incentive, but it seems more would be required. Other professions have shared regulation in the past, for example through the Financial Services Authority, but with little sense of a collective identity. Kinship and the affective connection to the parent discipline appear important throughout the case-studies discussed in this book, but it is less clear how this will continue to be reinforced, particularly if there is a greater organizational focus in professional educational and training following the 2011 review of legal education (BSB 2010).

These are key practical and strategic challenges for the legal profession, particularly for actors such as the Law Society who have an organizational interest in emphasizing the importance of the profession's collective identity. I suggest in the next section that how and when the collective identity is invoked will be on a far more contingent basis in the future. Paradoxically, this contingency may continue to successfully fuel the evolution of legal professionalism into the twenty-first century.

Towards a Contingent Legal Professionalism

The traditional collective mobility projects of Larson and Abel were located in the historically specific conditions of the late nineteenth and twentieth century. Thus, Larson highlights the increasing legitimacy of scientific knowledge, a heterogeneous clientele, an uncompetitive (although free) market and an affinity with the dominant ideology (1977: 47–9). As others argue, and as I have made clear in this book, these conditions are no longer in place, and thus their particular conception of professionalism appears less relevant as an explanation of the contemporary landscape (Abel 1989, Kritzer 1999). However, other writers have argued this sociological concept was always too narrow, and failed to take account of, for example, the evolving nature of the professions' 'contract' with the state (Paterson 1996), or that the public service claims of the profession had some empirical basis (Halliday 1987). More recently, others have argued that professionalism has changed and is now found in the occupational control that elite lawyers wield within the organizational context of the firm (Muzio and Ackroyd 2005, Faulconbridge and Muzio 2008).

  However, these examples of occupational control in elite professional services firms are only a partial explanation of the shifting nature of contemporary legal professionalism. Thus, for example, Muzio and Ackroyd's insightful analysis does not take account of the internal stratification within the profession which dictates that partners of many law firms demonstrate only a limited form of occupational control. Equally, however, the organizational focus (while a critical part of the developing picture), glosses over the ways in which there appear to be some enduring notions of collective professionalism which accommodate divergent models of professional advancement operating at the edge of law.

  In contrast to Larson's historical study, contemporary field conditions are characterized by a fragmented and heterogeneous profession, a fluid body of expert knowledge, an openly hostile state, increasingly powerful clients (of which the state is one), a fractured relationship with universities and an increasingly competitive and de-regulated marketplace. I argue that this has generated what might be described as a 'contingent legal professionalism'.[3] Today's fragmented, fluid and uncertain conditions give rise to a legal professionalism that is fragmented, fluid and uncertain because this is what the conditions of the field require. The precise nature of the professional strategies, ideologies and values that are invoked or will be acknowledged will be contingent upon a range of factors: the market's needs, the regulatory framework's requirements, the relative resources of professional actors, their field location in terms of their boundary bridging capabilities or

---

  3   Teodoro also invokes the term 'contingent professionalism'. However, he uses it to refer to 'mobility-contingent professionalism', whereby the ability of public sector professional bureaucrats to be entrepreneurial in developing new and risky policy innovations is contingent upon them moving regularly between jobs and agencies (2010: 455–6).

internal subordination and the likely responses of other professional actors both legal and non-legal (Webb 2004: 94–5).

Moreover, rather than this being the decline of professionalism (Abel 1989) or the end of lawyers (Susskind 2008), the continued rise (or at least evolution) of legal professionalism may be fuelled by the complexity of the field. The emergence of a range of divergent models of legal professionalism, some of which are moving away from traditional legal professionalism, may generate both momentum and resources for a much looser, more contingent form of legal professionalism. The tensions created and the negotiations demanded by the emergence of these different models of professionalism may enable the most convincing story to be delivered to the right audience in the right way, at the right time. Thus, as Greenwood, Suddaby and Hinings note in the context of Accountancy, it is easier for the professional association to claim 'public interest' motivations rather than individual firms (2002: 68). The presence of the different actors also enables the weight of the professional arguments to be enhanced. Thus the representations about the importance of the maintenance of the independent legal profession were made not only by the Law Society, but in concert with individual responses from powerful firms such as Clifford Chance and Allen & Overy and the City of London Law Society. Whether by strategic decision-making, or coalescence around the most efficient archetype, a contingent and fluid professionalism may bring the most efficient model for advancing the professional interests to the fore at a particular moment. The Law Society and STEP, for example, work together when it is in their interests to do so.[4]

Certainly, elements of this model invoke aspects of the internal stratification of Abbott (1988), Nelson and Trubek's competing arenas within which professional ideology is generated (1992b) and Muzio and Ackroyd's defensive professionalism (2005). However, what I propose is something altogether less certain and more complex, which both takes account, and is a product, of the uncertain, challenging and fluid conditions in which professional actors operate. In particular, the boundaries and alliances between different individuals and organizations are far less fixed than those implied in Nelson and Trubek's arenas, and the goal of a profession-wide solution is far less necessary or inevitable than Van Hoy (1993) suggests. It is a picture of complexity (Webb 2004).

Notwithstanding the shift from the profession wide framework, I argue that this remains professionalism because claims of expertise and status are still invoked to support market position. Thus, STEP, through their suite of educational qualifications and lobbying of governments and employers, assert the 'gold standard' of the expertise of their members and contrast it with the dangers posed to the public by unqualified will-writers. Similarly large corporate law firms sell

---

4   'In a joint initiative with the Society of Trust and Estate Practitioners, the Law Society has agreed a protocol with Nationwide Building Society to clarify and speed up the estate administration process. This is in addition to protocols already in place with Lloyds TSB and HSBC' (Law Society 2009c).

their services in a global market on the basis of the distinctive expertise that their firm offers; promising the 'best people at all levels ... and second to none resources' (www.cliffordchance.com/about_us/Our_promise_to_our_clients.html [accessed: 27 August 2010]). Status also appears important. For example, respondents in the STEP case-study reported the prestige attached to being Branch Chair, which enhanced their business. Conversely, legal executives consistently reported the ways in which their lack of university education marks them out as having followed a second-class route into the profession. Moreover, while access to the profession is premised upon ostensibly neutral criteria such as 'merit' and 'fit', the reality is that many aspirants from more disadvantaged socio-economic backgrounds struggle to accord to the ways in which these criteria operate in practice. Law firms which recruit from elite institutions, with an insistence on the most testing conceptions of 'excellent academics', are thus able to reinforce their position as high-status actors.

However, in contrast to traditional conceptions of professionalism, these strategies are deployed by a range of actors, often with little pretence that they will have benefit (or indeed, even relevance) for the wider profession. Critically, however, the ability of these individuals or organizations to deploy such strategies will be contingent upon market conditions, regulatory demands, and perhaps, above all, field location. These factors will also determine the extent to which they are invoked either on an individual or collective basis, or even alongside each other. Professionalism becomes a 'dance shaped ... by the relative autonomies of the players' (Webb 2004: 94), and these autonomies are shaped by field location. Thus, as discussed above, elite corporate law firms with the capacity to 'glide' between professional boundaries are less bound by institutional logics. Others, such as legal executives and outsider students, find it more difficult to challenge the prevailing exclusionary patterns of closure. While the elite actors are less bound by these disciplinary ties, the points of difference that they share with each other or indeed environing professions do not appear to represent the basis of 'thingness', or the establishment of a new social entity (Abbott 1995: 870). Their attachment to the traditional profession may be far looser and more contingent than in the past, but it remains.

Policy Implications

Despite its best efforts, the Law Society has consistently failed to make much progress in developing a profession-wide solution to the ongoing problems of diversity within the legal profession. The profession was too fragmented, the Law Society lacked credibility and the commercial interests of the large, powerful corporate law firms drove their decision-making (Braithwaite 2010). The case-studies on 'outsider' students and legal executives add a depressing weight to the conclusions of Sommerlad et al., which confirm 'biases against non-white professionals and those drawn from lower socio-economic groups' (2010: 6).

One of the regulatory objectives of the LSA, s.1(1)(f), is to 'encourage[e] an independent, strong, diverse and effective legal profession', and the Legal Services Board has taken this seriously, with one of its first actions being to respond to the Milburn Report (LSB 2009b). At the end of 2010 it announced plans to require Front-line Regulators to require firms to publish detailed diversity statistics (LSB 2010d). Arguably, this approach offers a better reading of the contemporary landscape through its organizational focus. However, I would argue that collective approaches to addressing the diversity problem need to be maintained, particularly for those organizations which do not operate in the elite corporate sector. Moreover, as the research discussed in Chapter 3 highlights, while there are issues that firms could address during the recruitment processes, the responses to tackling socio-economic disadvantage and its impact on social mobility need to be addressed in a co-ordinated way involving the government, the professions, universities and schools.

Building from Clementi's proposals for the regulation of Legal Disciplinary Practices to focus on the economic unit rather than the individual practitioner (2004b: 127), ss. 90–104 LSA 2007 address the regulation of Alternative Business Structures on an organizational basis. The Hunt Review's recommendations of Authorised Internal Regulation (AIR) within firms (2009: Rec. 42), is regulatory recognition of the multiplicity of professional actors. Moreover, Hunt's conceit that this could be a profession-wide solution (2009: 5) is a further example of the overlapping ways in which individual and collective models of professionalism operate. The final framework is, at time of writing, under consultation (SRA 2010b), and the extent to which the profession-wide solution (however tenuous) survives is likely to be contingent on its acceptability to the large corporate firms. Nick Eastwell's appointment as the SRA's 'Chief Advisor to City firms' may not be sufficient to quell the City's unease (Hollander 2010a). The disciplinary ties that I have discussed in this book are unlikely to be so strong as to hold them to a regulatory framework that they have long considered unfit for purpose (CLLS 2009b). Nicolson and Webb's suggestions of firm-based compliance officers within the largest firms and the development of an 'organisationally based ethic' (1999: 121), may be enhanced within the post-Hunt framework. However, the development of organizationally focused ethical values may further enhance the importance of individual models of professionalism (Francis 2005).

The history of the relationship between the legal profession and university Law Schools in England and Wales is fraught (Cownie and Cocks 2009). Although the Law Society, as the fulcrum of the collective professional project, has always tried to reflect the concerns of its members (JASB 2002a: 12), the large law firms, through the CLLS, have been increasingly vocal in pressing their own views over the nature and content of the Qualifying Law Degree (CLLS 2010a: 5). The three Front-line Regulators proposed a 'root and branch' review of legal education to begin in February 2011 (BSB 2010). In a recent speech, following the announcement of this review, David Edmonds, Chair of the LSB, indicated that 'for those leaving school and aiming for a legal career, we need to see the total length of time spent in education – and so the total amount of debt – shrink' (2010b: 24). This impetus, and concern over the mismatch between the number of traineeships available and the number of graduating law students, may see calls to collapse the training contract and LPC stages. Further contextual factors are the post-Browne funding arrangements for higher education which will see greater graduate contributions from students, particularly in the humanities and social sciences (such as Law), and the encouragement of private providers in the delivery of undergraduate degrees (Willets 2010). Two of these private providers, BPP and the College of Law, have both launched two-year, intensive practice-oriented law degrees.

Against this backdrop, it is possible to envisage a greater firm influence over legal education. Thus, the private providers may deliver the accredited route to a particular firm from degree onwards, in similar ways to the model that they already offer in respect of the LPC. However, such programmes offered without the benefits of research-led teaching may struggle to demonstrate that they can equip students with the broader contextual awareness and critical thought that the profession requires (see Chapter 3). Given that the existing qualification route has supported the market dominance of the elite firms, they may be content to push for clearer oversight of the Qualifying Law Degree. This may enhance the formal ties between universities and the professions (which is likely to be attractive to students in the post-Browne era). This is likely to provoke concern from some quarters of the academy (Bradney 2003). Thus, even the calls for increased ethics in the undergraduate curriculum are perceived as threats to the autonomy of university legal education (SLS 2010).

Conclusion

Analysis of the stories of those operating at the edge of law can enhance our understanding of the ways in which contemporary legal professionalism is responding to the challenges of the twenty-first century. Innovation and change can be found at the periphery to mainstream legal professionalism, but I argue that the capacity of actors to generate new patterns of professionalism (let alone shape the wider profession) is significantly affected by their location in the field. Some elites, such as corporate law firms, may glide between fields. Others, such as the Law Society, are more deeply embedded within the institutional logics of traditional professionalism. More marginalized actors such as 'outsider' students and legal executives find it difficult to advance along traditional professional lines or challenge the conditions of the field. Notwithstanding the profound changes within the marketplace, socio-economic disadvantage continues to exert a powerful exclusionary force within the legal profession.

As I made clear in Chapter 1, my selection of case-studies is inevitably partial. Future work would need to consider the applicability of this model to other branches of the legal profession, not least the barristers' profession, and needs to extend its geographical reach to the rest of the UK (at the very least). Others operating at the edge of law include claims management companies, unregulated will-writers and immigration advice providers, and further afield the management consultants and accountants operating in professional services alongside and in competition with the large corporate law firms. The precise impact of Alternative Business Structures can still only be guessed at, and the potential interaction of these new organizational forms with other developments such as the increasing sophistication of information technology and other business practices such as out-sourcing (Susskind 2008) will further test the ties between individual and collective models of professionalism. I am also interested in the way that 'kinship' operates as a disciplinary tie perhaps in a more affective way than formal codes of conduct and regulatory frameworks. Relatedly, generational changes within the profession may present further challenges.

The importance of field location, and of differentiation between and within sectors of the professions, appears central to our developing understanding of how professionalism will evolve in the future. I have argued that today's fragmented, fluid and uncertain conditions, give rise to a looser, far more complex notion of professionalism, which will be contingent upon the presence of different factors at any one time. Webb argues that 'a complexity perspective, by displacing competition with differentiation as its core function, opens up a far more complex, and yet unknowable future for the profession' (2004: 98). What is known is that the complex and contingent professionalism which is emerging requires us to pay close attention not simply to the elite professional actors, but also to those at the edge of law. Legal professionalism continues its fascinating evolution.

Bibliography

Abbott, A. 1988. *The System of the Professions: An Essay on the Division of Expert Labour*. London: University of Chicago Press.

Abbott, A. 1995. Things of Boundaries. *Social Research*, 62(4), 857–82.

Abel, R. 1985. Lawyers and the Power to Change. *Law and Policy*, 7(1), 5–18.

Abel, R. 1988. *The Legal Profession of England and Wales*. London: Basil Blackwell.

Abel, R. 1989. Between Market and State: The Legal Profession in Turmoil. *Modern Law Review*, 52(3), 285–325.

Abel, R. 2003. *English Lawyers between Market and State: The Politics of Professionalism*. Oxford: Oxford University Press.

Abel, R. 2004. The Professional is Political. *International Journal of the Legal Profession*, 11(1/2), 131–56.

Aldridge, M. 1996. Dragged to the market: being a profession in a post-modern world. *British Journal of Social Work*, 26(2) 177–94.

Allen & Overy 2004. *Review of the Regulatory Framework for Legal Services in England and Wales: Response by Allen & Overy LLP to the Consultation Published by the Independent Reviewer in March 2004* [Online, December]. Available at: http://webarchive.nationalarchives.gov.uk/+/http://www.legal-services-review.org.uk/content/consult/mccallum_resp.pdf [accessed: 24 August 2010].

Allen & Overy 2006. *Evidence to the Joint Committee on the Draft Legal Services Bill (EV24)* [Online]. Available at: http://www.parliament.the-stationary-office.co.uk/pa/jt200506/232/6062610.htm [accessed: 24 August 2010].

The American Lawyer (2010) *Associate Survey 2010* [Online, 1 September]. Available at: http://www.law.com/jsp/tal/PubArticleTAL.jsp?id=1202470848460&src=EMC-Email&et=editorial&bu=The%20American%20Lawyer&pt=Am%20Law%20Daily&cn=Am_Law_Daily_09012010&kw=www.americanlawyer.com%2Fassociates [accessed: 2 September 2010].

Ames, J. 2010. The Law Society: Chancery Lane. *The Lawyer* [Online, 29 November]. Available at: http://www.thelawyer.com/focus-the-law-society-chancery-lame/1006257.article [accessed: 15 December 2010].

Anderson-Gough, F., Grey, C. and Robson, K. 2000. In the name of the client: the service ethic in two professional services firms. *Human Relations*, 53 (9), 1151–74.

Anderson-Gough, F., Grey, C. and Robson, K. 2006. Professionals, Networking and the Networked Professional. *Research in the Sociology of Organizations*, 24, 231–56.

Archer, L. 2007. Diversity, equality and higher education: a critical reflection on the ab/uses of equity discourse within widening participation. *Teaching in Higher Education*, 12(5/6), 635–53.

Archer, M. 1995. *Realist Social Theory: The Morphogenic Approach*. Cambridge: Cambridge University Press.

Ashoka Foundation 2005. *John Richardson Profile* [Online]. Available at: http://www.ashoka.org/fellow/3672 [accessed: 26 July 2010].

Baksi, C. 2010a. High street firms 'fear for the future'. *Law Society Gazette* [Online, 23 August]. Available at: http://www.lawgazette.co.uk/news/high-street-firms-fear-future [accessed: 6 September 2010].

Baksi, C. 2010b. Law Society commences court action over tender process. *Law Society Gazette* [Online, 27 August]. Available at: http://www.lawgazette.co.uk/news/law-society-commences-court-action-over-tender-process [accessed: 6 September 2010].

Bańkowski, Z. and Mungham, G. 1976. *Images of Law*. London: Routledge.

Barclay, S. and Marshall, A.-M. 2005. Supporting a Cause, Developing a Movement and Consolidating a Practice: Cause Lawyers and Sexual Orientation Litigation in Vermont, in *The Worlds Cause Lawyers Make: Structure and Agency in Legal Practice*, edited by A. Sarat and S. Scheingold. Stanford: Stanford University Press, 171–202.

Bar Standards Board (BSB) 2010. *BSB to participate in review of legal education* [Online, 19 November]. Available at: http://www.barstandardsboard.org.uk/news/latest/611.html [accessed 16 December 2010].

Battilana, J. 2006. Agency and Institutions: The Enabling Role of Individuals' Social Position. *Organization*, 13(5), 653–76.

Bauman, Z. 2005. Chasing Elusive Society. *International Journal of Politics, Culture and Society*, 18, 123–41.

Beagan, B. 2001. Micro Inequities and Everyday Inequalities: 'Race', Gender, Sexuality and Class in Medical School. *Canadian Journal of Sociology*, 26(4), 583–610.

Beaverstock, J. 2004. 'Managing Across Borders': Knowledge Management and Expatriation in Professional Service Legal Firms. *Journal of Economic Geography*, 4(2), 157–79.

Beck, U. 1994. The Reinvention of Politics: Towards a Theory of Reflexive Modernization, in *Reflexive Modernization: Politics, Tradition and Aesthetics in the Modern Social Order*, edited by U. Beck, A. Giddens and S. Lash. Cambridge: Polity Press, 1–55.

Beck, U. 2005. The Cosmopolitan State: Redefining Power in the Global Age. *International Journal of Politics, Culture and Society*, 18, 143–59.

Behiels, M. 2010. Stephen Harper's Rise to Power: Will His 'New' Conservative Party Become Canada's 'Natural Governing Party' of the Twenty-First Century? *American Review of Canadian Studies*, 40(1), 118–45.

Bellow, G. and Charn, J. 1995. Paths Not Yet Taken: Some Comments on Feldman's Critique of Legal Services Practice. *Georgetown Law Journal*, 83(4), 1633–68.

Benson Commission 1979. *Royal Commission on Legal Services*. (Cmnd. 7648). London: HMSO.

Binns, C. 1987. The study of Soviet and East European elites, in *Research Methods for Elite Studies*, edited by G. Moyser and M. Wagstaffe. London: Allen and Unwin, 216–31.

Bishop, M. 2009a. *Barriers to Progress Still Remain for Legal Executives* [Online]. Available at: http:/www.ilex.org.uk/media/press_releases/press_release_archive/barriers_to_progress.aspx [accessed: 11 February 2010].

Bishop, M. 2009b. Reflections on my Year. *President's Blog Summer 2009* [Online]. Available at: http://www.ilex.org.uk/about_ilex/news/presidents_blog/reflections_on_a_year.aspx [accessed: 18 November 2010].

Black Lawyers Directory (BLD) 2008. *Saimo Chahal Profile* [Online, January]. Available at: http://www.Onlinebld.com/saimo_chahal_lawyerofthemonth_january2008.html [accessed: 26 July 2010].

Blomley, N. 2007. How to turn a beggar into a bus stop: Law, traffic, and the 'function of the place'. *Urban Studies*, 44(9), 1697–1712.

Boggan, S. 2006. Call Him Mr Loophole. *The Guardian* [Online, 27 January]. Available at: http://www.guardian.co.uk/world/2006/jan/27/law.transport [accessed: 21 January 2011].

Boltanski, L. and Chiapello, E. 1999. *Le nouvel esprit du capitalisme*. Paris: Gallimard.

Boltanski, L. and Chiapello, E. 2006. The New Spirit of Capitalism. *International Journal of Politics, Culture and Society*, 18(3/4), 161–88.

Bolton, S. and Muzio, D. 2007. Can't Live with 'Em; Can't Live Without 'Em: Gendered Segmentation in the Legal Profession. *Sociology*, 41(1), 47–61.

Boon, A. 2001. Cause Lawyers in a Cold Climate: The Impact(s) of Globalisation on the United Kingdom, in *Cause Lawyering and the State in a Global Era* edited by A. Sarat and S. Scheingold. Oxford and New York: Oxford University Press, 143–85.

Boon, A. 2004. Cause Lawyers and the Alternative Ethical Paradigm: Ideology and Transgression. *Legal Ethics*, 7(2), 250–68.

Boon, A. 2005. From Public Service to Service Industry: The Impact of Socialisation and Work on the Motivation and Values of Lawyers. *International Journal of the Legal Profession*, 12(2), 229–60.

Bourdieu, P. and Wacquant, L. 1992. *An Invitation to Reflexive Sociology*. Cambridge: Polity Press.

Bourdieu, P. 1977. *Outline of a Theory of Practice*. Cambridge: Cambridge University Press.

Bourdieu, P. 1984. *Distinction*. Cambridge, MA: Harvard University Press.

Bourdieu, P. 1987. The Force of Law: Toward a Sociology of the Juridical Field. *Hastings Law Journal*, 38(5), 805–53.

Bourdieu, P. 1990. *The Logic of Practice*. Stanford: Stanford University Press.

Bradney, A. 2003. *Conversations, Choices and Chances: The Liberal Law School in the Twenty-First Century*. Oxford: Hart Publishing.

Braithwaite, J. 2010. The strategic use of demand side diversity pressure on the solicitors' profession. *Journal of Law and Society*, 37(3), 442–65.

Braun, V. and Clarke, V. 2006. Using Thematic Analysis in Psychology. *Qualitative Research in Psychology*, 33(2), 77–101.

Brewin, A. and Govender, K. 2010. *Rights-Based Legal Aid: Rebuilding BC's Broken System*. Vancouver: CCPA/LEAF [Online, 9 November]. Available at: http://www.policyalternatives.ca/sites/default/files/uploads/publications/BC% 20Office/2010/11/CCPA_Legal_Aid_web.pdf [accessed: 6 January 2011].

Bridges, L. 1975. *Legal Services in Birmingham*. Birmingham: University of Birmingham.

British Columbia Civil Liberties Association (BCCLA) 2007. *Civil Liberties Update – February 2007* [Online]. Available at: http://www.bccla.org/Update/ Feb07update.htm [accessed: 6 January 2011].

British Columbia Health Atlas 2004 [Online]. Available at: http://www.chspr.ubc. ca/files/publications/2004/chspr04–12/Lifeexpectancy.pdf [accessed: 15 July 2010].

British Institute of Human Rights (BIHR) 2010. *BIHR Director awarded Pro Bono/Human Rights Lawyer of 2010* [Online, 17 May]. Available at: http:// www.bihr.org.uk/news/bihr-director-awarded-pro-bonohuman-rights-lawyer- of-2010 [accessed: 10 January 2011].

Brown, P. 1990. The 'Third Wave': education and the ideology of parentocracy *Sociology of Education*, 11(1), 65–86.

Browne, J. 2010. *An Independent Review of Higher Education Funding and Student Finance* [Online, 12 October]. Available at: http://www.independent. gov.uk/browne-report [accessed: 13 October 2010].

Bucher, R. and Strauss, E. 1961. Professions in Process. *American Journal of Sociology*, 66(4), 325–34.

Buck, A., Palmer, N. and Pleasance, P. 2005. Social Exclusion and Civil Law: Experience of Civil Justice Problems among Vulnerable Groups. *Social Policy and Administration*, 39(3), 302–22.

Burleigh, D. 2010. Question Time. *Legal Executive Journal* [Online, April]. Available at: http://www.ilex.org.uk/about_ilex/who_we_are/from_the_chief_ executive.aspx [accessed: 21 April 2010]. Online version no longer freely available.

Burrage, M. 1996. From a Gentleman's to a Public Profession –Status and Politics in the History of English Solicitors. *International Journal of the Legal Profession*, 3(1/2), 45–80.

Butler, P. 2010. Local charity cuts jeopardise David Cameron's 'big society'. *The Guardian* [Online, 23 July]. Available at http://www.guardian.co.uk/ society/2010/jul/23/charity-cuts-big-society [accessed: 6 January 2011].

Cain, M. 1994. The Symbol Traders, in *Lawyers in a Post-Modern World: Translation and Transgression*, edited by M. Cain and C. Harrington. Buckingham: Open University Press, 15–48.

Canadian Bar Association (CBA) 2009 *Code of Professional Conduct* [Online, August]. Available at: http://www.cba.org/CBA/activities/pdf/codeofconduct. pdf [accessed: 6 January 2011].

Carbado, D. and Gulati, M. 2000. Working Identity. *Cornell Law Review*, 85, 1259–1308.

Carbado, D. and Gulati, M. 2003. The Law and Economics of Critical Race Theory. *Yale Law Journal*,112, 1757–1828.

Carlin, J. 1962. *Lawyers on Their Own*. New Brunswick: Rutgers University Press.

Carr-Saunders, A. and Wilson, P. 1933. *The Professions*. Oxford: Clarendon Press.

Carter, S. 2007. Council Members' Report. *SOLO* [Online, November]. Available at: http://www.spg.uk.com/magazine/solomagpdf/12–2007.pdf [accessed: 6 September 2010].

Castree, N. 2010. Crisis, Continuity and Change: Neoliberalism, the Left and the Future of Capitalism. *Antipode*, 41(1), 185–213.

Charles, G. 2004. A Revolution in Legal Education. *The Lawyer* [Online, 22 March]. Available at: http://www.thelawyer.com/a-revolution-in-legal-education/109190.article [accessed: 11 November 2010].

Chellel, K. 2009. Law Society to Students: Legal Career May be Too Risky. *The Lawyer* [Online, 28 July]. Available at: http://www.thelawyer.com/law-society-to-students-legal-career-may-be-too-risky/1001544.article [accessed: 16 December 2010].

Chen, M. and Bargh, J. A. 1997. Non conscious behavioural confirmation processes: the self-fulfilling consequences of automatic stereotype activation. *Journal of Experimental Social Psychology*, 33, 541–60.

City Firms Working Group 2008. Minutes of the Meeting of the 30th July 2008. *Sub-Committee of the Legal Affairs and Policy Board of the Law Society* [Online]. Available at: http://www.lawsociety.org.uk/aboutlawsociety/how/ committees/view=viewmeeting.law?MEETINGID=3020&COMMITTEE ID=11513 [accessed: 26 August 2010].

City of London Law Society (CLLS) 2007a. *Commons 2nd Reading Briefing* [Online, 30 June]. Available at: http://www.citysolicitors.org.uk/FileServer. aspx?oID=283&lID=0 [accessed: 25 August 2010].

City of London Law Society (CLLS) 2007b. *House of Commons Suggested Amendments* [Online, 1 July]. Available at: http://www.citysolicitors.org.uk/ FileServer.aspx?oID=284&lID=0 [accessed: 25 August 2010].

City of London Law Society (CLLS) 2007c. *City of London Law Society Briefing on the New York Bar proposed Conflicts Rule Change* [Online, 23 October]. Available at http://www.citysolicitors.org.uk/FileServer.aspx?oID=202&lID=0 [accessed: 7 September 2010].

City of London Law Society (CLLS) 2009a. *Review of the Regulation of Corporate Legal Work - Letter to Nick Smedley, 8 January 2009* [Online 14 January]. Available at: http://www.citysolicitors.org.uk/FileServer.aspx? oID=498&lID=0 [accessed: 9 January 2011].

City of London Law Society (CLLS) 2009b. *Initial Response to Evidence – Letter to Lord Hunt, 30 June 2009* [Online, 1 July]. Available at: http://www.citysolicitors.org.uk/FileServer.aspx?oID=606&lID=0 [accessed: 9 January 2011].

City of London Law Society (CLLS) 2010a. *Response to SRA's Consultation on Outcomes Focused Regulation (23rd July)* [Online, 30 July]. Available at http://www.citysolicitors.org.uk/FileServer.aspx?oID=823&lID=0 [accessed: 9 January 2011].

City of London Law Society (CLLS) 2010b. *Response to SRA consultation 'The architecture of change: the SRA's new Handbook'* [Online, 20 August]. Available at:http://www.citysolicitors.org.uk/FileServer.aspx?oID=840&lID=0 [accessed: 7 September 2010].

City of London Law Society Professional Rules and Regulation Committee (CLLS PRRC) 2009. *Minutes of October Meeting* [Online, 1 December]. Available at: http://www.citysolicitors.org.uk/FileServer.aspx?oID=806&lID=0 [accessed: 17 December 2010].

City of London Law Society Professional Rules and Regulation Committee (CLLS PRRC) 2010. *Minutes of April Meeting* [Online, 19 May]. Available at: http://www.citysolicitors.org.uk/FileServer.aspx?oID=807&lID=0 [accessed: 17 December 2010].

Clementi, D. 2004a. *Consultation Paper on the Review of the Regulatory Framework for Legal Services in England and Wales* [Online, March]. Available at: http://webarchive.nationalarchives.gov.uk/+/http://www.legal-services-review.org.uk/content/consult/review.htm [accessed: 24 August 2010].

Clementi, D. 2004b. *Review of the Regulatory Framework for Legal Services in England and Wales: The Final Report* [Online, December]. Available at: http://webarchive.nationalarchives.gov.uk/+/http://www.legal-services-review.org.uk/content/report/report-chap.pdf [accessed: 23 August 2010].

Clifford Chance 2007. *What is Law? Graduate Opportunities and Vacation Schemes* [Online]. Available at http://gradsuk.cliffordchance.com/media/pdf/clifford_chance_graduates_2007.pdf [accessed: 25 June 2008].

Clifford Chance 2010. *Clifford Chance launches Academy Development Centre.* [Online, 21 April]. Available at: http://www.cliffordchance.com/newsandevents/news/2010/04/launches_academ.html [accessed: 4 February 2011].

Cole, B. 2000. *Trends in the Solicitors' Profession: Annual Statistical Report 1999.* London: The Law Society.

Cole, B. 2004. *Trends in the Solicitors' Profession: Annual Statistical Report 2003.* London: The Law Society.

Cole, B. 2009. *Trends in the Solicitors' Profession: Annual Statistical Report 2008.* London: The Law Society.

Collier, R. 2005. 'Be Smart, Be Successful, Be Yourself'? Representations of the Training Contract and the Trainee Solicitor in Advertising by Large Law Firms. *International Journal of the Legal Profession*, 12(1), 51–92.

Cook, A. Faulconbridge, J. and Muzio, D. 2010. A Legal Aristocracy? Recruitment Practices and Elite Reproduction in English Global Law Firms. *Professional Education Working Papers* [Online]. Available at: http://www.lancs.ac.uk/professions/professional_ed/docs/a_legal_aristocracy.pdf [accessed: 8 January 2011].

Cooper, D. and Robson, K. 2006. Accounting, professions and regulation: Locating the sites of professionalization. *Accounting, Organizations and Society*, 31 (4–5), 415–44.

Cooper, D. J., Hinings, B., Greenwood, R. and Brown, J. L. 1996. Sedimentation and Transformation in Organizational Change: The Case of Canadian Law Firms. *Organization Studies*, 17(4), 623–47.

Costello, C. 2004. Changing Clothes: Gender Inequality and Professional Socialization. *NWSA Journal*, 16(2) 138–55.

Costello, C. 2005. *Professional Identity Crisis: Race, Class, Gender, and Success at Professional Schools*. Nashville: Vanderbilt University Press.

Cousins, M. 1994. The politics of legal aid – a solution in search of a problem. *Civil Justice Quarterly*, 13 (Apr), 111–32.

Cownie, F. and Cocks, R. 2009. *'A Great and Noble Occupation!' The History of the Society of Legal Scholars*. Oxford: Hart Publishing.

Crenshaw, K. 1989/1993. Demarginalizing the Intersection of Race and Sex: A Black Feminist Critique of Antidiscrimination Doctrine, Feminist Theory and Antiracist Politics, in *Feminist Legal Theory: Foundations*, edited by X. Weinberg. Philadelphia: Temple University Press, 383–95.

Crewe, I. 1974. Introduction: studying elites in Britain, in *British Political Sociology Yearbook, Volume 1: Elites in Western Democracy*, edited by I. Crewe. London: Croom Helm, 9–54.

Currie, A. 2000. Legal Aid Delivery Models in Canada: Past Experience and Future Developments. *British Columbia Law Review*, 33(2), 285–318.

Curtis, S. and Shani, N. 2002. The Effect of taking Paid Employment during Term-Time on Students' Academic Performance. *Journal of Further and Higher Education*, 26(1), 129–38.

Davies, C. 1995. *Gender and the Professional Predicament in Nursing*. Buckingham: Open University Press.

Davies, M. 1999. Can the Office for the Supervision of Solicitors Expect a Happy Birthday? A Short Review of the First Three Years. *Professional Negligence*, 15(3), 173–84.

Davies, M. 2010. The Demise of Professional Self-Regulation: Evidence From the 'Ideal Type' Professions of Medicine and Law. *Professional Negligence*, 26(1), 3–38

Davies, P. 1999. Half Full, Not Half Empty: A Positive Look at Part-time Education. *Higher Education Quarterly*, 53(2), 141–55.

Davis, A. 2010. A new approach to Law firm Regulation. *The American Lawyer* [Online, 22 July]. Available at http://www.law.com/jsp/tal/PubArticleTAL.jsp?id=1202463792675&hbxlogin=1 [accessed 22 January 2011].

Dean, J. 2010a. Law Society seeks to block privilege for non-lawyers. *Law Society's Gazette* [Online, 6 May]. Available at: http://www.lawgazette.co.uk/news/law-society-seeks-block-privilege-non-lawyers [accessed: 29 January 2011].

Dean, J. 2010b. Freshfields reports fall in turnover. *Law Society's Gazette* [Online, 8 July]. Available at: http://www.lawgazette.co.uk/news/freshfields-reports-fall-turnover [accessed: 7 September 2010].

Denzin, N. and Lincoln, Y. 1994. Introduction: Entering the Field of Qualitative Research, in *Handbook of Qualitative Research*, edited by N. Denzin and Y. Lincoln. London: Sage, 1–29.

Department for Business Innovation and Skills (BIS) 2009. *Higher Ambitions: The Future of Universities in a Knowledge Economy* [Online]. Available at: http://www.bis.gov.uk/assets/biscore/corporate/docs/h/09–1447-higher-ambitions.pdf [accessed: 18 November 2010].

Department for Constitutional Affairs (DCA) 2003. *Competition and Regulation in the legal services market* [Online, July]. Available at: http://www.dca.gov.uk/consult/general/oftreptconc.htm [accessed: 24 August 2010].

Department for Constitutional Affairs (DCA) 2005. *The Future of Legal Services: Putting Consumers First.* (CM6679). London: DCA.

Devonald, L. 1994. An endangered species. *Law Society's Gazette*, 29 June, 2.

Dezalay, Y. 1991. Turf Battles and Tribal Wars. *Modern Law Review*, 54(6), 792–809.

Dezalay, Y. 1995. 'Turf Battles' or 'Class Struggles': The Internationalization of the Market for Expertise in the 'Professional Society'. *Accounting, Organizations and Society*, 20(5), 331–44.

Dezalay, Y. and Garth, B. 1996. Fussing about the Forum: Categories and Definitions as Stakes in a Professional Competition, *Law and Social Inquiry*, 21(2), 205–312.

Dezalay, Y. and Garth, B. 2004. The Confrontation between the Big Five and Big Law: Turf Battles and Ethical Debates as Contests for Professional Credibility. *Law and Social Inquiry*, 29(3), 615–38.

Dezalay, Y. and Trubek, D. 1994. Global Restructuring and the Law: Studies of the Internationalization of Legal Fields and the Creation of Transnational Arenas. *Case Western Law Review*, 44(2), 407–98.

Dimaggio, P. and Powell, W. 1991. The Iron Cage Revisited: Institutional Isomorphism and Collective Rationality in Organizational Fields, in *The New Institutionalism in Organizational Analysis*, edited by P. Dimaggio and W. Powell. Chicago: University of Chicago Press, 1–38.

Dingwall, R. 1997. Accounts, Interviews and Observations, in *Context and Method in Qualitative Research*, edited by R. Dingwall and G. Miller. London: Sage, 51–65.

Dodd, V. and Lewis, P. 2010. Ian Tomlinson death: police officer will not face criminal charges. *The Guardian* [Online, 22 July]. Available at: http://www.

guardian.co.uk/uk/2010/jul/22/ian-tomlinson-police-not-charged   [accessed: 6 January 2011].

Dowell, K. 2010. The Optima-Capita deal: how the SRA arrived at its 'severe reprimand'. *The Lawyer* [Online, 16 August]. Available at: http:// www.thelawyer.com/the-optima-capita-deal-how-the-sra-arrived-at-its-%E2%80%98severe-reprimand%E2%80%99/1005296.article   [accessed: 3 September 2010].

D'Souza, E. Revealed: the contents of the City LPC. *The Lawyer* [Online, 12 March]. Available at: http://www.thelawyer.com/revealed-the-contents-of-the-new-city-lpc/100028.article [accessed: 30 June 2011].

Duff, E., Shiner, M. and Boon, A. 2000. *Entry into the Legal Professions: The Law Student Cohort Study Year 6*. (Research Study 39). London: The Law Society.

Eby, D. 2006. The Power of the Affidavit. *Presentation to ESRC HIV-AIDS and Law Seminar* [Online]. Available at: http://www.keele.ac.uk/research/lpj/Law_HIV-AIDSProject/Pres_Papers.htm [accessed: 15 July 2010].

EcoJustice 2009. Court victory forces Canada to report pollution data for mines. *Press Release* [Online, 24 April]. Available at: http://www.ecojustice.ca/media-centre/press-releases/court-victory-forces-canada-to-report-pollution-data-for-mines/ [accessed: 26 January 2011].

Edmonds, D. 2010a. Address to the Council of the Law Society. [Online, 8 June]. Available at: http://www.legalservicesboard.org.uk/news_publications/speeches_presentations/2010/2010_06_08_Law_Society_Council.pdf [accessed: 25 August 2010].

Edmonds, D. 2010b. *Upjohn Lecture* [Online, November]. Available at: http://www. legalservicesboard.org.uk/news_publications/speeches_presentations/2010/de_lord_upjohn_lec.pdf [accessed: 2 December 2010].

Eekelaar, J., Maclean, M. and Beinart, S. 2000. *Family Lawyers: The Divorce Work of Solicitors*. Oxford: Hart Publishing.

Elliot, Mr 1956. President's Address. *Solicitors' Managing Clerks Association Gazette* (June).

Empson, L. (ed.) 2007. *Managing the Modern Law Firm: New Challenges, New Perspectives*. Oxford: Oxford University Press.

Etzioni, A. 1969. *The Semi-Professions and Their Organisations: Teachers, Nurses and Social Workers*. New York: Free Press.

Falkenberg, L. 1990. Improving the accuracy of stereotypes within the workplace. *Journal of Management*, 16(1), 107–18.

Faulconbridge, J. and Muzio, D. 2008. Organizational Professionalism in Globalizing Law Firms. *Work, Employment and Society*, 22(1), 7–25.

Feldman, M. 1995. Political Lessons: Legal Services for the Poor. *Georgetown Law Journal*, 83(4), 1529–1632.

Fleming, J. 2003. Dispute Warning Over Conflicts. *Law Society Gazette* [Online, 6 June]. Available at: http://www.lawgazette.co.uk/news/dispute-warning-over-conflicts [accessed: 26 August 2010].

Flood, J. 1991. Doing Business: The Management of Uncertainty in Lawyers' Work, *Law and Society Review*, 25(1), 41–71.

Flood, J. 1995. The Cultures of Globalization: Professional Restructuring for the International Market, in *Professional Competition and Professional Power: Lawyers, Accountants, and the Social Construction of Markets*, edited by Y. Dezaley and D. Sugarman. London: Routledge, 139–69.

Flood, J. 1996. Megalawyering in the Global Order: The Cultural, Social and Economic Transformation of Global Legal Practice. *International Journal of the Legal Profession*, 3(1/2), 169–214.

Flood, J. 2007. Partnership and Professionalism in Global Law Firm: Resurgent Professionalism?, in *Redirections in the Study of Expert Labour: Established Professions and New Expert Occupations*, edited by D. Muzio and S. Ackroyd with J.-F. Chanlat. Basingstoke: Palgrave Macmillan, 52–74.

Flood, J. 2008. Will There Be Fallout from Clementi? The Global Repercussions for the Legal Profession after the UK Legal Services Act 2007 (April 2008). *Miami-Florida European Union Center Jean Monnet/Robert Schuman Paper Series*, 8(6); *U. of Westminster School of Law Research Paper*, 08-03 [Online]. Available at SSRN: http://ssrn.com/abstract=1128398 [accessed: 12 October 2010].

Flood, J. 2010. From Ethics to Regulation: The Re-Landscaping and Re-Professionalization of Large Law Firms in the 21st Century (Version 2). [Online, 9 August]. Available at SSRN: http://ssrn.com/abstract=1650760 [accessed 10 August 2010].

Flood, J. and Whyte, A. 2009. Straight There, No Detours: Direct Access to Barristers. *International Journal of the Legal Profession*, 16 (2/3), 131–52.

Fontana, A. and Frey, J. 1994. Interviewing: The Art of Science, in *Handbook of Qualitative Research*, edited by N. Denzin and Y. Lincoln. London: Sage, 361–76.

Fournier, V. 1999. The appeal to 'professionalism' as a disciplinary mechanism. *Sociological Review*, 47 (2), 280–307.

Fowler, B. 1997. *Pierre Bourdieu and Cultural Theory: Critical Investigations*. London: Sage

Fowler, B. and Wilson, F. 2004. Women Architects and Their Discontents. *Sociology*, 38(1), 101–19.

Francis, A. 2000. Lawyers, CABx and the Community Legal Service: A New Dawn for Social Welfare Law Provision? *Journal of Social Welfare and Family Law*, 22(1), 59–75.

Francis, A. 2002. Legal Executives and the Phantom of Legal Professionalism: The Rise and Rise of the Third Branch of the Legal Profession? *International Journal of the Legal Profession*, 9(1), 5–25.

Francis, A. 2004. Out of Touch and Out of Time: Lawyers, their Leaders and Collective Mobility in the Legal Profession. *Legal Studies*, 24(4), 322–48.

Francis, A. 2005. Legal Ethics, the Marketplace and the Fragmentation of Legal Professionalism. *International Journal of the Legal Profession*, 12(2), 173–99.

Francis, A. 2006. 'I'm not one of those women's libber type people but …': Gender, Class and Professional Power within the Third Branch of the English Legal Profession. *Social and Legal Studies*, 15(4), 475–93.

Francis, A. and McDonald, I. 2005. Part-time Law Students: The Forgotten Cohort? *The Law Teacher*, 39(3), 277–98.

Francis, A. and McDonald I. 2006. Preferential Treatment, Social Justice and the Part-time Law Student – the Case for the Value Added Part-time Law Degree. *Journal of Law and Society*, 33(1), 92–108.

Francis, A. and McDonald, I. 2009. After Dark and Out in the Cold: Part-time Law Students and the Myth of 'Equivalency'. *Journal of Law and Society*, 36(2), 220–47.

Franklin, A. and Lee, R. 2007. The Embedded Nature of Rural Legal Services: Sustaining Service Provision in Wales. *Journal of Law and Society*, 34(2), 218–43.

Fredman, S. 2002. *Discrimination Law*. Oxford: Oxford University Press.

Freidson, E. 1970. *The Profession of Medicine: A Study of the Sociology of Applied Medicine*. New York: Dodd Mead and Co.

Freidson, E. 1992. Professionalism as Model and Ideology, in *Lawyers' Ideals/ Lawyers Practices: Transformations in the American Legal Profession*, edited by R. Nelson, D. Trubek and R. Solomon. Ithaca and London: Cornell University Press, 215–29.

Freidson, E. 1994. *Professionalism Reborn: Theory, Prophecy and Policy*. Cambridge: Polity Press.

Freidson, E. 2001. *Professionalism: The Third Logic*. Cambridge: Polity Press.

Gabel, P. and Harris, P. 1982–3. Building Power and Breaking Images: Critical Legal Theory and the Practice of Law. *New York University Review of Law and Social Change*, 11, 369–412.

Galanter, M. and Palay, T. 1991. *The Tournament of Lawyers: The Transformation of the Big Law Firm*. Chicago: University of Chicago Press.

Galanter, M. and Roberts, S. 2008. From kinship to Magic Circle: the London commercial law firm in the twentieth century. *International Journal of the Legal Profession*, 15(3), 143–78.

Ghose, K. 2005. *Beyond the Courtroom: A Lawyers Guide to Campaigning*. London: Legal Action Group.

Giddens, A. 1984 *The Constitution of Society: Outline of the Theory of Structuration*. Cambridge: Polity Press.

Gieryn, T. F. 1983. Boundary-work and the demarcation of science from non-science: strains and interests in professional ideologies of scientists. *American Sociological Review*, 48(6), 781–95.

Ginsburg, T. and Wolf, J. 2004. The Market for Elite Law Firm Associates. *Florida State Law Review*, 31 (2003–04), 909–64.

Glaser, B. and Strauss, A. 1967. *The Discovery of Grounded Theory*. Chicago: Aldine.

Goffman, E. 1968. *Asylums: Essays on the Social Situation of Mental Patients and Other Inmates.* Harmondsworth: Penguin/Peregrine.

Goldthorpe, J. 2003. The myth of education-based meritocracy. *New Economy*, 10(4), 234–9.

Goriely, T. 1996. Law for the Poor: the relationship between advice agencies and solicitors in the development of poverty law. *International Journal of the Legal Profession*, 3(1/2) 215–48.

Grabham, E. 2006. Taxonomies of Inequality: Lawyers, Maps and the Challenge of Hybridity. *Social and Legal Studies*, 15(1), 5–23.

Granfield, R. 1994. Do Law Students Abandon Their Ideals?: The Crisis of Idealism in the Age of Affluence. *Legal Studies Forum*, 18(1), 53–74.

Granfield, R. and Koenig, T. 1992. The Fate of Elite Idealism: Accommodation and Ideological Work at Harvard Law School. *Social Problems*, 39(4), 315–31.

Granfield, R. and Koenig, T. 2003. 'It's hard to be a human being and a lawyer': Young Attorneys and the Confrontation with Ethical Ambiguity in Legal Practice. *West Virginia Law Review*, 105(2), 495–524.

Greenwood, R. and Hinnings, C. R. 1993. Understanding Strategic Change: The Contribution of Archetypes. *Academy of Management Journal*, 36(5), 1052–81.

Greenwood, R. and Suddaby R. 2001. Colonizing Knowledge: Commodification as a Dynamic of Jurisdictional Expansion in Professional Service Firms. *Human Relations*, 54(7) 933–53.

Greenwood, R. and Suddaby, R. 2006. Institutional Entrepreneurships in Mature Fields: The Big Five Accounting Firms. *Academy of Management Journal*, 49(1), 27–48.

Greenwood, R., Suddaby, R. and Hinings, C. 2002. Theorizing Change: The Role of Professional Associations in the Transformation of Institutionalized Fields. *Academy of Management Journal*, 45(1), 58–80.

Griffiths-Baker, J. 2002. *Serving Two Masters: Conflicts of Interest in the Modern Law Firm.* Oxford: Hart Publishing.

Hagan, J. and Kay, F. 1995. *Gender in Practice: A Study of Lawyers' Lives.* Oxford: Oxford University Press.

Halliday, T. 1987. *Beyond Monopoly.* Chicago: University of Chicago Press.

Halpern, D. 1994. *Entry into the Legal Professions – The Law Student Cohort Study Years 1 and 2.* London: The Law Society.

Hanley, L. 2007. Don't Tell Me that GCSEs are Too Easy when Millions are Failing. *The Guardian* [Online, 20 August]. Available at: http://www.guardian.co.uk/commentisfree/2007/aug/20/comment.politics?intcmp=239 [accessed: 21 January 2011].

Hanlon, G. 1999. *Lawyers, The State and the Market: Professionalism Revisited.* Basingstoke: Macmillan.

Hansard (Lords) 1999. *House of Lords Weekly Hansard, Vol. 596: 1175–1178, 28th January.* London: The Stationary Office.

Hansard (Commons) 2007. Criminal Justice and Immigration Bill (16th Sitting). *Public Bills Committees* [Online, 29 November]. Available at http://www. publications.parliament.uk/pa/cm200708/cmpublic/criminal/071129/ pm/71129s12.htm [accessed: 10 December 2010]

Harris, G. 2008. Aamer Anwar on his battle with the law. *The Sunday Times*, 11 May. Paywall now in place.

Harris, J. 2003. *The Last Party: Britpop, Blair and the Demise of British Rock.* London: Harper Perennial.

Harris, J. 2006a. City Law Society Calls for Redraw of Legal Services Bill, *The Lawyer* [Online, 19 June]. Available at: http://www.thelawyer.com/city-law-society-calls-for-redraw-of-legal-services-bill/120463.article [accessed: 25 August 2010].

Harris, J. 2006b. Law Society President Woolf Moves to Appease City Critics. *The Lawyer* [Online, 24 July]. Available at: http://www.thelawyer.com/ law-society-president-woolf-moves-to-appease-city-critics/121143.article [accessed: 25 August 2010].

Harris, P. and Beinart, S. 2005. A Survey of Law Schools 2004. *The Law Teacher*, 39(3), 299–366.

Heinz, J., Nelson, R., Sandefur, R. and Laumann, E., 2005. *Urban Lawyers: The New Social Structure of the Bar.* Chicago and London: University of Chicago Press.

Helm, T. and Stratton, A. 2011. Ed Miliband claims notion of the 'big society' for Labour. *The Guardian* [Online, 15 January]. Available at: http://www.guardian. co.uk/politics/2011/jan/15/ed-miliband-attack-blair-brown [accessed: 20 January 2011].

Herald Scotland 2008. Judgment in the Aamer Anwar contempt case, *Herald Scotland* [Online, 1 July]. Available at: http://www.heraldscotland.com/ judgment-in-the-aamer-anwar-contempt-case-1.883698 [accessed: 6 January 2011].

Her Majesty's Court Service (HMCS) 2010. *Costs Guidelines for Summary Assessment.* [Online]. Available at: http://www.hmcourts-service.gov.uk/ publications/guidance/scco/previous_rates.htm#costs2010 [accessed: 15 November 2010].

Heslett, R. 2010a. The Law Society is Meeting the Needs of Members in Difficult Times. *Law Society Gazette* [Online, 1 July]. Available at: http://www. lawgazette.co.uk/opinion/president039s-podium/the-law-society-meeting-needs-members-difficult-times [accessed: 25 August 2010].

Heslett, R. 2010b. *The Legal Landscape – Looking with New Eyes' (Speech at Said Business School, Oxford University)* [Online, 26 May]. Available at: http:// www.guardian.co.uk/law/2010/may/26/robert-heslett-speech-said-business-school [accessed: 23 January 2011].

Hilbink, T. 2004. You Know the Type: Categories of Cause Lawyering. *Law and Social Inquiry*, 29(3), 657–98.

Hirsch, A. 2010. Fury as 'Superb' Training Scheme for Legal Aid Lawyers Faces Axe. *The Guardian* [Online, 11 July]. Available at http://www.guardian.co.uk/law/2010/jul/11/legal-aid [accessed: 7 January 2011].

Hodgart, A. 2008. Legal Services Act will judge the quick and the dead. *The Lawyer* [Online, 16 June]. Available at: http://www.thelawyer.com/legal-services-act-will-judge-the-quick-and-the-dead/133339.article [accessed: 3 September 2010].

Hollander, G. 2010a. SRA picks ex-Linklaters star to build bridges with City. *The Lawyer* [Online, 18 October]. Available at: http://www.thelawyer.com/sra-picks-ex-linklaters-star-to-build-bridges-with-city/1005814.article [accessed: 4 February 2011].

Hollander, G. 2010b. Linklaters raids Freshfields for restructuring star Howard. *The Lawyer* [Online, 22 November]. Available at: http://www.thelawyer.com/linklaters-raids-freshfields-for-restructuring-star-howard/1006186.article [accessed: 13 January 2011].

Honneth, A., Kicyba, H. and Schwibbs, B. 1986. The Struggle for Symbolic Order: An Interview with Pierre Bourdieu. *Theory, Culture and Society*, 3(3), 35–51.

Hughes, E. 1981. *Men and their Work*. Westport: Greenwood Press (orig. pub. 1958).

Hunt, Lord 2009. *The Hunt Review of the Regulation of Legal Services*, London, The Law Society [Online, October]. Available at: http://www.lawcentres.org.uk/uploads/Legal_Regulation_Report_October_2009.pdf [accessed 30 June 2011].

Hyslop, L. 2010. Winter Olympics on slippery slope after Vancouver crackdown on homeless. *The Guardian* [Online, 3 February]. Available at: http://www.guardian.co.uk/world/2010/feb/03/vancouver-winter-olympics-homeless-row [accessed: 15 July 2010].

ILEX 1976a. *Council Minutes: 22nd October.* Bedford. ILEX.

ILEX 1976b. *Council Minutes: 25th November*. Bedford: ILEX.

ILEX 1978. *Policy Committee Minutes: 20th October*. Bedford: ILEX.

ILEX 2003. *Moving Forward, Staying Ahead.* Bedford: ILEX.

ILEX 2009. Milburn Report fails to tackle non-graduate social mobility. *Press Release, pr038.09* [Online, 21 July]. Available Online at http://www.ilex.org.uk/media/press_releases/milburn_report_response.aspx [accessed: 11 February 2010].

ILEX 2010a. *Joint consultation of ILEX and IPS on Probate rights: 07.10.* [Online]. Available at: http://www.ilex.org.uk/PDF/IPS%20con%20doc%20probate%20rights.pdf [accessed: 19 November 2010].

ILEX 2010b. First Legal Executive Fellow Judge Appointed, *Press Release* [Online, 12 August]. Available at: http://www.ilex.org.uk/media/press_releases/first_legal_executive_judge.aspx [accessed: 19 November 2010].

ILEX/IPS 2010. *Rule Change Application Made by ILEX Professional Standards to the Legal Services Board Under Schedule 4, Part 3, Paragraph 20(1) Legal Services Act 2007* [Online]. Available at: http://www.legalservicesboard.org.

uk/what_we_do/regulation/pdf/ilex_professional%20_standards_code_of_ conduct_application_annexes.pdf [accessed: 9 January 2011].

ILEX/ The Law Society 1979. *Minutes of the Joint Committee: 16th November.* Bedford: ILEX.

The Independent 2002. Gareth Peirce: Tough Case. *The Independent* [Online, 4 August]. Available at: http://www.independent.co.uk/news/people/profiles/ gareth-peirce-tough-case-638748.html [accessed: 6 January 2011].

Irvine, Lord 1998. New Rights of Audience for Legal Executives, *Lord Chancellor's Department Press Release* (105/98, 23 April).

Jacob, M.-A. 2009. The Shared History: Unknotting Fictive Kinship and Legal Process, *Law & Society Review*, 43(1), 95–126.

Jamous, H. and Peloille, B. 1970. Changes in the French University-Hospital System, in *Professions and Professionalization*, edited by J. Jackson. Cambridge: Cambridge University Press, 109–52.

Johnson, N. and Johnstone, K. 2009. *Offshore Evolution: Transparency and Solutions in Cross Border Wealth Structuring – Executive Summary* [Online, July]. Available at: http://www.step.org/pdf/FiveFuturesSTEPExtracts.pdf [accessed: 13 January 2011].

Johnson, T. 1972. *Professions and Power.* London: Macmillan.

Johnstone, Q. and Flood, J. 1982. Paralegals in American and English Law Offices. *Windsor Yearbook of Access to Justice*, 2, 152–90.

Johnstone, Q. and Hopson, D. 1967. *Lawyers and Their Work: An Analysis of the Legal profession in the United States and England.* Indianapolis: Bobbs-Merril and Co.

Joint Academic Stage Board of the Law Society and Bar Council (JASB) 2002a. *The Academic Stage of Training for Entry to the Legal Profession: Standards, Content and related issues.* (July). London: The Law Society.

Joint Academic Stage Board of the Law Society and Bar Council (JASB) 2002b. *A Joint Statement issued by the Law Society and the General Council of the Bar on the Completion of the Initial or Academic Stage of Training by Obtaining an Undergraduate Degree* [Online]. Available at: http://www.sra. org.uk/documents/students/academic-stage/academicjointstate.pdf [accessed: 19 November 2010].

Joint Committee on the Draft Legal Services Bill (JCLSB), 2006. *Report.* [Online]. Available at: http://www.publications.parliament.uk/pa/jt200506/jtselect/ jtlegal/232/232i.pdf [accessed: 19 November 2010].

Jones, L. 2005. Exploring the Sources of Cause and Career Correspondence, in *The Worlds Cause Lawyers make: Structure and Agency in Legal Practice*, edited by A. Sarat and S. Scheingold. Stanford: Stanford University Press, 203–38.

Jopson, N. 2001. Solicitors under Pressure. *New Law Journal*, 151 (6974, 9 March), 330–1.

Kennedy, D. 1998. Legal Education as Training for Hierarchy, in *The Politics of Law: A Progressive Critique*, edited by D. Kairys. New York: Basic Books, 54–75.

Kennedy, H. 1992. *Eve was Framed: Women and British Justice*. London: Chatto & Windus.

Kendrick, R. 2005. Law Soc. Deputy Vice President is an SP. *SOLO*, January, 4.

Kiang, M. 2009. 'Unique Model' for Public Service Work. *The Lawyers' Weekly* [Online, 22 May]. Available at: www.lawyersweekly.ca/index.php?section=art icle&articleid=925 [accessed: 16 July 2010].

Kirkpatrick, I. and Ackroyd, S. 2003. Archetype Theory and the Changing Professional Organization: A Critique and Alternative. *Organization*, 10(4), 731–50.

Kostiner, I. 2003. Evaluating Legality: Toward a Cultural Approach to the Study of Law and Social Change. *Law and Society Review*, 37(3), 323–68.

Krathwohl, D., Bloom, B. and Masia, B. 1964. *Taxonomy of Education Objectives: The Classification of Education Goals: Handbook II: The Affective Domain*. New York: Longman.

Kritzer, H. 1999. The Professions are Dead, Long Live the Professions: Legal Practice in a Postprofessional World. *Law and Society Review*, 33(1), 713–59.

Kritzer, H. 2001. The Fracturing Legal Profession: the Case of Plaintiffs' Personal Injury Lawyers. *International Journal of the Legal Profession*, 8(3), 225–50.

Laffin, M. 1990. The engineering profession: from self-regulation to state sponsored collaboration, in *Corporatism and Accountability: Organized Interests in British Public Life*, edited by C. Crouch and R. Dore. Oxford: Clarendon Press, 125–48.

Laffin, M. 1998. Conclusion, in *Beyond Bureaucracy: The Professions in the Contemporary Public Sector*, edited by M. Laffin. Aldershot: Ashgate, 218–26.

Laffin, M. and Entwistle, T. 2000. New Problems, Old Professions? The Changing National World of Local Government Professions. *Policy and Politics*, 28(2), 207–20.

Landau, D. 2009. Steve Cohen. *Red Pepper* [Online, March]. Available at: http://www.redpepper.org.uk/Steve-Cohen/ [accessed: 8 January 2011].

Larson, M. 1977. *The Rise of Professionalism: a Sociological Analysis*. London: University of California Press.

Law Centres Federation (LCF) 2010. *Law Centres' Calls to the Next Government* [Online]. Available at: http://www.lawcentres.org.uk/uploads/Law_Centre_ Calls_-_Print_Version.pdf [accessed: 23 January 2011].

Law Society 1961. *Council Minutes: 5th May*. London: The Law Society.

Law Society 1962. *Council Minutes: 2nd November*. London: The Law Society.

Law Society 1963. *Council Minutes: 20th December*. London: The Law Society.

Law Society 1998. *MDPs: Why? Why not?* London: The Law Society.

Law Society 1999. *Multi-disciplinary Practices: Proposals for the way forward: 13th October 1999*. London: The Law Society.

Law Society 2000a. *Consultation Document: A new Law Society for a changing profession* [Online]. Available at: http://www.lawsociety.org.uk/secure/meeting/157284/New_Law_Society_For_a_Changing_Profession.pdf [accessed: 24 August 2010].

Law Society 2000b. *Competition Restrictions in the Profession: The Law Society's Response to the Office of Fair Trading.* London: The Law Society.

Law Society 2000c. *MDPS: An interim report: 13th July.* London: The Law Society.

Law Society 2002a. *Quality, Choice and the Public Interest: Response to the consultation paper 'In the Public Interest?' published by the Lord Chancellor's Department* (November). London: The Law Society.

Law Society 2002b. *Quality, Choice and the Public Interest: Response to the consultation paper 'In the Public Interest?' published by the Lord Chancellor's Department: Exposure Draft 14th October 2002.* London: The Law Society.

Law Society 2003. Extending Competition. *Press Release*, 24th July 2003. No longer available Online. On file with author.

Law Society 2004. *Independence and Quality: The Law Society's response to the consultation paper on the review of the regulation of legal services in England and Wales, June 2004.* London: The Law Society [Online]. Available at: http://www.lawsociety.org.uk/secure/file/145431/d:/teamsite-deployed/documents/templatedata/Internet%20Documents/Non-government%20proposals/Documents/independenceandqualityfinal.pdf [accessed: 15 December 2005].

Law Society 2005. *Council Minutes – 20th January* [Online]. Available at: http://www.lawsociety.org.uk/secure/meeting/134350/4_ii_Final_Council_Minutes_-_20_January_2005.doc [accessed: 17 December 2010].

Law Society 2006. *Independent regulation, empowered consumers: The Law Society's response to the White Paper: The Future of Legal Services – Putting Consumers First (January).* London: The Law Society.

Law Society 2007. *The Great Quality of Life Debate (17th July)* [Online]. Available at: http://www.lawsociety.org.uk/newsandevents/news/majorcampaigns/view=newsarticle.law?CAMPAIGNSID=317737#groups [accessed: 3 September 2010].

Law Society 2008a. *Council Minutes 12th November* [Online]. Available at http://www.lawsociety.org.uk/secure/meeting/177416/Meeting_2_-_12_November2008__Part_1__amended_post_Dec_Meet%C3%A2%C2%80%C2%A6.pdf [accessed: 17 December 2010].

Law Society 2008b. *Council Minutes 17th December* [Online]. Available at: http://www.lawsociety.org.uk/secure/meeting/177613/Meeting_3_-__17_December2008__Part_1_.pdf [accessed: 17 December 2010].

Law Society 2008c. *Minutes of the Membership Board, 27th November* [Online]. Available at: http://www.lawsociety.org.uk/secure/meeting/177187/Membership_Board_27_November_2008_Part_1_Mins.pdf [accessed 23 January 2011].

Law Society 2009a. *Initial response to evidence by Lord Hunt: Response to the consultation 30 June 2009* [Online]. Available at: http://www.lawsociety.org. uk/regulatory-review.page [accessed: 27 August 2010].

Law Society 2009b. *Annual Report* 2009 [Online]. Available at: http://www. lawsociety.org.uk/new/documents/2010/financialreport_2009.pdf [accessed: 7 September 2010].

Law Society 2009c. Estate Administration with Nationwide: New Protocol. *Press Release* [Online, 21 August]. Available at: http://www.lawsociety.org.uk/ newsandevents/news/view=newsarticle.law?NEWSID=422246 [accessed: 18 January 2011].

Law Society 2010a. *Election Manifesto* [Online]. Available at: http://www. lawsociety.org.uk/new/documents/2010/manifesto2010.pdf [accessed: 3 September 2010].

Law Society 2010b. *SRA consultation on transforming the regulation of legal services: Law Society response* [Online, 3 August]. Available at: http://www. lawsociety.org.uk/secure/file/187345/e:/teamsite-deployed/documents// templatedata/Internet%20Documents/Non-government%20proposals/ Documents/lsresponse_sraconsultationregulation270710.pdf [accessed: 7 September 2010].

Law Society 2010c. *July Council Meeting, Papers (including Chief Executive's Report, and RAB report)* [Online]. Available at: http://www.lawsociety.org.uk/ secure/meeting/187612/P1_papers_post_meeting.pdf [accessed: 17 December 2010].

Law Society 2010d. *June Council Meeting* [Online]. Available at: http://www. lawsociety.org.uk/secure/meeting/187284/Meeting_7_-_8–9_June_2010___ Part_1__amended_post_July_mtg.pdf [accessed: 17th December 2010].

Law Society of British Columbia 2004. *Minutes of the July Meeting* [Online]. Available at: http://www.lawsociety.bc.ca/about/docs/minutes/04–07–09.pdf [accessed: 6 January 2011].

Law Society's Gazette (LSG) 1962a. Status and Training – A new scheme. *The Law Society's Gazette*, January, 26.

Law Society's Gazette (LSG) 1962b. Letters: Institute of Legal Executives, *The Law Society's Gazette*, March, 165.

The Lawyer 1998a. Snubbed LawSoc head quits for Ilex. *The Lawyer* [Online, 9 January]. Available at: http://www.thelawyer.com/snubbed-lawsoc-head-quits-for-ilex/94844.article [accessed: 18 November 2010].

The Lawyer 1998b. Government to force MDPs on Law Society. *The Lawyer* [Online, 11 October]. Available at: http://www.thelawyer.com/government-to-force-mdps-on-law-society/89395.article [accessed: 24 August 2010].

The Lawyer 1999a. Law Society rivals sling mud as presidential race starts. *The Lawyer* [Online, 8 July]. Available at: http://www.thelawyer.com/law-society-rivals-sling-mud-as-presidential-race-starts/81741.article [accessed: 24 August 2010].

The Lawyer 1999b. Papering over the Cracks. *The Lawyer.* [Online, 11 August]. Available at: http://www.thelawyer.com/papering-over-the-cracks/87383. article [accessed: 26 August 2010].

The Lawyer 2000a. Davies Arnold Cooper takes back legal executive to head up department. *The Lawyer* [Online, 15 May]. Available at: http://www.thelawyer. com/dac-takes-back-legal-executive-to-head-dept/87130.article [accessed: 18 November 2010].

The Lawyer 2000b. Napier proposes Law Society City forum. *The Lawyer* [Online, 19 June]. Available at: http://www.thelawyer.com/napier-pledges-law-society-city-forum/86892.article [accessed: 26 August 2010].

The Lawyer 2000c. Conflicts rules under fire from City Law Society. *The Lawyer* [Online, 3 July]. Available at: http://www.thelawyer.com/conflicts-rules-under-fire-by-city-law-society/87099.article [accessed: 26 August 2010].

The Lawyer 2007. A Tough Act to Follow. *The Lawyer* [Online, 19 July]. Available at: http://www.thelawyer.com/a-tough-act-to-follow/127389.article [accessed: 2 September 2010].

The Lawyer 2009. Focus: Beachcroft, Going Public. *The Lawyer* [Online, 27 July]. Available at: http://www.thelawyer.com/focus-beachcroft-going-public/1001497.article [accessed: 2 September 2010].

The Lawyer 2010. A tale of two clans: ABS row divides legal profession north of the border. *The Lawyer* [Online, 5 April]. Available at http://www.thelawyer. com/a-tale-of-two-clans-abs-row-divides-legal-profession-north-of-the-border/1003994.article [accessed: 20 January 2011].

Layder, D. 1993. *New Strategies in Social Research.* Cambridge: Polity Press.

Leask, P. 1985. Law Centres in England and Wales. *Law and Policy.* 7(1), 61–76.

Leca, B. and Naccache, P. 2006. A Critical Realist Approach to Institutional Entrepreneurship. *Organization*, 13(5), 627–51.

Lee, L. 2010. Professional solidarity will be essential in year ahead. *Law Society Gazette* [Online, 5 August]. Available at: http://www.lawgazette.co.uk/ opinion/president039s-podium/professional-solidarity-will-be-essential-year-ahead [accessed: 7 September 2010].

Lee, R. 1992. From Profession to Business: The rise and rise of the City Law Firm. *Journal of Law and Society*, 19(1), 31–48.

Lee, R. 1999. *Firm Views – Work of and Work in the Largest Law Firms*, Research Study No. 35. London: The Law Society.

The Legal Executive 1999. Viewpoint. *The Legal Executive*, September, 44.

The Legal Executive 2005a. Viewpoint, *The Legal Executive*, March, 4.

The Legal Executive 2005b. Viewpoint, *The Legal Executive*, August, 30.

Legal Services Board (LSB) 2009a. *Section 30 Internal Governance Rules* [Online]. Available at: http://www.legalservicesboard.org.uk/what_we_do/ regulation/pdf/internal_governance_rules_2009.pdf [accessed: 25 August 2010].

Legal Services Board (LSB) 2009b. *Response to the Government's Panel for Fair Access to the Professions* [Online, 23 March]. Available at: http://www.

legalservicesboard.org.uk/what_we_do/responses_to_consultations/pdf/
response_230309.pdf [accessed: 18 January 2011].

Legal Services Board (LSB) 2010a. *Workshop on consumers' experience of will-writing services* [Online]. Available at: http://www.legalservicesboard.org.uk/
news_publications/events/will_writing_workshop.htm [accessed: 26 August
2010].

Legal Services Board (LSB) 2010b. *Alternative business structures: approaches
to licensing. Guidance to licensing authorities on the content of licensing rules*
[Online]. Available at: http://www.legalservicesboard.org.uk/what_we_do/
consultations/closed/pdf/abs_guidance_on_licensing_rules_guidance.pdf
[accessed: 2 September 2010].

Legal Services Board (LSB) 2010c. *Final LSB Decision Notice 6th May 2010:
Institute of Legal Executives Professional Standards Ltd's application for
approval of amendments to its Code of Conduct* [Online]. Available at: http://
www.legalservicesboard.org.uk/what_we_do/regulation/pdf/final_decision_
notice_ips_code_of_conduct_6_may_2010.pdf [accessed: 19 November
2010].

Legal Services Board (LSB) 2010d. *LSB announces proposals on workforce
diversity transparency* [Online, 15 December]. Available at: http://
www.legalservicesboard.org.uk/news_publications/press_releases/2010/
pdf/20101213_workforce_transparency2.pdf [accessed: 20 December 2010].

Legal Services Board ABS Implementation Group 2010. *Minutes of the July
Meeting* [Online]. Available at: http://www.legalservicesboard.org.uk/Projects/
abs/pdf/minutes_of_the_ninth_meeting-of_the_abs_implementation_group.
pdf [accessed: 2 September 2010].

Legal Services Commission (LSC) 2010. *SWL and Family Services Information
for Applicants Annexes Version 2nd February 2010* [Online]. Available at:
http://www.legalservices.gov.uk/docs/civil_contracting/Annexes_Combined_
v2.pdf [accessed: 10 July 2010].

Leicht, K. and Fennel, M. 1997. The Changing Organizational Context of
Professional Work. *Annual Review of Sociology*, 23 (August), 215–31.

Leicht, K. and Lyman, E. 2006. Markets, Institutions, and the Crisis of Professional
Practice. *Research in the Sociology of Organizations*, 24, 17–44.

Liaschenko, J. and Peter, E. 2004. Nursing Ethics and Conceptualisations of
Nursing: Profession, Practice and Work. *Journal of Advanced Nursing*, 46(5),
488–95.

Lin, A. 2010. Chinese M&A on the Rise. *American Lawyer Daily* [Online, 19
August]. Available at: http://amlawdaily.typepad.com/amlawdaily/2010/08/
china-ma.html [accessed: 19 August 2010].

Lind, S. 2010. SRA relaxes conflicts rules after review of use of Chinese walls.
Legal Week [Online, 27 July]. Available at: http://www.legalweek.com/
legal-week/news/1724910/sra-relaxes-conflicts-rules-review-chinese-walls
[accessed: 27th August 2010].

Liveley, K. 2000. Reciprocal emotion management: Working together to maintain stratification in private law firms. *Work and Occupations*, 27(1), 32–63.

Lord Chancellor's Department 2002. *In the Public Interest? A consultation by the LCD following the OFT report on Competition in the Professions* (CP 07/02). London: LCD.

Lounsbury, M. 2002. Institutional Transformation and Status Mobility: The Professionalization of the Field of Finance. *Academy of Management Journal*, 43(1), 255–66.

Lounsbury, M. 2007. A Tale of Two Cities: Competing Logics and Practice Variation in the Professionalizing of Mutual Funds. *Academy of Management Journal*, 50(2), 289–307.

Lovell, T. 2000. Thinking Feminism with and against Bourdieu, in *Reading Bourdieu on Society and Culture*, edited by B. Fowler. Oxford: Blackwell, 27–48.

Luban, D. 1988. *Lawyers and Justice: An Ethical Study*. Princeton: Princeton University Press.

MacDonald, K. 1995. *The Sociology of the Professions*. London: Sage.

Mackay, Lord. 1992. Inevitable legal changes. *New Law Journal*, 142(6574, 30 October), 1505–8.

Manchester Law Society 2009. Small Firms' Forum. *Messenger*, July

Manderson, D. and Turner, S. 2006. Coffee House: *Habitus* and Performance among Law Students. *Law and Social Inquiry*, 31(3), 649–76.

Manley, J. 1995. Sex-Segregated Work in the System of Professions: The Development and Stratification of Nursing. *The Sociological Quarterly*, 36(2), 297–314.

Mansfield, M. 2009. *Memoirs of a Radical Lawyer*. London: Bloomsbury Publishing.

Marcos, F. 2000. The storm over our heads: the rendering of legal services by audit firms in Spain. *International Journal of the Legal Profession*, 7(1), 7–21.

Marquis, C. and Lounsbury, M. 2007. Vive La Résistance: Competing Logics and the Consolidation of U.S. Community Banking. *Academy of Management Journal*, 50(4) 799–820.

Marriott, A., Sexton, L. and Staley, D. 1994. Components of Job Satisfaction in Psychiatric Social Workers. *Health and Social Work*, 19(3), html only.

Marsh, S. 1983. The CNAA Law Degree. *The Law Teacher*, 17(2), 73–123.

Martin, R. 1985. The Law Union of Ontario. *Law and Policy*, 7(1), 51–60.

Mason, P. and Hughes, N. with Hek, R., Spalek, B., Ward N. and Norman, A. 2009. *Access to Justice: A Review of Existing Evidence of the Experiences of Minority Groups based on Ethnicity, identity and Sexuality.* (07/09). London: Ministry of Justice.

Mather, L., McEwen, C. and Maiman, R. 2001. *Divorce Lawyers at Work: Varieties of Professionalism in Practice*. New York: Oxford University Press.

Maynard, R. 1992. Are mature students a problem? *Journal of Access Studies*, 17(2), 106–11.

Mayson, S. 2008. *External Ownership and Investment: Issues and Challenges* (College of Law, Legal Services Policy Institute) [Online]. Available at: http://www.college-of-law.co.uk/uploadedFiles/core/Assets/External%20 Ownership%20and%20Investment%20Discussion%20Paper.pdf [accessed: 2 September 2010].

Mayson, S. 2010a. *If ABS are the Answer, what's the Question?* (College of Law, Legal Services Policy Institute) [Online, May 2010]. Available at: http://www.college-of-law.co.uk/uploadedFiles/core/About_the_College/ Legal_Services_Policy_Institute/Mayson%20%282010%29%20If%20ABSs %20are%20the%20answer,%20what%27s%20the%20question.pdf [accessed: 2 September 2010].

Mayson, S. 2010b. *Regulation of Legal Services - Reserved Legal Services: History and Rationale* (College of Law, Legal Services Policy Institute) [Online]. Available at: http://www.college-of-law.co.uk/uploadedFiles/core/About_ the_College/Legal_Services_Policy_Institute/LSI%20%282010%29%20 Reserved%20legal%20activities%20final%20100820.pdf [accessed: 2 September 2010].

McIntosh, D. 2009. Chairman's Column. *City Solicitor*, (Summer), Issue 67, 4–5.

McIntosh, D. 2010. Chairman's Column. *City Solicitor*, (Summer), Issue 70, 8–9.

McLeod-Roberts, L. 2009a. Law Soc and SRA in face-off over board selection. *The Lawyer* [Online, 16 June]. Available at: http://www.thelawyer.com/ law-soc-and-sra-in-face-off-over-board-selection/1001031.article [accessed: 25 August 2010].

McLeod-Roberts, L. 2009b. SRA names members of revamped board. *The Lawyer* [Online, 18 August]. Available at: http://www.thelawyer.com/sra-names-members-of-revamped-board/1001713.article [accessed: 25 August 2010].

McLeod-Roberts, L. 2010a. Top firms reject candidates with 'working class accents'. *The Lawyer* [Online, 21 December]. Available at: http://www.thelawyer. com/top-firms-reject-candidates-with-working-class-accents/1006459.article [accessed: 17 January 2011].

McPartland, C. 2009a. Shoosmiths to withdraw training contracts. *The Lawyer* [Online, 30 March]. Available at: http://www.thelawyer.com/shoosmiths-to-withdraw-training-contracts/1000257.article [accessed: 4 April].

McPartland, C. 2009b. Legal executives: an easier route into a career in law? *The Lawyer* [Online, 15 June]. Available at: http://www.thelawyer.com/legal-executives-an-easier-route-into-a-career-in-law?/1001067.article [accessed: 18 November 2010].

McPartland, C. 2009c. Legal exec aims for top job after making partner at Glaisyers, *The Lawyer* [Online, 20 July]. Available at: http://www.thelawyer. com/legal-exec-aims-for-top-job-after-making-partner-at-glaisyers/1001455. article [accessed: 19 November 2010].

McPartland, C. 2010. CC's fast-track LPC adds to two-tier fears, *The Lawyer* [Online, 20 September]. Available at: http://www.thelawyer.com/

cc%E2%80%99s-fast-track-lpc-adds-to-two-tier-fears/1005535.article [accessed: 16 December 2010].

McRobie, H. 2010. George Osborne can't cherry pick from Canada's cuts model. *The Guardian* [Online, 8 June]. Available at: http://www.guardian.co.uk/commentisfree/2010/jun/08/george-osborne-canada-cuts-model [accessed: 20 January 2011].

McVea, H. 2002. Predators and the Public Interest – the 'Big Four' and Multi-Disciplinary Practices. *Modern Law Review*, 65(6), 811–33.

Melville, A. and Laing, K. 2007. 'I just drifted into it': constraints faced by publicly funded family lawyers. *International Journal of the Legal Profession*, 14(3), 281–300.

Milburn, A. 2009. *Unleashing Aspirations: The Final Report of the Panel on Fair Access to the Professions* [Online]. Available at: http://www.cabinetoffice.gov.uk/media/227102/fair-access.pdf [accessed: 19 November 2010].

Miller, R., Action, C., Fullerton, D. and Maltby, J. 2002. *SPSS for Social Scientists*. Basingstoke: Palgrave Macmillan.

Millerson, G. 1964. *The Qualifying Associations: A Study in Professionalisation*. London: Routledge and Kegan Paul.

Ministry of Justice (MoJ) 2009. *Study of Legal Advice at Local Level*. London: Ministry of Justice [Online, June 2009]. Available at: http://www.justice.gov.uk/publications/docs/legal-advice-local-level.pdf [accessed: 6 January 2011].

Ministry of Justice (MoJ) 2010. Clarke unveils plans for radical reform of justice. *Press Release* [Online, 15 November]. Available at: http://www.justice.gov.uk/news/newsrelease151110b.htm [accessed: 21 December 2010].

Moorhead, R. 1998. Legal Aid in the Eye of a Storm: Rationing, Contracting, and a New Institutionalism. *Journal of Law and Society*, 25(3), 365–87.

Moorhead, R. 2001. Third way regulation? Community legal services partnership. *Modern Law Review*, 64(6), 543–62.

Moorhead, R. 2004. Legal aid and the decline of private practice: blue murder or toxic job? *International Journal of the Legal Profession*, 11(3),159–90.

Moorhead, R. 2010. Lawyer Specialization – Managing the Professional Paradox. *Law and Policy*, 32(2), 226–59.

Morgan, D. 1992. *Discovering Men*. London: Routledge.

Morley, L. 2007. The X factor: employability, elitism and equity in graduate recruitment. *21st Century Society*, 2(2), 191–207.

Moyser, G. and Wagstaffe, M. 1987. Studying elites: theoretical and methodological issues, in *Research Methods for Elite Studies*, edited by G. Moyser and M. Wagstaffe. London: Allen and Unwin, 1–24.

Murray, J. 1950. A short history of the SMCA. *Solicitors Managing Clerks' Association Gazette*, November.

Murray, J. 1951. A short history of the SMCA: contd., *Solicitors Managing Clerks' Gazette*, February.

Mutch, A., Delbridge, R. and Ventresca, M. 2006. Situating Organizational Action: The Relational Sociology of Organizations. *Organization*, 13(5), 607–25.

Muzio, D. and Ackroyd, S. 2005. On the Consequences of Defensive Professionalism: Recent Changes in the Legal Labour Process. *Journal of Law and Society*, 32 (4), 615–42.

Muzio, D., Faulconbridge, J. and Cook, A. 2010. Learning to be a Lawyer: English Legal Education and Law Firms in an International Perspective. *Presentation to the Legal Service Board* [Online, June]. Available at http://www.legalservicesboard.org.uk/what_we_do/Research/research_events/pdf/learning_to_be_a_lawyer_muzio_et_al.pdf [accessed: 8 January 2011].

Nelson, R. and Trubek, D. 1992a. New Problems and New Paradigms in Studies of the Legal Profession, in *Lawyers' Ideals/Lawyers Practices: Transformations in the American Legal Profession*, edited by R. Nelson, D. Trubek and R. Solomon. Ithaca and London: Cornell University Press, 1–27.

Nelson, R. and Trubek, D. 1992b. Arenas of Professionalism, in *Lawyers' Ideals/Lawyers Practices: Transformations in the American Legal Profession*, edited by R. Nelson, D. Trubek and R. Solomon. Ithaca and London: Cornell University Press, 177–214.

Nicolson, D. 2005. Demography, Discrimination and Diversity: A New Dawn for the British Legal Profession? *International Journal of the Legal Profession*. 12(2), 201–28.

Nicolson, D. and Webb, J. 1999. *Professional Legal Ethics*. Oxford: Oxford University Press.

Norman, L. 2004. *Career Choices in Law: A Survey of Law Students (Research Study 50)*. London: The Law Society.

Oakley, J. and Cocking, D. 2006. *Virtue Ethics and Professional Roles*. Cambridge: Cambridge University Press.

Office of Fair Trading 2001. *Competition in Professions* (March, OFT328) [Online]. Available at: http://www.oft.gov.uk/shared_oft/reports/professional_bodies/oft328.pdf [accessed: 24 January 2011].

Park, G. and Lippert, R. 2008. Legal aid's logics. *Studies in Law, Politics and Society*, 45, 177–201.

Pateman, C. 1988. *The Sexual Contract*. Oxford: Polity Press.

Paterson, A. 1996. Professionalism and the Legal Services Market, *International Journal of the Legal Profession*, 3 (1/2), 137–68.

Peppet, S. 2005. Lawyers' Bargaining Ethics, Contract and Collaboration: The End of the Legal Profession and the Beginning of Professional Pluralism. *Iowa Law Review*, 90, 475–538.

Perkin, H. 1969. *Origins of Modern English Society 1780–1880*. London: Routledge & Kegan Paul.

Perkin, H. 1990. *The Rise of Professional Society: England since 1880*. London and New York: Routledge.

Perrin, L. 2000. Perrin's View. *The Lawyer* [Online, 7 August]. Available at: http://www.thelawyer.com/perrins-view/85474.article [accessed: 26 August 2010].

Pierce, J. 1995. *Gender Trials: Emotional Lives in Contemporary Law Firms*. Berkeley: University of California Press.

Pinnington, A. and Morris, T. 2003. Archetype Change in Professional Organizations: Survey Evidence from Large Law Firms. *British Journal of Management*, 14(1), 85–99.

Pitcher, J. and Purcell, K. 1998. Diverse expectations and access to opportunities: is there a graduate labour market? *Higher Educational Quarterly*, 52(2), 179–203.

Pivot 2002. *To Serve and Protect: A Report on Policing in Vancouver's Downtown Eastside.* Vancouver: Pivot Legal Society [Online]. Available at: http://www.pivotlegal.org/pdfs/toserveandprotect.pdf [accessed: 6 January 2011].

Pivot 2006. *Cracks in the Foundation: Solving the Housing Crisis in Canada's Poorest Neighbourhood.* Vancouver: Pivot Legal Society [Online]. Available at: http://www.pivotlegal.org/pdfs/CracksinFoundation.pdf [accessed: 6 January 2011].

Pivot 2009. Methadone patients protected by tenancy laws, Supreme Court rules. *Press Release* [Online, 2 December]. Available at: http://www.pivotlegal.org/News/09–12–02--Methadone-patients-protected.html [accessed: 26 January 2011].

Pleasance, P., Balmer, N., Tam, T., Buck, A. and Patel, A. 2008. *Findings of the 2007 Civil and Social Justice Survey.* London: Legal Services Research Centre.

Polikoff, N. 1996. Am I My Client? The Role Confusion of a Lawyer Activist. *Harvard Civil Rights – Civil Liberties Law Review*, 31, 443–71.

Powell, M. 1993. Professional Innovation: Corporate Lawyers and Private Lawmaking, *Law & Social Inquiry*, 18(3), 423–52.

PricewaterhouseCoopers (PWC) 2007. *Annual Law Firm Survey – Executive Summary* [Online]. Available at: http://www.pwc.co.uk/eng/publications/16th_law_firms_survey.html [accessed: 15 August 2009]. No longer Online. On file with author

PricewaterhouseCoopers (PWC) 2009. *Annual Law Firm Survey – Executive Summary 18th Annual Law Firms' Survey 2009* [Online]. Available at: http://www.pwc.co.uk/eng/publications/18th_law_firms_survey.html [accessed: 23 January 2011].

Pringle, R. 1989. *Secretaries Talk: Sexuality, Power and Work.* London: Verso.

QAA 2007. *Quality Matters: A Briefing Paper – The Classification of Degree Awards* [Online]. Available at: http://www.qaa.ac.uk/enhancement/qualityMatters/QMApril07.pdf [accessed: 10 November 2010].

Reay, D. 2004. 'It's all becoming habitus': Beyond the habitual use of habitus in educational research. *British Journal of the Sociology of Education*, 25(4), 431–44.

Reay, D., David, M. and Ball, S. 2005. *Degrees of Choice: social class, race and gender in higher education.* Stoke-on-Trent: Trentham Books.

Regulatory Affairs Board (RAB) 2009a. *Minutes of 21st May Meeting.* London: The Law Society [Online]. Available at: http://www.lawsociety.org.uk/secure/meeting/183887/05._RAB_Note_of_meeting_21_May_2009.pdf [accessed: 17 December 2010].

Regulatory Affairs Board (RAB) 2009b. *Minutes of the 25th June Meeting.* London: The Law Society [Online]. Available at: http://www.lawsociety. org.uk/secure/meeting/181481/06._RAB_minutes_-_25_June_2009.pdf [accessed: 17 December 2010].

Regulatory Affairs Board (RAB) 2009c. *Minutes of the 13th October Meeting.* London: The Law Society [Online]. Available at: http://www.lawsociety.org. uk/secure/meeting/182139/02._RAB_minutes_-_13_Oct_2009.pdf [accessed: 17 December 2010].

Richardson, J. 2005. Advocating Change. *Pivot Post,* 1 (April), 6–8 [Online]. Available at: http://www.pivotlegal.org/pdfs/PivotPost1.pdf [accessed: 23 January 2011].

Rigby, B. and Hancock, A. 2010. What the Legal Services Reforms Could Mean for City Law Firms. *Law Society Gazette* [Online, 19 May]. Available at: http://www.lawgazette.co.uk/features/what-legal-services-reforms-could-mean-city-law-firms [accessed: 16 July 2010].

Ripplinger, S. 2007. Ann Livingston of VANDU is wearied by death. *Holly's Fight for Justice* [Online, 13 December]. Available at: http://fightforjustice. blogspot.com/2008/01/ann-livingston-of-vandu-is-wearied-by.html [accessed: 23 January 2011].

Robbins, D. 1991.*The World of Pierre Bourdieu: Recognising Society.* Milton Keynes: Open University Press.

Robbins, D. 2005. The Origins, Early Development and Status of Bourdieu's Concept of Cultural Capital. *British Journal of Sociology,* 56(1), 13–30.

Robins, J. 2007. Legal executives set to close the gap on solicitors. *Law Society Gazette* [Online, 25 January]. Available at: http://www.lawgazette.co.uk/ features/legal-executives-set-close-gap-solicitors [accessed: 12 November 2010].

Robins, J. 2008. Shifting Sands. *Law Society Gazette* [Online, 15 May]. Available at: http://www.lawgazette.co.uk/features/shifting-sands-1 [accessed: 6 January 2011].

Roslender, R. 1992. *Sociological Perspectives on Modern Accountancy.* London: Routledge.

Rothwell, R. 2010a. Co-op in new drive to promote legal services to food shoppers. *Law Society Gazette* [Online, 22 April]. Available at: http://www. lawgazette.co.uk/news/co-op-new-drive-promote-legal-services-food-shoppers [accessed: 7 September 2010].

Rothwell, R. 2010b. Small firms will be 'resilient' in the face of ABSs. *Law Society Gazette* [Online, 15 July]. Available at: http://www.lawgazette.co.uk/ news/small-firms-will-be-resilient-face-abss [accessed: 3 September 2010].

Rothwell, R. 2010c. Law Society should open to non-solicitors, council member proposes, *Law Society Gazette* [Online, 6 December]. Available at: http:// www.lawgazette.co.uk/news/law-society-should-open-non-solicitors-council-member-proposes [accessed: 16th December 2010].

Sarat, A. and Scheingold, S. 2005. The Dynamics of Cause-Lawyering: Constraints and Opportunities', in *The Worlds Cause Lawyers Make: Structure and Agency in Legal Practice*, edited by A. Sarat and S. Scheingold. Stanford: Stanford University Press, 1–34.

Savage, N. 2002. Professional Status and the Training Contract. *Solicitors Journal*, 146(35), 818.

Scheingold, S. and Bloom, A. 1998. Transgressive Cause Lawyering: Practice Sites and the Politicization of the Professional. *International Journal of the Legal Profession*, 5(2/3), 209–53.

Scheingold, S. and Sarat, A. 2004. *Something to Believe In: Politics, Professionalism and Cause Lawyering*. Stanford: Stanford University Press.

Schleef, D. 2006. *Managing Elites: Professional Socialization in Law and Business Schools*. Lanham and Oxford: Rowman and Littlefield Publishers.

The Sentinel 2009. Care homes lawyer clear of misconduct. *The Sentinel* [Online, 19 September]. Available at: http://www.thisisstaffordshire.co.uk/news/care-homes-lawyer-clear-misconduct/article-1352493-detail/article.html [accessed: 6 January 2011].

Seron, C. and Ferris, K. 1995. Negotiating Professionalism: The Gendered Social Capital of Flexible Time. *Work and Occupations*, 22(1), 22–47.

Shamir, R. and Chinski, S. 1998. Destruction of Houses and Construction of a Cause: Lawyers and Bedouins in the Israeli Courts, in *Cause Lawyering: Political Commitments and Professional Responsibilities*, edited by A. Sarat and S. Scheingold. Oxford and New York: Oxford University Press, 227–57.

Sharpe, A. 2007. Structured Like a Monster: Understanding Human Difference Through a Legal Category. *Law and Critique*, 18(2), 207–28.

Sherer, P. and Lee, K. 2002. Institutional Change in Large Law Firms: A Resource Dependency and Institutional Perspective. *Academy of Management Journal*, 45(1), 102–19.

Sherr, A. 1994. Come of Age. *International Journal of the Legal Profession*, 1(1) 3–12.

Shils, E. 1975. *Center and Periphery: Essays in Macrosociology*. London and Chicago: University of Chicago Press.

Sidaway, J. and Punt, T. 1997. *Paralegal Staff Working in Solicitors' Firms*. London: The Law Society.

Siddiqui, N., Ismail, S. and Allen, M. 2008. *Safe to Return? Pakistani women, domestic violence and access to refugee protection – A report of a trans-national research project conducted in the UK and Pakistan* [Online]. Available at: http://www.smlc.org.uk/waspcontents.htm [accessed: 23 January 2011].

Silverman, D. 1993. *Interpreting Qualitative Data: Methods for Analysing Talk, Text and Interaction*. London: Sage.

Simon, W. 1978. The Ideology of Advocacy: Procedural Justice and Professional Ethics. *Wisconsin Law Review*, 1, 29–144.

Slaughter and May 2008. *Trainee Graduate Recruitment* [Online]. Available at: http://www.slaughterandmay.com/brochures/brochures/general/trainee_recruitment_brochure_london.pdf [accessed: 23 April 2008].

Smedley, N. 2009. *Review of the Regulation of Corporate Legal Work* [Online, March]. Available at: http://www.legalregulationreview.com/corporatereview.html [accessed: 27 August 2010].

Smedley, N. Perrin, C. and Rozenberg, J. *Interview 26th March 2009* – [Online]. Available at: http://www.lawsociety.org.uk/newsandevents/pressreleases/view=newsarticle.law?NEWSID=418667 [accessed: 26 August 2010].

Smith, A. 2006. Vicious (magic) circle. *Legal Ethics*, 9(2), 152–6.

Smith, D. and Saunders, M. 1991 *Other Routes: Higher Education Policy*. Buckingham: SRHE/Open University Press, Cutting Edge series.

Smith, M. and Tam, T. 2007. *Findings from the Legal Advice Sector Workforce Surveys*. London: Legal Services Research Centre.

Society of Legal Scholars (SLS), 2010. *SLS Response on Legal Ethics* [Online]. Available at: http://www.legalscholars.ac.uk/pubdocs/responses/SLS_Comments_on_Legal_Ethics.doc [accessed: 16 December 2010].

Society of Trusts and Estates Practitioners (STEP) 2008a. Non-Doms - HMRC Clarifications Welcome - Consultation Continues - Deferral Needed. *Press Release* [Online, 12 February]. Available at http://www.step.org/news/press_releases/2008/non-doms_-_hmrc_clarifications.aspx [accessed: 13 January 2011].

Society of Trusts and Estates Practitioners (STEP) 2008b. *Annual Report 2008*. London: STEP [no longer available Online]

Society of Trusts and Estates Practitioners (STEP) 2010a. *Trusted Advisor – The Future: A report on the future of UK trust and estate practice.* [Online, July]. Available at: http://www.step.org/pdf/STEP%20Trusted%20Advisor%20The%20Future%20FINAL.pdf [accessed: 13 January 2011].

Society of Trusts and Estates Practitioners (STEP) 2010b. Survey Reveals Incompetence and Dishonesty of 'Cowboy' Will Writers. *Press Release* [Online, 9 August]. Available at: http://www.step.org/default.aspx?page=1645 [accessed: 13 January 2011].

Society of Trusts and Estates Practitioners (STEP) 2010c. STEP Sets the Standard in Will Writing Education. *Press Release* [Online, 2 September]. Available at: http://www.step.org/news/press_releases/2010/step_ww_qualification_launch.aspx [accessed: 13 January 2011].

Society of Trusts and Estates Practitioners (STEP) 2010d. STEP launches Diploma for Accountants and Tax Practitioners. *Press Release* [Online, 11 November]. Available at: http://www.step.org/news/press_releases/2010/step_launches_diploma_for_acco.aspx [accessed: 26 January 2011].

Socio-Legal Studies Association (SLSA) 2009. *SLSA Statement of the Principles of Ethical Research Practice.* [Online, January]. Available at: http://www.slsa.ac.uk/images/slsadownloads/ethicalstatement/slsa%20ethics%20statement%20_final_%5B1%5D.pdf [accessed: 4 January 2011].

The Solicitors' Journal 1962. Letters. *The Solicitors' Journal*, 16 February, 132.

The Solicitors' Journal 1963. Letters. *The Solicitors' Journal*, 26 July, 590.

Solicitors' Managing Clerks' Association (SMCA) 1956. Professional Status for Managing Clerks. *Solicitors' Managing Clerks' Association Gazette*, November, 129–132.

Solicitors' Managing Clerks' Association (SMCA) 1961. Editorial. *Solicitors' Managing Clerks' Gazette*, May, 80.

Solicitors Regulation Authority (SRA) 2007. *Annual Report 2006/2007* [Online]. Available at: http://www.sra.org.uk/documents/annual-reports/annual-report-2006–2007.pdf [accessed: 26 August 2010].

Solicitors Regulation Authority (SRA) 2009a. *SRA response to Legal Services Board consultation on proposed rules under section 30 of the Legal Services Act (Part 1)* [Online, 1 June]. Available at: http://www.sra.org.uk/sra/consultations/consultation-responses/response-legal-services-board-consultation-section-30-part-1.page [accessed: 25 August 2010].

Solicitors Regulation Authority (SRA) 2009b. *SRA response to the Review of the Regulation of Corporate Legal Work* [Online, 30 June]. Available at: http://www.sra.org.uk/sra/consultations/consultation-responses/response-review-regulation-corporate-legal-work-june-2009.page [accessed: 26 August 2010].

Solicitors Regulation Authority (SRA) 2010a. *Completing the academic stage of training: Guidance for providers of recognised law programmes* [Online, August]. Available at: http://www.sra.org.uk/documents/students/academic-stage/academicstageguide.pdf [accessed: 18 November 2010].

Solicitors Regulation Authority (SRA) 2010b. *The Architecture of Change Part 2 – the new SRA Handbook – feedback and further consultation* [Online, October]. Available at: http://www.sra.org.uk/documents/SRA/consultations/handbook/october-consultation-paper.pdf [accessed: 29 November 2010].

SOLO 2001. *The Magazine of the Sole Practitioners Group of the Law Society* [Online, July]. Available at: http://www.spg.uk.com/magazine/solomagpdf/7–2001.pdf [accessed: 3 September 2010].

SOLO 2005. *The Magazine of the Sole Practitioners Group of the Law Society*, 20 [Online, April]. Available at: http://www.spg.uk.com/magazine/solomagpdf/4-2005.pdf [accessed: 30 June 2011].

Sommerlad, H. 1995. Managerialism and the legal profession: a new professional paradigm. *International Journal of the Legal Profession*, 2(2/3), 159–85.

Sommerlad, H. 1999. The implementation of quality initiatives and the New Public Management in the legal aid sector in England and Wales: bureaucratisation, stratification and surveillance. *International Journal of the Legal Profession*, 6, 311–43.

Sommerlad, H. 2001. 'I've lost the plot': An Everyday Story of Legal Aid Lawyers. *Journal of Law and Society*, 28(3), 335–60.

Sommerlad, H. 2002. Women Solicitors in a Fractured Profession: Intersections of Gender and Professionalism in England and Wales. *International Journal of the Legal Profession*, 9(3), 213–34.

Sommerlad, H. 2003. Can Women Lawyer Differently?, in *Women in the World's Legal Professions*, edited by U. Schultz and G. Shaw. Oxford: Hart Publishing, 191–224.

Sommerlad, H. 2007. Researching and Theorizing the Processes of Professional Identity Formation. *Journal of Law and Society*, 34 (2), 190–217.

Sommerlad, H. and Sanderson, P. 1998. *Gender, Choice and Commitment: Women Solicitors in England and Wales and the Struggle for Equal Status*. Farnham: Ashgate.

Sommerlad, H. and Sanderson, P. 2009. *Training and Regulating Providers of Publicly Funded Legal Advice: A Case-Study of Civil Provision* (08/09). London: Ministry of Justice.

Sommerlad, H., Webley, L., Duff, L., Muzio, D. and Tomlinson, J. with Parnham, R. 2010. *Diversity in the Legal Profession in England and Wales: A Qualitative Study of Barriers and Individual Choices*. London: Legal Services Board [Online]. Available at: http://www.legalservicesboard.org.uk/what_we_do/Research/Publications/pdf/lsb_diversity_in_the_legal_profession_final.pdf [accessed: 11 November 2010].

Southwark Law Centre 2007. *Report on the work of the Possession Prevention Project April 2004 – April 2007*. Southwark Law Centre/Blackfriars Advice Centre [Online, July]. Available at: http://www.plenet.org.uk/data/files/possession-prevention-project-2007–8.pdf [accessed: 20 January 2011].

Southworth, A. 1998. Lawyers and the 'Myth of Rights' in Civil Rights and Poverty Practice. *Public Interest Law Journal*, 8 (1998–99), 469–520.

Sturges, C. 2002. How Fringe became mainstream, *The Independent* [Online, 5 August]. Available at: http://www.independent.co.uk/arts-entertainment/theatre-dance/features/how-fringe-became-mainstream-638917.html [accessed: 20 December 2010].

Suddaby, R., Gendron, Y. and Lam, H. 2009. The Organizational Context of Professionalism in Accounting. *Accounting, Organizations and Society*, 34(3–4), 409–27.

Sugarman, D. 1995a. Who colonized whom? Historical reflections on the intersection between law, lawyers and accountants, in *Professional Competition and Professional Power: Lawyers, Accountants, and the Social Construction of Markets*, edited by Y. Dezaley and D. Sugarman. London: Routledge, 226–37.

Sugarman, D. 1995b. *A Brief History of the Law Society*. London: The Law Society.

Sugarman, D. 1996. Bourgeois Collectivism, Professional Power and the Boundaries of the State. The Public and Private Life of the Law Society, 1825–1914. *International Journal of the Legal Profession*, 3(1/2), 83–135.

Susskind, R. 2008. *The End of Lawyers? Rethinking the Nature of Legal Services*. Oxford: Oxford University Press.

Sutton, C. 2007. Alternative Business Structures (ABS) and the Legal Services Bill. The Last Lap. *SOLO*, 10–11 [Online, November]. Available at: http://www.spg.uk.com/magazine/solomagpdf/12–2007.pdf [accessed: 3rd September 2010].

Sutton, C. 2009. SPG in Action! *SOLO*, 20–21 [Online, December]. Available at: http://www.spg.uk.com/magazine/solomagpdf/12–2009.pdf [accessed: 3 September 2010].

Sutton, C. 2010. *What Matters – Please vote, implementation of Alternative Business Structures* [Online, 4 August]. Available at: http://www.spg.uk.com/article/archive/?type=0 [accessed: 3 September 2010].

Sweetman, P. 2003. Twenty-first Century Dis-ease? Habitual Reflexivity or the Reflexive Habitus. *Sociological Review* 51(4), 528–49.

Swift, J. 2010. Aussie firm Slater & Gordon posts turnover rise after acquisitive year. *The Lawyer* [Online, 19 August]. Available at: http://www.thelawyer.com/1005338.article#comments [accessed: 3 September 2010].

Tasker, G. 2010. *The Story of STEP - From a Vision to Global Reality* [Online]. Available at: http://www.step.org/about_step/the_story_of_step.aspx [accessed: 25 November 2010].

Teodoro, M. 2010. Contingent Professionalism: Bureaucratic Mobility and the Adoption of Water Conservation Rates. *Journal of Public Administration Research and Theory*, 20(2), 437–59.

Thomson, D. 2005. Negotiating Cause Lawyering Potential in the Early Years of Corporate Practice, in *The Worlds Cause Lawyers Make: Structure and Agency in Legal Practice*, edited by A. Sarat and S. Scheingold. Stanford: Stanford University Press, 274–303.

Thornton, M. 1996. *Dissonance and Distrust: Women in the Legal Profession*. Melbourne: Oxford University Press.

Timmons, H. 2010. Outsourcing to India Draws Western Lawyers. *New York Times* [Online, 4 August]. Available at: http://www.nytimes.com/2010/08/05/business/global/05legal.html?_r=1&scp=1&sq=%E2%80%98Outsourcing%20to%20India%20Draws%20Western%20Lawyers%E2%80%99%20New%20York%20Times%20&st=cse [accessed: 6 August 2010].

Trubek, L. 1996. Embedded Practices: Lawyers, Clients and Social Change. *Harvard Civil Rights – Civil Liberties Law Review*, 31, 415–41.

Tsang, L. 1999. Faith and law – how does the holding of religious beliefs affect practice as a solicitor? A look at the opportunities for work and the perils of religious discrimination. *Law Society Gazette* [Online, 25 August]. Available at: http://www.lawgazette.co.uk/news/faith-and-law-how-does-holding-religious-beliefs-affect-practice-a-solicitor-a-look-opportuniti [accessed: 20 January 2011].

Vancouver 2006. *Downtown Eastside Community Monitoring Report 2005–2006*. Vancouver: Vancouver City Council, 10th Edition [Online]. Available at: http://vancouver.ca/commsvcs/planning/dtes/pdf/2006mr.pdf [accessed: 23 January 2011].

Van Hoy, J. 1993. Intraprofessional Politics and Professional Regulation: A Case-Study of the ABA Commission on Professionalism. *Work and Occupations*, 20(1), 90–109.

Vignaendra, S., Williams, M. and Garvey, J. 2000. Hearing Black and Asian Voices – An Exploration of Identity, in *Discriminating Lawyers*, edited by P. Thomas. London: Cavendish, 121–54.

Wasserstrom, R. 1975. Lawyers as Professionals: Some Moral Issues. *Human Rights*, 5, 1–20.

Webb, J. 1999. Post-Fordism and the Reformation of Liberal Legal Education, in *The Law School – Global Issues, Local Questions*, edited by F. Cownie. Aldershot: Ashgate, 228–60.

Webb, J. 2004. Turf wars and market control: competition and complexity in the market for legal services. *International Journal of the Legal Profession*, 11(1), 81–102.

Webley, L. and Duff, L. 2007. Women Solicitors as a Barometer for Problems within the Legal Profession: Time to Put Values Before Profits? *Journal of Law & Society* 34(3), 374–402.

Wilensky, H. 1964. The Professionalization of Everyone. *American Journal of Sociology*, 70, 137–58.

Wilkins, D. and Gulati, M. 1998. Reconceiving the Tournament of Lawyers: Tracking, Seeding and Information Control in the Internal Labor Markets of Elite Law Firms. *Virginia Law Review*, 84, 1581–1681.

Willets, D. 2010. Statement on higher education funding and student finance. *House of Commons* [Online, 3 November]. Available at: http://www.bis. gov.uk/news/speeches/david-willetts-statement-on-HE-funding-and-student-finance [accessed: 17 January 2011].

Williams, C. 1989. *Gender Differences at Work: Women and Men in Nontraditional Occupations*. Berkeley: University of California Press.

Witz, A. 1992. *Professions and Patriarchy*. London: Routledge.

Zander, M. 1978. *Legal Services in the Community*. London: Maurice Temple-Smith Ltd.

Zemans, F. 2000. The Community Legal Clinic Quality Assurance Program: An Innovative Experience in Quality Assurance in Legal Aid. *British Columbia Law Review*, 33, 243–83.

Zimdars, A. 2010. The Profile of Pupil Barristers at the Bar of England and Wales 2004–2008. *International Journal of the Legal Profession*, 17(2), 117–34.

Index